"THE KID"

BLASTS A WINNER

About the Author

Bill Nowlin grew up in the Boston area and saw Ted Williams play often, even touching one of Ted's home runs in Fenway Park's center-field bleachers. Later, Bill was one of the first fans to the mound when Jim Lonborg induced the final out and the Red Sox won the 1967 pennant. He was elected as SABR's Vice President in 2004 and has served on the Board of Directors since that time. Bill is also the author or co-author of dozens of books on the Red Sox or Red Sox players, including six prior books on Ted Williams, along with one in the works on Ted Williams and the Jimmy Fund. He has written more than 1,000 articles for SABR and edited or co-edited more than 100 books in all. Bill is also co-founder of Rounder Records of Cambridge, Massachusetts. He's traveled to more than 100 countries, but says there's no place like Fenway Park.

"THE KID" BLASTS A WINNER

Ted Williams's 110 Game-Deciding Home Runs

Bill Nowlin

SUMMER
GAME
BOOKS

ISBN: 978-1-955398-16-9 (print)
ISBN: 978-1-955398-17-6 (ebook)

For information about permissions, bulk purchases, or additional distribution, write to

Summer Game Books
P. O. Box 818
South Orange, NJ 07079

or contact the publisher at www.summergamebooks.com

A different version of much of the content of this book was published on the Society for American Baseball Research website.

The photo on page xii of this book is used with permission from the National Baseball Hall of Fame and Museum. Other photos in the book are as credited. Uncredited photos come from the author's personal collection.

Other Books by Bill Nowlin

WORKING A "PERFECT GAME": CONVERSATIONS WITH UMPIRES (Summer Game Books, 2020)

BOSTON RED SOX IN 5's and 10s (The History Press, 2020)

THE BOSTON RED SOX KILLER B's: BASEBALL'S BEST OUTFIELD, by Jim Prime and Bill Nowlin (Sports Publishing, 2019)

RED SOX vs. YANKEES by Bill Nowlin and David Fischer (Sports Publishing, 2019)

BOSTON RED SOX IQ: HALL OF FAME EDITION (Black Mesa Books, 2018)

TED WILLIAMS – FIRST LATINO IN THE BASEBALL HALL OF FAME (Rounder Books, 2018)

TOM YAWKEY: PATRIARCH OF THE BOSTON RED SOX by Bill Nowlin (University of Nebraska Press, 2018)

SO YOU THINK YOU'RE A RED SOX FAN? by Bill Nowlin (Skyhorse, 2017)

THE BOSOX CLUB: 50 YEARS by Bill Nowlin (Rounder Books, 2017)

FROM THE BABE TO THE BEARDS by Bill Nowlin and Jim Prime (Skyhorse Publishing, 2014)

DON'T LET US WIN TONIGHT: AN ORAL HISTORY OF THE 2004 BOSTON RED SOX'S IMPOSSIBLE PAYOFF RUN by Allan Wood and Bill Nowlin (Triumph Books, 2014)

521: THE STORY OF TED WILLIAMS' HOME RUNS (Rounder Books, 2013)

FENWAY PARK DAY BY DAY: THE FIRST HUNDRED YEARS (Rounder Books, 2012)

FENWAY PARK AT 100: BASEBALL'S HOMETOWN by Bill Nowlin and Jim Prime (Skyhorse Publishing, 2012)

AMAZING TALES FROM THE RED SOX DUGOUT by Jim Prime and Bill Nowlin (Skyhorse Publishing, editions in 2012, 2017, and 2020)

FENWAY PARK TRIVIA (Rounder Books, 2012)

CURSE IN THE REARVIEW MIRROR (Black Mesa, 2011)

THE GREAT RED SOX SPRING TRAINING TOUR OF 1911: SIXTY-THREE GAMES, COAST TO COAST (McFarland & Co., 2010)

PUMPSIE & PROGRESS (Rounder Books, 2010)

RED SOX BY THE NUMBERS by Bill Nowlin and Matt Silverman (Skyhorse, 2010)

BOSTON RED SOX IQ: THE ULTIMATE TEST OF TRUE FANDOM (Black Mesa Books, 2009)

THE ULTIMATE RED SOX HOME RUN GUIDE by Bill Nowlin and David Vincent (Rounder Books, 2009)

RED SOX THREADS: ODDS AND ENDS FROM RED SOX HISTORY by Bill Nowlin (Rounder Books, 2008)

THE RED SOX WORLD SERIES ENCYCLOPEDIA (No Longer the World's Shortest Book) with Jim Prime (Rounder Books, 2008)

WHEN BASEBALL WENT TO WAR edited by Todd Anton and Bill Nowlin (Triumph Books, 2008)

TED WILLIAMS AT WAR by Bill Nowlin (Rounder Books, 2007)

LOVE THAT DIRTY WATER: The Standells and the Improbable Anthem of the Boston Red Sox by Chuck Burgess and Bill Nowlin (Rounder Books, 2007)

DAY BY DAY WITH THE BOSTON RED SOX by Bill Nowlin (Rounder Books, 2006)

THE 50 GREATEST RED SOX GAMES by Cecilia Tan and Bill Nowlin (John Wiley, 2006)

BLOOD FEUD: THE RED SOX, THE YANKEES, AND THE STRUGGLE OF GOOD VERSUS EVIL by Bill Nowlin and Jim Prime (Rounder Books, 2005)

THE KID: TED WILLIAMS IN SAN DIEGO edited by Bill Nowlin (Rounder Books, 2005)

MR. RED SOX: THE JOHNNY PESKY STORY by Bill Nowlin (Rounder Books, 2004)

FENWAY LIVES by Bill Nowlin (Rounder Books, 2004)

THE FENWAY PROJECT, edited by Bill Nowlin & Cecilia Tan (Rounder Books, 2004)

TED WILLIAMS: THE PURSUIT OF PERFECTION by Jim Prime and Bill Nowlin (Sports Publishing, 2002)

MORE TALES FROM THE RED SOX DUGOUT: YARNS FROM THE SOX by Jim Prime and Bill Nowlin (Sports Publishing, 2002)

TED WILLIAMS: A SPLENDID LIFE by Bill Nowlin and Jim Prime (Triumph Books, 2002)

TALES FROM THE RED SOX DUGOUT by Jim Prime with Bill Nowlin (Sports Publishing, Inc., 2000)

FENWAY SAVED with Mike Ross and Jim Prime (Sports Publishing, 1999)

TED WILLIAMS: A TRIBUTE by Jim Prime and Bill Nowlin (Masters Press, 1997)

THE EARLY DAYS OF BLUEGRASS (Rounder Books, 2019)

THE ROUNDER BOOK OF BLUEGRASS MUSIC TRIVIA (Rounder Books, 2016)

ALEXANDER BERKMAN, ANARCHIST – LIFE, WORK, IDEAS (Christie Books, 2014)

WOODY GUTHRIE, AMERICAN RADICAL PATRIOT (Rounder Books, 2013)

WHEN FOOTBALL WENT TO WAR by Todd Anton and Bill Nowlin (Triumph Books, 2013)

Bill is editor or co-editor of an additional 50 or so books.

Table of Contents

"THE KID"
BLASTS A WINNER

(With permission from the National Baseball Hall of Fame and Museum.)

Ted Williams on Hitting

"I said it 30 years ago and I steadfastly believe it today. In fact I've said it so often it could probably serve as my epitaph: Hitting a baseball is the single most difficult thing to do in sport."[1]

Williams's three golden rules of hitting were: *"(1) get a good ball to hit; (2) proper thinking at the plate; (3) be quick with the bat."*[2]

"It takes more than natural ability to excel as a hitter," he stressed. *"You've got to be smart. Hitting is 50% from the neck up, and knowing what's going on is 50% of the battle."*[3]

Introduction

There is no question that Ted Williams emphasized the mental part of the game. Fifty years after publication, his book *The Science of Hitting* remains something of a Bible for batters.

Based on what research we do not know, he wrote in *The Science of Hitting*, "I had a higher percentage of game-winning home runs than Babe Ruth."[4]

That was an intriguing assertion. Was it true? Winning a game, however one does it, is a good thing – for the winner. Ted Williams hit 521 home runs during his major-league career. How many of them were game-winning home runs? And how many did Babe Ruth have?

For that matter, what *is* a game-winning home run? Certainly, a home run hit in the bottom of the ninth inning that gives your team at least a one-run margin of victory is a game-winning homer. Likewise, a solo home run in the top of the first inning would be the game-winning home run if the game ends with the score 1-0. But there are many other possibilities that present themselves.

According to the definition I decided to use, the first game-winning homer Ted Williams hit was on May 4, 1939 in Detroit. It was in the 10th game of his career. He hit it in the top of the fifth inning. The 20-year-old rookie had already hit a two-run homer in the fourth. That one cut the Tigers' lead to 4-2. Now he was up again in the very next inning. Joe Cronin had just singled in two and tied the score. "The Kid" hit a three-run homer that drove in two other Hall of Famers – Jimmie Foxx and Cronin – and gave the Red Sox a 7-4 lead in the game. The final score was 7-5. Clearly, a game-winning homer.

How am I defining a "game-winning home run?"

A "game-winning home run" is defined as a home run that provides the final margin of victory in the game, at least one more run than the opposing team scored.

It is not my goal to create a new statistic here, but only to explore something that struck me as worth exploring.

What this is not intended to be is a rehash of a short-lived official statistic from a few decades ago known as the "game-winning RBIs." There was a statistic by that name which was introduced by the Elias Sports Bureau and used from 1980-1988 and then abandoned. It was defined in Rule 1004-a as "the <u>RBI</u> that gives a club the lead it never relinquishes."

It calculated things in a different way. That definition would say that Ted Williams provided the game-winning RBI in the game of September 23, 1939, when he hit a two-run home run in the third inning. That gave Boston a 2-0 lead. It was a lead they never lost. The Red Sox added seven more runs in the bottom of the fifth. But the final score was Boston 10, Philadelphia Athletics 8. Obviously, many more runs scored after the first two. His two-run homer gave the Red Sox a lead they never lost, but the hit that drove in the ninth Boston run – the run that ultimately made the difference between a win and a loss – was Bob Johnson's sacrifice fly in the seventh inning.

The "game-winning RBI stat" was criticized for not being sufficiently dramatic and not capturing clutch hitting. I'm not sure it was intended to do either, but it seemed to fall short on more than one basis. Two articles bearing on the 1980s stat appeared in the *New York Times*[5] and in Baseball Prospectus.[6]

I don't know what definition Ted Williams may have been using when he wrote his book.

Using my definition, I asked Tom Ruane of Retrosheet if he could provide a listing of Ted Williams homers that fit the bill. He could, and he did. The list is 110 home runs long.

Each one is written up in this book in capsule form. A lengthier version of each one has been written for SABR's Games Project and can be found, by date, on the SABR website here: https://sabr.org/gamesproject. Scroll down on the page and look under "Browse the Games Project." Looking first at the decade in question, you will be able to find the writeups. Most of them are ones that I wrote, but there are a few which others in SABR wrote up before I started on this book. All of the entries in this book were written by myself and specifically for this book.

Hopefully, reading through these games will prove enjoyable. Red Sox fans in particular may enjoy this book, given that every game here is, by definition, a Red Sox win. Reading of 110 Red Sox wins will, for many, be an enjoyable experience. Writing them was.

Ted Williams himself – despite being a player for the Red Sox in four decades (his career began in 1939 and ended in 1960) – never saw the Red Sox win the World Series. He was born in San Diego and was only 12 days old when the Red Sox won the 1918 World Series. He died in July 2002, 27 months before the end of the magical 2004 Red Sox season.

But he won a lot of games for the team. He won games in different ways – sometimes a single did the trick. Once it was on a bases-loaded walk. But there were 110 times that he won a game with a home run – a solo homer, a two-run shot, a three-run homer, or a grand slam. One of the solo homers was an inside-the-park home run, and that one clinched the American League pennant in 1946.

A higher percentage than Babe Ruth? Of Ted Williams's 521 home runs, 110 of them were game-winners. That translates to 21.11% – just over 20% of the homers he hit were game-winning homers. Using the definition I supplied, Tom Ruane also provided statistics comparable to Williams for the other 500 home run hitters. Herm Krabbenhoft calculated all of Ruth's home runs.

Yes, Ted Williams had a higher percentage than Babe Ruth. In fact, we see that only one player on the 500+ homer list topped Ted Williams – Eddie Murray – which is interesting because Murray always had the reputation of being a clutch hitter.

Digging more deeply and considering all who hit 400 or more home runs, we find two other players who reached the 20% threshold: Adrian Beltre (97/477 = 20.33%) and Willie Stargell (93/465) = 20.00%.

Of course, for a team to win a game, it takes more than one person hitting a home run. Even a grand slam in the bottom of the ninth doesn't itself win the game if your pitching has given the opposition more than a four-run lead. A solo home run might win a game that had been 3-3, but those earlier three runs had to have scored before your solo homer could make the difference. Naturally, playing on a mediocre team is not going to help put you in a position to win as many games in this fashion. The contributions of your teammates – pitching, defense, and offense – all are part of the picture.

Rank	First	Last	GW HR	Tot HR	Pct GW
1	Eddie	Murray	116	504	23.02%
2	Ted	Williams	110	521	21.11%
3	Reggie	Jackson	118	563	20.96%
4	Mickey	Mantle	112	536	20.90%
5	Albert	Pujols*	141	679	20.77%
6	Gary	Sheffield	103	509	20.24%
7	Willie	McCovey	105	521	20.15%
8	Mike	Schmidt	109	543	20.07%
9	Henry	Aaron	151	755	20.00%
10	Jim	Thome	121	612	19.77%
11	Mel	Ott	101	511	19.77%
12	Harmon	Killebrew	112	573	19.55%
13	Willie	Mays	124	660	18.79%
14	Eddie	Mathews	94	512	18.36%
15	Frank	Robinson	106	586	18.09%
16	Manny	Ramirez	100	555	18.02%
17	Babe	Ruth	126	714	17.65%
18	David	Ortiz	94	541	17.38%
19	Jimmie	Foxx	92	534	17.23%
20	Sammy	Sosa	101	609	16.58%
21	Ernie	Banks	83	512	16.21%
22	Barry	Bonds	122	762	16.01%
23	Mark	McGwire	92	583	15.78%
24	Ken	Griffey, Jr	99	630	15.71%
25	Rafael	Palmeiro	85	569	14.94%
26	Alex	Rodriguez	98	696	14.08%

*Includes 2021 season. Between the Dodgers and Angels, Pujols hit 17 home runs in 2021, but none was a game-winner.

1939

Preseason

The first game-winning home run that Ted Williams hit in a Red Sox uniform came on his very first at-bat in New England. It was a first-inning grand slam hit in Worcester, Massachusetts during a preseason exhibition game at Fitton Field, the Red Sox playing against the Holy Cross Crusaders baseball team on April 14, 1939.

On base were Jimmie Foxx, Joe Cronin, and Jim Tabor. Bobby Doerr was on deck. "The Kid" faced Holy Cross pitcher Mike Klarnick.

Williams homered, and it was "no towering, wind-blown fly. On the contrary, Ted's thump ... sailed over the head of Hank Ouelette, playing a deep center field, and carried to the reaches of the football gridiron."[i] It was, wrote the *Worcester Gazette*, "one of the longest seen at Fitton Field."[ii]

The final score was 14-2, Red Sox. The grand slam was the game-winning hit. Williams drove in another run later in the game.

---

i   J. Earl Chevalier, "Red Sox Beat Holy Cross, 14-2, in Exhibition," *Springfield* (Massachusetts) *Republican*, April 15, 1939: 9.

ii "Circuit Blow by Williams Routs Purple," *Worcester Evening Gazette*, April 15, 1939: 8.

Despite Williams being full of confidence, his head-down home run trot was the picture of modesty. (Leslie Jones photograph, Boston .Public Library)

1939

Rookie Explodes on the Scene

Since winning the World Series back in 1918, the Red Sox had spent 15 years never getting higher in the standings than fifth place. After they had begun to rebuild under new owner Tom Yawkey, and a couple of fourth-place finishes in 1934 and 1935, they reached second place in 1938. Things were looking up. The 1939 season was Ted Williams's rookie year and he arrived at Spring Training a highly touted and brash 20-year-old kid from San Diego. The year before, he had won the Triple Crown with the Minneapolis Millers in the American Association, batting .366 with 43 homers and 114 RBIs.

Could he live up to the press hype in Boston? He certainly could. Williams put up one of the best freshman seasons of all time, setting a set a rookie for RBIs in a season that still stands. Joe Cronin (107) and Jimmie Foxx (105) both drove in over 100 as well, and "The Kid" hit 31 homers (8 game-winners). Boston won 89 games, but they still finished a distant second, 17 games behind the Yankees, who completed the year with their fourth consecutive championship.

Red Sox 7
Detroit Tigers 6

May 4, 1939 — Briggs Stadium, Detroit

Boston Red Sox rookie Ted Williams was 20 years old when he first played in a game at Detroit's Briggs Stadium. It quickly became his favorite ballpark in which to hit.

Williams — "The Kid" — had won the Triple Crown in the American Association in 1938, with 43 home runs among his contributions to the Minneapolis Millers. Williams batted left-handed and was a pull hitter. The overwhelming number of home runs he hit went to right field, or right-center.

Over his first eight games in the major leagues, the only home run he had hit was on April 23, his fourth game, off Bud Thomas of the Philadelphia Athletics at Fenway Park. It was a two-run homer in the first inning of a game the Red Sox lost, 12-8.

Williams faced right-hander Roxie Lawson in the 10th game of his career. Lawson was pitching in his eighth year in the big leagues and had more than 600 innings of experience under his belt.

His first time up, in the first inning, Williams hit one out of Briggs Stadium — up and over the right-field roof, but "foul by inches."[7] He then lined out to center.

Hitting a ball over the right-field roof was quite a feat in itself, even if foul. It was 325 feet to right field and 440 feet to straightaway center, with right-center listed at 375 feet. And the rooftop was more than 100 feet above field level.[8]

On a 3-and-2 count in the fourth inning, with Boston player-manager Joe Cronin on base, Ted's "towering smash landed atop the right-field roof, nearer center field than right, and bounded back into the playing field only because the eaves of the roof slant downward in that sector. As the crow flies, that belt was good for 360 feet without even figuring altitude."[9] The *Boston*

Herald agreed: The ball had "landed on top of the 120-foot-high third and last deck of the grandstand in right-center, above a spot on the field 360 feet from home."[10] In perspective, 120 feet is about triple the height of Fenway Park's "Green Monster."

Ted Williams Scores Five
Runs With Two Homers

It was a dramatic drive, a two-run homer that halved the Tigers' lead to 4-2.

Ted came up again in the fifth inning. Lawson had walked Doc Cramer, given up a single to Joe Vosmik, and walked Jimmie Foxx. Cronin hit a bases-loaded single to score two runs and tie the game. Bob Harris was brought in to relieve. He had only 15-2/3 innings of major-league experience, but had been with Toledo in the American Association in 1938 and certainly knew about Ted Williams. The righty, who had turned 24 just three days earlier, pitched around Williams, and the count went to 3-and-0.

Harris likely had seen "Titanic Ted's" first two drives out of the park, one foul and one fair. Tigers catcher Rudy York certainly saw them. Harris, on in relief with the score 4-4, had to worry about Foxx and Cronin on base. Williams recounted the story to reporters after the game: "When the count was three and oh, I got the sign from Joe to take a shot at the next one, cripple though it was. [Detroit catcher Rudy] York was kidding me all along. Now he says, 'Three and nothing, kid. What are you going to do? Hit?' and I answered him that I always told the truth and that I was going to hit the next pitch. He didn't believe it, called for the fast one, it was in there and I hit it."[11]

This one hadn't landed on the roof; it went clear out of the park. The *Globe* described it: "It was a climbing liner — as much a liner as a drive could be which cleared a 120-foot barrier, straight as a string, over the whole works in right field, about a dozen feet fair. According to eye-witnesses outside the park, it landed across adjoining Trumbull Ave. and bounded against a taxi company garage on the other side on the first hop."[12]

"So you weren't kidding, after all?" said York as Williams crossed home plate.[13]

At 120 feet, the Briggs Stadium upper deck was the "tallest barrier in either league to clear and one that the game's greatest sluggers from Babe Ruth down had tried and never accomplished."[14] Detroit writers called it the longest homer ever hit at the stadium.

The three-run homer gave the Red Sox a 7-4 lead. Detroit scored one run in the fifth and one in the seventh. The final was 7-6 Boston, and Ted Williams had the first game-winning home run of his career, to be followed by 109 more.

It was reportedly 17 years before another batter hit one out of Detroit's ballpark. That batter was Mickey Mantle.

Williams hit 521 homers, 248 of them at Fenway Park. Of the 273 he hit on the road, more than 20 percent were hit in Detroit. The 55 home runs he hit at Briggs Stadium far outpaced the 35 he hit at Shibe Park and the 35 he hit at Cleveland Stadium. Only one visiting player hit more; Babe Ruth hit 60 home runs in Detroit. It's no wonder Ted called Detroit his favorite park in which to hit. One wonders how many homers he would have hit had he been a Tiger his whole career.[15]

Boston Red Sox 10
St. Louis Browns 8
(10 innings)

May 9, 1939 — Sportsman's Park, St. Louis

Williams's first game-winner in extra innings came five days later in St. Louis.

The early-season Tuesday afternoon game drew only 1,589 – or 2,134 per the *St. Louis Globe-Democrat*.[16] Jack Kramer was starting pitcher for the St. Louis Browns, only the fourth start of what became a 12-year major-league career for Kramer; he was 2-0 coming into the game.

Williams Homer in 10th With Two on Gives Sox 10-8 Win Over Browns

Kramer gave up one run in the first inning and one run in the second. Shockingly, Ted Williams struck out both in the first inning and again in the second, with the bases loaded both times.

Kramer continued to struggle in the third inning, and the Red Sox scored two more runs. Harry Kimberlin relieved Kramer.

On four base hits and a sacrifice fly, with an error mixed in, the Browns got three runs back in their half of the third off Boston's Jim Bagby Jr.

Neither side scored in the fourth or fifth.

The Red Sox extended their lead to 7-3 in the top of the sixth when Jimmie Foxx hit a three-run 450-foot homer "into the distant center-field bleachers."[17]

In the bottom of the seventh, the Browns scored twice. Harlond Clift singled and Beau Bell homered. It was 7-5, Red Sox.

St. Louis rallied for two more runs in the bottom of the eighth, thanks to a couple of pinch-hitters. Former Red Sox outfielder Mel Almada singled off Bagby's heel. Billy Sullivan pinch-hit for the pitcher, swung at the first pitch, and homered onto the roof of the right-field pavilion.[18] The game was tied, 7-7.

In the top of the 10th, Joe Vosmik singled to right field.[19] So did Foxx, who was held to a single on a ball hit off the right-field screen. Cronin struck out and was so angry with himself that, as Gerry Moore noted in his game story, he nearly threw the bat into the dugout.

Williams batted with two on and one out. He had been slumping. After his game-winning home run he'd hit on May 4, he'd gone 1-for-15. Williams's swing was on target. He homered off reliever Ed Cole, a three-run blow. On a full count, Williams "caught an inside pitch and lined it onto the chummy rightfield roof. It barely cleared the screen."[20] It was 10-7, Red Sox.

Needing three outs to close out the win, Heving got one, but then gave up a single and a double. Suddenly, St. Louis had something going, and one run scored on an infield out. Two relievers, one after the other, were pressed into duty. The third Red Sox pitcher of the inning walked the first man he faced. Two on, two out, a two-run lead. Clift hit a "towering smash" to left-center field.

"With one last effort the speeding Joe [Vosmik] stuck out his glove while still going full tilt. Somehow it landed and stuck in there and the near distraught Cronin threw away his cap and raced out into left field to hug Vosmik."[21]

The Browns had amassed 17 base hits, but got only two bases on balls. The trio of Thompson, Heffner, and Bell accounted for 10 of the 17 hits. Bell had three RBIs. Foxx and Williams each had three RBIs, all on home runs. Each team left 12 men on base.

In the end, the 10th-inning Ted Williams homer and the former Brownie Vosmik's catch resulted in a 10-8 win for the Red Sox.

Boston Red Sox 7
New York Yankees 3

July 2, 1939 — Fenway Park, Boston
(first game of a doubleheader)

This game's win was secured by Ted Williams's first game-winning home run off a future Hall of Famer.[22]

New York's Lefty Gomez (four 20-win seasons to his credit) opposed Lefty Grove, with eight 20-win seasons. The first-place Yankees were 12½ games ahead of second-place Boston.[23]

The Yankees scored first, and Grove lost his batterymate in the first inning due to a collision at home plate. Gene Desautels was "knocked cold and forced to retire for the rest of the day."[24] Johnny Peacock took his place. The injury was the first of seven for both teams in the doubleheader.[25] Adding a second run in the fourth, New York led until Jimmie Foxx walked to lead off the bottom of Boston's fourth. Williams flied out to left field, but Joe Cronin hit a two-run homer high into the net above the left-field wall that tied the game, 2-2. Each side scored one run in the sixth.

Grove led off the bottom of the seventh and Gomez struck him out. Tom Carey singled but was forced at second on Cramer's grounder to shortstop. Foxx walked to put two on with two outs.

This set the stage for Ted Williams. Gomez got two strikes on him, but then "The Kid" hit a three-run home run to deep right field. The ball carried into the right-field bleachers, "a drive that went with a favoring wind, just clearing the fence as Henrich backed into the wall."[26] Henrich dropped as he crashed and had to be assisted off the field. "Blood trickled from a cut on the right side of his head."[27]

The Red Sox added an insurance run in the bottom of the eighth. Joe Vosmik walked and was sacrificed to second by Jim Tabor. Peacock atoned in some measure for a pair of errors earlier, singling in Vosmik.

The 7-3 score held as Grove set down the side in the ninth, the final batter being a pitcher (Red Ruffing) pinch-hitting for Gomez. Ruffing struck out.[28]

It wasn't yet the Fourth of July, but young Williams already had 61 runs batted in. He set a rookie record in 1939, never matched before or since, by driving in 145 runs. [Note: see the section at the end of this section entitled "How many RBIs did Ted Williams have in 1939?"]

The Yankees won the second game, 9-3. Williams was 0-for-2 and walked twice. He walked 107 times in 1939.

The two games together took as long to play as some single games take in the second decade of the twenty-first century: 1:53 and 2:00. In 2019 the average Red Sox-Yankees game lasted 3:24.[29]

Boston Red Sox 9
Cleveland Indians 5

July 15, 1939 — Cleveland Stadium

The Red Sox were riding a nine-game winning streak.

Cleveland starter Willis Hudlin got bombed for five runs in the top of the first inning. With one out and runners on second and third, Williams was walked intentionally.[30] Hudlin then walked shortstop/manager Joe Cronin for the first run. A second scored on a groundout. Jim Tabor drove in two more with a single and Boston pitcher Fritz Ostermueller singled in another.

The Indians picked up three in the third on a bases-clearing double by Moose Solters, the third run on an error by right-fielder Williams who "wasted so much time looking for the handle that all three runners scored."[31] He did get an outfield assist, finally getting ahold of the ball and throwing out Solters who had tried to reach third base.

For the second game in a row, the Red Sox had taken a 5-0 lead but then lost it. The Indians tied it up in the bottom of the fifth on a double and an RBI single. Reliever Emerson Dickman replaced Ostermueller. Two more singles followed.

Still tied, 5-5, in the top of the eighth, Jimmie Foxx grounded out. Ted Williams blasted Johnny Broaca's first pitch for "a vicious clout into the far-off right-field stands"[32] which gave Boston the lead and proved sufficient for the ultimate 9-5 win. The *Cleveland Plain Dealer* said it landed about six rows into the stands, not far from the foul pole. The *Boston Herald* agreed, to the row, describing "Ted the Terror" slamming the ball and rejuvenating the Red Sox.[33] It was 6-5, but the next two batters combined to produce one more run. Joe Cronin singled to left, getting to second base on an error by Solters. Joe Vosmik singled over second base and into center, which drove in Cronin.

The Red Sox added two more in the top of the ninth. With one out, Bobby Doerr singled to left field. Doc Cramer hit a triple to right-center. Foxx hit a sacrifice fly nearly to the warning track in center field and Cramer tagged and scored to make it 9-5. Williams grounded out to first base unassisted. Foxx's drive would have been a home run in many parks; it was caught 20 feet in front of Cleveland Stadium's center-field barrier which stood some 470 feet from home plate.

Bruce Campbell pinch-hit for Allen, but grounded out to second base. Rollie Hemsley got his fifth hit, a single to left-center. Weatherly tried to bunt for a base hit, but popped up to the pitcher. Chapman grounded into a force play, Doerr to Cronin covering second base.

With 4 2/3 innings of relief work, allowing four scattered hits and no runs, Dickman earned a well-deserved win, improving his record to 4-1 with his third win in eight days.

The outcome gave the Red Sox their 10th win in a row; they won their next two games, too, sweeping the July 16 doubleheader in Detroit, 9-2 and 3-0.

Boston Red Sox 8
Washington Senators 6

August 19, 1939 — Griffith Stadium, Washington
(first game of a doubleheader)

Ted Williams's first grand slam won this game for the Red Sox. The pitchers for the first game were two rookies: right-hander Joe Haynes for the Senators and Lefty Lefebvre (as one might intuit, a left-hander) for the Red Sox.

Neither team scored in the first three innings. Jimmie Foxx, Boston's first baseman, hit a solo homer "high into the centerfield bleachers" to kick off the fourth.[34]

The Senators took a 2-1 lead in the bottom of the fifth on a single, a force out, and three more singles, the third by Johnny Welaj, driving in two runs. The Senators added another run in the sixth and a leadoff double and Johnny Bloodworth's single.

Boston tied it up in the top of the seventh. Third baseman Jim Tabor drew a base on balls. With one out, Lou Finney pinch-hit for Lefebvre and doubled down the right-field line, driving in Tabor and cutting Washington's lead to 3-2. Bobby Doerr stepped in. On back-to-back wild pitches, Finney took third and then scored.

Joe Heving relieved for Boston. He retired the side in the seventh but after a double and walk in the bottom of the eighth, it was his turn for a wild pitch. Both runners advanced and he intentionally walked Bloodworth. Another pinch-hitter came through, this time for the Senators. Taft Wright pinch-hit for Vernon and doubled down the right-field line, scoring two runners.

Three outs from defeat, the Red Sox came to bat in the top of the ninth. Tabor singled to center and Peacock singled to right. Pete Appleton relieved Haynes. Heving bunted too hard and the lead runner was thrown out at third. Doerr surprised the Senators by laying down a bunt on the third-base line for a single. The bases were loaded.

Doc Cramer hit a fly ball to center field, but it wasn't deep enough for Peacock to tag and score. The Red Sox were down to their last out.

Jimmie Foxx walked, forcing in a run to narrow the Senators' lead to 5-4.

Williams came up. In his first four plate appearances, the rookie phenom had fouled out to first base, flied out to center, singled to right field, and grounded out to first base.

Williams was still a little more than a week from turning 21 years old.[35]

WILLIAMS HOMER GIVES SOX SPLIT

Ted's Grand Slam in Ninth
With 2 Out Nips Nats, 8-6

The first pitch was an outside fastball. "The Kid" pounced on Appleton's second pitch – a slow curve – and hit a grand slam over Griffith Stadium's 35-foot-high right-field wall, clearing it by several yards. The wall was about 350 feet from the plate, cleared by what Shirley Povich of the *Washington Post* called "an enormous clout."[36] Right fielder George Case didn't even bother to turn around.[37] The *Boston Globe*'s sportswriter said the ball landed "in a lone tree whose top is just visible above the fence."[38] Boston had rallied to an 8-5 lead, which they held.

Williams's first career grand slam got him into triple digits in RBIs for the season. He went on to hit 17 grand slams as a major leaguer, but few were more instrumental to a Red Sox win than his first – when one swing transformed defeat into victory on a Saturday afternoon in Washington, DC, in 1939.

Boston Red Sox 6
Cleveland Indians 5

August 28, 1939 — League Park, Cleveland

Of the eight game-winning homers Ted Williams hit in his rookie year, three of them were hit in Cleveland, all in a 45-day span. He'd homered on July 15 at the larger-capacity Cleveland Stadium, then this Monday afternoon one at League Park and another the very next day.

Mel Harder had won his last six decisions for the Indians. He faced submarining Elden Auker.

In the third inning, the Red Sox scored first. Third baseman Jim Tabor led off with a triple. Harder struck out Auker, but Doc Cramer singled to left field.

Harder drew a one-out walk in the bottom of the third. Shortstop Lou Boudreau doubled to right field. Indians right fielder Bruce Campbell singled to left and both runners scored, giving Cleveland a 2-1 lead.

The Indians added one in the bottom of the sixth, on a one-out triple to left by first baseman Jeff Heath who tripled to left field and an infield grounder from Ken Keltner. On a close play at the plate, Heath was ruled safe and it was 3-1.

Ted Williams led off the top of the seventh with a broken-bat single to left field. Joe Cronin singled and Williams went first to third. Lou Finney pinch-hit for catcher Gene Desautels and came through with a single, scoring Williams.

The score stood 3-2, Indians, but not for long. The Tribe added two more runs in the bottom of the seventh. Moe Berg took over catching duties for the Red Sox. Auker walked Ben Chapman and Hal Trosky hit a two-run homer over the right-center-field wall, giving the Indians a 5-2 edge.

With one out in the top of the eighth, Doc Cramer doubled off the right-field wall. Joe Vosmik walked. Jimmie Foxx knocked in Cramer with a single to center. On a 3-1 count, Williams swung hard and missed Harder's curveball by a foot. He hit the next pitch over League Park's "chummy right-field screen...a long high fly that scaled the close barrier in right with plenty to spare."[39] Suddenly, it was 6-5, Red Sox. It was Williams's 20th home run. His 110 runs batted in led the American League.

It was still a one-run game. Campbell hit a ball to the center-field wall, hauled in by Cramer. After Dickman allowed back-to-back one-out singles to both Chapman and Trosky, the Indians had runners on first and third with just the one out. Cronin called on Jack Wilson to relieve Dickman. On a 3-0 count, Heath fouled out to Berg. Keltner walked and that loaded the bases. The tying run was at third, the go-ahead run at second, but there were two outs. On a 2-2 count, pinch-hitter Odell Hale popped up to second baseman Doerr in short right field.

The next day's *Boston Globe* quoted Joe Cronin as saying, "The Kid has lived up to his advance notice. I guess that's so even if he doesn't drive in another run for the rest of the year."[40] After readers of the August 29 *Globe* put down their morning paper, Williams did drive in another run – five of them – that very day.

Boston Red Sox 7
Cleveland Indians 4

August 29, 1939 — League Park, Cleveland

Another grand slam, and Ted Williams had a game-winner for the second day in a row.

Even fewer spectators turned out for the Tuesday afternoon game on August 29 – some 1,500. The starting pitchers were Lefty Lefebvre for the Red Sox, in just his third career appearance and his second of 1939, and Harry Eisenstat for the Indians.

The game was scoreless through the first four innings.

Joe Cronin doubled to lead off the fifth. Jim Tabor flied out deep to right; Cronin tagged and took third. Desautels singled to Boudreau at short; Cronin prudently remained at third. Lefebvre walked to load the bases.

Cramer grounded out to third baseman Ken Keltner for the second out of the inning, the throw going to first base as Cronin scored. Vosmik walked, again loading the bases.

Jimmie Foxx grounded to Boudreau, who misplayed the ball and was assessed an error. Desautels scored an unearned run for a 2-0 Red Sox lead. The bases remained loaded.

That brought up Ted Williams. On a 2-and-1 count, the "smiling stringbean rookie sensation" hit a grand slam that "traveled at least 400 feet over the right-center field wall."[41] Sportswriter Eugene J. Whitney of Cleveland's *Plain Dealer* explained that the ball "ricocheted off electric light wires on the south side of Lexington Avenue and bounced into a parking lot."[42]

Suddenly, it was 6-0, Red Sox.

The Indians got one off Lefebvre in the bottom of the fifth on a one-out walk, a two-out single, and then another single by Jeff Heath.

Williams Lashes Homer With Bases Full to Beat Tribe Again

Williams came up again with the bases loaded in the sixth. This time, he drew a walk.

Lefebvre may have run out of steam. The first three Indians singled in the bottom of the eighth, the third one producing a run. Joe Heving relieved Lefebvre. The runners moved up on a wild pitch, and a run scored on a sacrifice fly by "Bad News" Hale. Bruce Campbell tripled and it was 7-4, but that was all they got.

Heving retired the Indians in order in the bottom of the ninth.

Lefebvre got the win, his first major-league decision.[43]

On this day in Cleveland, Ted Williams added five more RBIs to the three he had had the day before, for a total of 115. By season's end, he had an official 145 RBIs, the first time a rookie had led the majors in runs batted in.

This all happened the day before Williams's 21st birthday – but no one in baseball knew it. He had declared his birthday to be October 30, so that it would not come up during the baseball season and become a distraction. He confessed this to sportswriter Harold Kaese of the *Boston Globe*: "I didn't want to celebrate my birthday during the playing season."[44] Baseball cards were among those sources that perpetuated the October 30 date; it was not until 1956 that a card – from Topps – reflected the August 30 date, the one that is on his military records.[45]

Boston Red Sox 10
Philadelphia Athletics 7

September 10, 1939 — Shibe Park, Philadelphia
(first game of a doubleheader)

The 1939 Boston Red Sox were in second place but 17½ games behind the Yankees, with the White Sox just 1½ games behind them. Boston had lost seven games in a row. The hosting Athletics were in seventh. Manager Connie Mack started Bill Beckmann. Joe Cronin started Broadway Charlie Wagner.

Both pitchers gave up two-run homers in the first inning. After Ted Williams singled to left, Joe Cronin followed with a homer "into the left-field stands."[46]

A's right fielder Wally Moses singled off Wagner, also to left, and third baseman Joe Gantenbein homered over the right-field fence. The 2-2 score held through four, though it was notable that Ted Williams tripled, again to left, in the third.

The Red Sox broke out with four runs in the top of the fifth. Lou Finney singled, stole second, and scored on Doc Cramer's double off the center-field scoreboard. Ted Williams walked. Cronin singled, scoring Cramer for a 4-2 lead, while Williams took second base. Left fielder Joe Vosmik sacrificed, advancing both runners. That promptly paid off as Tabor singled to left field and drove them both in.

Philadelphia's new pitcher, Chubby Dean, retired the Sox in the sixth.

The Indians got one in the sixth, and one in the seventh, both on sacrifice flies. In the sixth, Gantenbein doubled, advanced on a grounder, and scored on Frankie Hayes' sac fly. In the seventh, Gantenbein was the one who hit the sacrifice fly, scoring Dario Lodigiani, who had walked and then moved up on Dean's infield single and on a groundout.

The Red Sox broke the game open in the top of the ninth. Finney reached on an error by Dick Siebert at first base. With two outs, Williams hit a two-run homer "far over the right field barrier," pushing the Red Sox lead to 8-4.[47] Cronin followed with a double. The next two Red Sox batters walked, loading the bases. Doerr came through with a two-run single to center field for a 10-4 advantage.

The Athletics weren't done yet, but the six-run deficit loomed large. Bob Johnson, who had gone out to play left field after pinch-hitting in the sixth, homered to left field. Pinch-hitter Dee Miles singled. So did Dean, still in the game. Miles scored on a groundout.

Gantenbein doubled down the right-field foul line and Dean scored with ease. But Dickman got the next two batters to fly out and the game was over, a 10-7 Red Sox victory.

With the Williams home run producing Boston's seventh and eighth runs, he had the game-winning base hit. It was the 25th home run of the young rookie's career.

Even with 17 runs scored, it only took one minute over two hours to complete the game.

How many RBIs did Ted Williams have in 1939?

As of this writing in October 2021, Ted Williams is credited with 145 runs batted in for the year 1939. It's particularly notable because, as mentioned above, it's an all-time rookie record for RBIs. The 145 is listed that way in all the record books, and in Ted Williams summary pages on both Retrosheet.org and Baseball-Reference.com. See:

https://www.baseball-reference.com/players/w/willite01.shtml

https://www.retrosheet.org/boxesetc/W/Pwillt103.htm

But if one looks at the game logs, on both sites, the total shows as 144. See:

https://www.baseball-reference.com/players/gl.fcgi?id=willite01&t=b&year=1939

https://www.retrosheet.org/boxesetc/1939/Iwillt1030011939.htm

If he had "only" 144 RBIs, he would still hold the rookie record, but he would share it with teammate Walt Dropo, a rookie with the 1950 Red Sox.

Why the difference? Looking at the play-by-play for the game of August 18, 1939 in Washington, I am told that the official totals have Cronin with one RBI and Williams with one. But it's hard to figure out where the Williams RBI comes from. He was 0-for-3 in the game, with two walks. There was an intentional walk in the first inning, He was the second batter up in the fourth and the sixth and made outs both times. There was no runner on base in the fourth. In the sixth, Jimmie Foxx was on second base with nobody out, but he scored on Joe Cronin's single after Williams made the out. In the seventh, he grounded out, for the final out of the inning. He was the third batter up in the ninth and walked, loading the bases. The batter that followed him was Cronin, who walked, thus picking up a second run batted in.

Four newspapers agree Cronin had 2 and Williams had 0 – see the game accounts in the *Boston Globe, Boston Herald, Evening Star* of Washington, and *Washington Post*.

Why would these two databases present what appears to be internally conflicting information? They have no control over what are deemed to be "official" records. Those, they simply report. Dedicated volunteers for Retrosheet have assembled the game logs, based on whatever evidence they have available – daily records from official scorers, but also newspaper accounts.

Even though the "official" record is 145, it does appear that the correct figure should be 144.

A jubilant Williams crosses home after a 1939 home run against the Yankees. (Leslie Jones photograph, Boston Public Library)

1940

What's a "Sophomore Slump?"

In his sophomore season, Ted Williams showed 1939 was no fluke. A student of the game and opposing pitchers from day 1, he was getting to know the opposition better and how to improve his game. The Red Sox moved him from right field to left field, where he remained the rest of his career. Williams bumped up his batting average from .327 to .344 and got on base a league-leading 44.2% of the times he came to the plate.

His 23 HR and 113 RBIs were both second on the team to Jimmie Foxx (36 and 119)—in fact Boston had four 100-RBI batters that year—but mediocre pitching held them back, as it so often did. The Red Sox end up tied for fourth in the AL with an 82-72 record, eight games behind the Tigers.

Only two of Williams's home runs were game-winners, the fewest of any full season of his career, but he got on base and he led both leagues in runs scored with 134. He was named an All-Star for the first time.

Boston Red Sox 4
Chicago White Sox 3
(12 innings)

June 16, 1940 — Comiskey Park, Chicago
(first game of a doubleheader)

Ted Williams greatly respected future Hall of Fame White Sox pitcher Ted Lyons. He cited him as one of the least predictable pitchers he had faced, "moving the ball all the time, giving you something here, then a curve there, then a little extra on the fastball, moving the ball all the time. Much tougher to guess with. A guy like Lyons would fool you because you'd have him figured and he'd come right back and cross you up. Ninth inning, wind blowing out, you have just hit his fastball the last time up, you know he can't throw a fast ball now, and sure enough he'd throw it and then come right back and throw it again. Lyons was that exception they told me about when I first came up: Don't guess with this guy. Hit what you see. It was fun for a young hitter to face a guy like Lyons. I often wish I could do it all over again."[48]

Ted Lyons pitched all 12 innings against the visiting Red Sox in the first game of a Sunday doubleheader at Comiskey Park. Boston manager Joe Cronin started his own future Hall of Famer – Lefty Grove.

Neither team scored until the bottom of the fifth when Chicago shortstop Luke Appling singled and left fielder Moose Solters followed with a home run to the stands in right-center field. The ChiSox added a run in the seventh. Taft Wright led off with a triple to left-center. Appling hit a sacrifice fly to right.

Lyons had given up just one base hit in the game, a scratch single back in the first inning. In the top of the eighth, Ted Williams tripled – not something he did often. He hit 14 triples in 1940, but never reached double digits again. Joe Cronin followed with a single to center.

The Red Sox tied the game in the top of the ninth. Doc Cramer walked. With two outs, Williams reached on a throwing error by the second baseman and was able to get to second base. Cronin singled and scored them both.

Ted Williams' Long Blow Wins Opener In 12th

Jim Bagby Jr. had replaced Grove, but Lyons kept on pitching. Neither team scored in the 10th or 11th, though Chicago managed the rare feat of combining two doubles with two walks and still coming up empty.

Leading off the 12th, Williams hit a home run, "a terrific drive into the upper right-field stands."[49]

Bagby induced an infield fly and two foul popups and the game was over.

It was a two-triple day for Ted. He hit another in the second game of the Sunday doubleheader, and hit a double, too. The Red Sox won the second game, 14-5.

Boston Red Sox 9
Washington Senators 4

July 5, 1940 — Griffith Stadium, Washington

This wasn't a well-played game. Shirley Povich of the *Washington Post* started his story saying that the Senators simply "had out-disgraced the Red Sox."[50] The Senators had 12 base hits (10 of them singles) to 14 by the Red Sox. Travis had three of the 12, two singles and a double. They left 11 men on base. Eight of Boston's 14 hits were for extra bases. Both Williams and Foxx had a double and a home run. The game-winning hit was Williams's fifth-inning home run.

Facing Willis Hudlin, the Red Sox took an early 3-0 lead in the top of the second. Right fielder Lou Finney singled to center field. With one out, he took second on a wild pitch. Joe Cronin walked. Cronin walked and catcher Gene Desautels singled, driving in Finney. Pitcher Jim Bagby helped with the bat; he singled and drove in Cronin from second base. Desautels scored the third run on a sacrifice fly by second baseman Bobby Doerr.

In the top of the third, Jimmie Foxx hit a home run "into the distant left-field bleachers" to lead off for Boston, his 20th homer of the 1940 season.[51] Ted Williams doubled – but was picked off second. It was 4-0, Red Sox.

The Senators scored once in the bottom of the third. Neither team scored in the fourth inning.

Bosox Batter
Washington, 9-4

Williams and Foxx
Hit for Circuit

With one out in the top of the fifth, Foxx doubled off the left-field wall. This brought up Ted Williams, who had that third-inning double to his credit but he had also committed the first-inning fielding error and had been picked off second base. Reliever Walt Masterson fooled him on one pitch, fooling him so badly that Williams swung hard but completely missed it by "a mile and the bat slipped out of his hands, sailing clear out into right field for a new intercollegiate record for bat throwing."[52] No doubt angry with himself, Williams got a firmer grip on the bat and connected with the next pitch. He "bashed his 11th homer over the garden wall in right," driving in the fifth and sixth runs for the Red Sox.[53] It was, wrote the Washington *Evening Star*, a "handle" hit. The paper said, "Had he caught it cleanly there's no telling where it would have gone."[54]

Finney singled. Tabor doubled to left field, Finney scoring from first. Cronin singled – also to left – and Tabor scored.

Meanwhile, the Senators got two runs back in the bottom of the fifth and after Boston scored once in the seventh on a leadoff triple by Jim Tabor and a single by Cronin, Washington added another in the eighth, a solo home run over the right-field wall by Jake Early.

POSTSCRIPT

It's not clear what pitch Masterson threw on the one which fooled Williams so badly, or the one he threw next. Williams was thinking of subsequent at-bats, perhaps following a strikeout or a weak foul popup, when he wrote, "Nothing pleased me more than to get a second chance at a pitcher who got me out on something he thought had fooled me. I couldn't *wait* to get up again, because I knew he would throw it again."[55]

One of Williams's most quoted statements from *The Science of Hitting* was: "Hitting is 50 per cent from the neck up." He was biased, of course. Pitchers were the enemy, in a sense. "I don't say pitchers lack intelligence, but I do say most of them aren't smart about the game." The reason, he thought, that it was sometimes not so difficult to out-guess a pitcher was that starters only worked every four or five days. They had "long activity lulls." Times have changed. With all the money involved, more than 60 years after

Williams played, and with all the tools available – for instance, video and computerized analytics – it is perhaps less likely he would find pitchers as lacking in determination and information as might once have been the case.

1941

.406 and Much, Much More

This was the year Williams hit .406. Eighty years later, no other batter has played in 100 or more games and hit .400. Feared at the plate, he was walked 147 times and recorded a phenomenal .553 on-base percentage, which remains an American League record. He was only struck out 27 times in over 600 plate appearances. His .735 slugging percentage was almost 100 points higher than second-place Joe DiMaggio (.643), and overshadowed Foxx's .505. He combined an amazing ability to get on base with a league-leading 37 homers. Only three other American Leaguers hit 30 or more—all of whom were on the Yankees.

The Red Sox climbed back to second place in the American League standings, but were a full 17 games behind the first-place Yankees, who allowed nearly a run less per game than did the Bosox.

Williams hit eight game-winning homers, five of them at Fenway Park. Six of the game-winners were in the books by June 17, at which time he was batting .424.

The end of another home run trot. (Leslie Jones photograph, Boston Public Library)

Boston Red Sox 4
Chicago White Sox 3
(11 innings)

May 7, 1941 — Comiskey Park, Chicago

It took two Ted Williams homers for The Kid to win this game. They were widely separated, the first one coming in the top of the third inning and the second one not until the 11th.

Williams had started the season pinch-hitting in six of his first seven games. He'd played four games in left field and then three in right; he was back in left field for this game.

The pitchers were John Rigney for the White Sox and Charlie Wagner for the Red Sox.

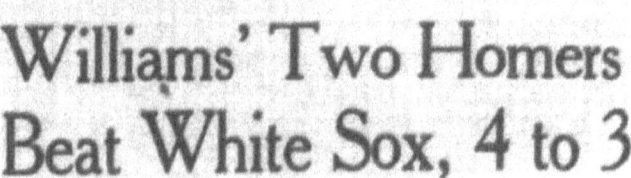

Williams' Two Homers
Beat White Sox, 4 to 3

Williams drove in the first run of the game, a first-inning single to right after Stan Spence's double to center field. In the third, Dom DiMaggio singled to center and Wagner scored. With Williams at the plate, DiMaggio was picked off first so Ted only got one RBI when he "lashed a homer well up into the seats in the upper grandstand in right-center."[56] The Red Sox led, 3-0.

The White Sox got two in the bottom of the fourth, helped by three Red Sox errors in the inning.

Neither team scored again until the bottom of the sixth, when the White Sox tied the game on a home run into the right-field stands hit by Joe Kuhel.

Both Rigney and Wagner buckled down. After Williams's third-inning homer, Rigney only allowed three scattered singles until the 11th inning. There were threats here and there; Chicago, for instance, had runners in scoring position in both the seventh and ninth.

The White Sox loaded the bases with one out in the 10th, but a ball that glanced off Wagner's glove and fortuitously went right to Cronin triggered a double play.

Charlie Wagner remembered the game years later, telling the author, "[Ted] said, 'If you'll tell me now that you'll hold 'em, I'll hit one out of here.' I said I would, and he hit the ball over the roof and the whole works, an incredible hit. We won the game. That's the kind of player he was."[57]

In the top of the 11th, Spence struck out. Ted Williams left the on-deck circle and stepped into the batter's box. He hit a ball to the same area as his first home run, but one that was hit about 50 feet higher and "onto the top of the double-deck stands...Ted's blow must have covered 450 at least and was the proverbial mile high."[58] The *Boston Herald* wrote that the ball went "to the very top of the right-centerfield grandstand upper roof," adding, "A conservative estimate of the distance the drive would have gone, on the level, was 500 feet." It gave the Red Sox the lead. The *Globe* called it "a prodigious home run swat" and said, "The roof of the upper deck in right field is nearly 400 feet from the batter's box. Williams's drive was a lift far above the top of the upper grandstand roof, which in turn must be 70 feet above the playing field. When it landed on the roof the ball bounded at least 50 feet in the air, and then disappeared to parts unknown."[59] Williams had driven in three of Boston's four runs.

Wagner held back Chicago for a 4-3 win.

Both starting pitchers had gone the distance.

Ted Williams, of course, finished the 1941 season batting .406, the last time a player in either the American or National League hit .400. Going 3-for-4 in this game helped.

Boston Red Sox 5
Philadelphia Athletics 2

May 27, 1941 — Fenway Park
(first game of a doubleheader)

During the time he spent with the big-league club, Charlie Wagner was Ted Williams's roommate. When he first arrived in Florida for spring training in 1938, "The Kid" asked manager Joe Cronin for someone who didn't smoke, didn't drink, liked to get to bed early and wake up early. Cronin pointed him to Charlie Wagner and both ballplayers frequently said it was a very good fit.[60]

On May 7, 1941 Williams had hit a home run in the top of the 11th inning, giving Wagner his first win of the 1941 season. Twenty days later, Williams hit another game-winning homer and Wagner had his second win of the season.

Manager Connie Mack started longtime veteran Bump Hadley in the May 27 game.

The Red Sox scored once in the first inning, once in the second inning, and once in the third inning. In the first, Dom DiMaggio doubled to left, took third base on Lou Finney's grounder to shortstop, and scored when Williams grounded to second.

The run in the second came on a walk to Cronin, Skeeter Newsome's groundout which advanced Cronin to second, and catcher Frankie Pytlak's double down the right-field line.

The Red Sox scored their third run on a two-out solo home run to right field by Ted Williams. DiMaggio had singled, leading off the inning, but (as in the May 7 game), he was erased on the basepaths – caught stealing. Finney flied out, but Williams homered. Where the ball came down was not entirely clear. The *Boston Herald* wrote, "Ted the Kid lofted one of his magnificently high homers into the right-field bleachers, right over the Red Sox bull-pen."[61] It scored the third Red Sox run.

In the bottom of the fifth inning, the Red Sox added to their total. Pytlak singled to center, his second hit of the game. DiMaggio tripled, making it 4-0. Finney fouled out to third base and Williams walked. Shortstop Al Brancato dropped a popup hit to him by Jimmie Foxx, and DiMaggio scored a fifth run, unearned.

In the sixth, Philadelphia's Benny McCoy walked with one out. Bob Johnson singled and McCoy went to second base. Dick Siebert fouled out, but center fielder Sam Chapman doubled to right field. No longer a shutout, the score was 5-1, Red Sox.

There were threats by both teams in the seventh, but the only other run to score in the game was by the Athletics in the eighth. Johnson led off with a walk and Siebert doubled to right-center field, driving him in.

Both pitchers worked complete games.

Both teams had seven base hits. DiMaggio had three of Boston's seven – a single, a double, and a triple. He also drew a walk.

In the day's second game, the Red Sox only mustered three base hits off Phil Marchildon – singles by DiMaggio, Pete Fox, and Williams. The single by Williams extended his hitting streak to 13 games. He was hitting an even .400 at the end of the day. Philadelphia won, 11-1.

Two days later, Williams hit another game-winning homer against the Athletics.

Boston Red Sox 6
Philadelphia Athletics 4

May 29, 1941 — Fenway Park

After going 3-for-4 in this Thursday afternoon game (the 37th game of the 1941 season), Ted Williams was hitting .421. This game-winning homer came right after the seventh-inning stretch. In between the two wins, the Sox had lost an 11-1 game to the Athletics (the second game of the May 27 doubleheader) and another extra-inning game (a 16-inning loss, 8-6) the day before. The Athletics were hot, having won nine of their last 11 games.

Jack Knott pitched for Philadelphia, Joe Dobson for Boston. Before the game, Knott's ERA was 5.55 and Dobson's was 7.56.

The first three runs were scored by the Red Sox. In the second, Pete Fox singled to left and so did Jim Tabor, Fox taking third. He scored on Skeeter Newsome's groundout to shortstop.

In the third, Lou Finney walked. Ted Williams singled, Finney to third. Joe Cronin hit a liner to right and Finney tagged and scored. Fox singled to first baseman Dick Siebert who flipped the ball to Knott covering, but Knott muffed the play and Williams got all the way to third base. Tabor singled to center field, and the Red Sox had their third run.

The Athletics put their first run on the board in the top of the fifth. A one-out triple off the wall in left-center field by catcher Frankie Hayes set up the run. Pete Suder saw Williams back up against the wall catching a fly to left, and Hayes tagged and scored.

They added two more runs – tying the score at 3-3 – in the top of the sixth on a single by Wally Moses and doubles by Bob Johnson and Sam Chapman, one to the flagpole in center and the other down the left-field line.

It was Dobson himself who kicked things off in the bottom of the seventh, singling sharply off the wall in left field. Dom DiMaggio bunted him to second. A groundout moved him to third, but what base he was on proved moot when Ted Williams swung at a 1-0 pitch and poled a long ball that landed in the "runway between the right field bleachers and the end of the grandstand."[62] A home run. That made it Boston 5, Philadelphia 3.

Skeeter Newsome made it 6-3 with an eighth-inning homer into the left-field screen. The Athletics got a fourth and final run on a Frankie Hayes double off the center-field wall and a single from pinch-hitter Dee Miles.

It was Dobson's first win as a member of the Red Sox. Later in the year, he reeled off seven wins in a row starting in mid-August and finished the season 12-5. As we shall see, no pitcher benefitted more from Ted Williams game-winning homers than Joe Dobson.

Boston Red Sox 6
Chicago White Sox 3

June 6, 1941 — Comiskey Park, Chicago

The White Sox were home at Comiskey Park. On May 7, Ted Williams had hit a game-winning homer off starter Johnny Rigney, who was 3-3 with a 2.33 ERA coming into this game. Joe Dobson started for Boston, 2-1, just coming off a 9-1 four-hit victory against the Tigers four days earlier.

Boston first baseman Jimmie Foxx ruined Rigney's ERA in the top of the first inning. Rigney got the first two Red Sox to make outs, but Ted Williams doubled to left-center field, Cronin walked on a full count, and "Double X" hit a three-run homer, a "400-foot liner into the bottom tier of the left-field bleachers."[63]

Dom DiMaggio walked, leading off the third inning for Boston. Lou Finney flied out, but Williams took Rigney deep again with a two-run homer into the upper deck of the right-field seats.[64]

Another home run off Rigney kicked off the fourth inning, a leadoff homer by Jim Tabor, a "terrific clout just to the left of the centerfield seats, a wallop that must have traveled 420 feet."[65] The Red Sox held a 6-0 lead. Buck Ross relieved Rigney, and in the five innings he worked, the Red Sox only mustered one base hit – a one-out single to left field by Jim Tabor in the sixth inning.

To that point, Dobson had allowed but two White Sox base hits. The White Sox recovered a bit and got three runs in their half of the sixth on three singles, a base on balls, and another single. Mike Ryba took over for the Red Sox and got the final out of the inning. He only allowed one hit, a single in the eighth.

There was no further scoring in the game.

It was only June 6, but after this 400-foot two-run home run into Comiskey Park's upper-right field deck, Rigney had already been victim to four Ted Williams home run swings in 1941, two of them game-winners. Foxx and Tabor homered, too, producing all the other Red Sox runs, but Ted's was the one that provided the margin of victory.

Between the three of them, Foxx, Tabor, and Williams had 25 home runs, more than the entire White Sox team at this point of the season.

The *Chicago Tribune*'s Irving Vaughan noted the proclivity for Red Sox batters to homer off Rigney, twice dubbing him Boston's "cousin" in the first paragraph of his game account, saying that surrendering home runs to Red Sox batters was Rigney's "specialty against the Bostonese."[66]

This day was the 22nd day of Ted Williams's consecutive-game hitting streak. June 7 was the 23rd and last game in the streak. At game's end on June 6, he was batting at a .436 clip. This home run was also the third game-winning homer in the 10-day stretch running from May 27 through June 6. His homers had won games on May 27, May 29, and then this one on June 6. Six days later he hit another one to win another game.

Boston Red Sox 3
St. Louis Browns 2

June 12, 1941 — Sportsman's Park, St. Louis
(second game of a doubleheader)

In the first game of this day's doubleheader, the Red Sox scored four runs in the top of the first – until Bob Muncrief replaced starter Bob Harris. Muncrief didn't allow another run the rest of the game, throwing 8 1/3 innings of relief. Joe Dobson started for Boston and he never got even one of the Browns out. He was charged with five runs. In the end, St. Louis won, 9-4.

Johnny Niggeling faced Red Sox left-hander Earl Johnson in the second game. All the scoring took place in the first four innings. In the top of the first, Lou Finney tripled and, after Ted Williams struck out, Joe Cronin singled. That gave Boston their first run. The Browns tied the score in the bottom of the inning, a triple factoring into their scoring, too. Right fielder Chet Laabs hit a two-out double and shortstop Johnny Berardino followed with a triple,

Leading off the third inning, Finney singled. Wielding a new bat (he'd been angry at himself for striking out in the first inning and broke his bat on the plate), Ted Williams hit a two-run home run. Swinging at a 3-0 pitch, "Tall Ted teed off and belted the next pitch over the roof of the right-field pavilion and onto Grand Boulevard."[67] "The "winning wallop" went "a mile over the roof in right field" according to Hy Hurwitz of the *Boston Globe*.[68] The Red Sox took a 3-1 lead.

With three consecutive singles, the third one driving in a run, the Browns knocked Johnson out of the game in the fourth. Mike Ryba relieved.

The score stood Boston 3, St. Louis 2.

The score never changed.

Williams walked in the fifth and again in the seventh. In the latter inning, he was thrown out trying to steal second. Williams did steal two bases in 1941. His most productive years at stealing bases were 1940 and 1948, with four steals each year. Over the course of his career, Williams stole 24 and was caught 17 times. Remarkably, he stole at least one base in four different decades – two in 1939, 14 in the 1940s, seven in the 1950s, and one in 1960.

The Williams home run back in the third inning was the winning hit. It was his fourth game-winning home run in a 17-day stretch. The others had been on May 27 and 29, and June 6.

Boston Red Sox 14
Detroit Tigers 6

June 17, 1941 — Fenway Park
(first game of a doubleheader)

The first pitcher who Ted Williams took deep in the major leagues was Luther "Bud" Thomas, on April 23, 1939.[69]

June 17 is Evacuation Day in Boston, celebrating the victorious Battle of Bunker Hill in the Revolutionary War, after which British troops left the city. The Tigers were in town and ready to play a holiday doubleheader.

The Red Sox were only three games out of first place in the American League. The Tigers were in fifth, but just two games behind the Red Sox.

There was some jostling of sorts in the first three innings. Thanks to three Joe Dobson walks and a single, the Tigers scored once in the top of the first. The Red Sox responded with three runs off Floyd Giebell, who gave up a mixture of three singles and three walks.

A second-inning grand slam by Detroit first baseman Rudy York went "far over everything in left field."[70] It was 5-3, Detroit, and Boston manager Joe Cronin called on Jack Wilson to relieve Dobson, adjudged "wild and ineffective."[71] Detroit added a run in the third on a single, sacrifice bunt, and Pat Mullin's single.

The Sox cut the margin to one when Bobby Doerr singled, Jimmie Foxx doubled, and (after Bud Thomas came in to relieve) Jim Tabor singled, followed by a run-scoring groundout by Johnny Peacock.

Three innings passed without a score until the bottom of the seventh. Right fielder Lou Finney reached when Mullin simply dropped a fly ball to center.

Facing Thomas, Ted Williams "pulled the second pitch into the right field wing of the grandstand, in about a dozen rows, not far fair. This put the Sox ahead, where they stayed."[72] He had given his team a 7-6 lead.

The team wasn't finished yet, though. Cronin doubled to right field. Foxx singled to left. Tabor reached on an infield single and Cronin scored from third base. Doerr singled to center and Foxx scored. Hal Newhouser relieved Thomas. He gave up three singles, a sacrifice fly, watched another error committed, and walked Williams, Cronin, and Foxx all in succession. Eight runs scored and Boston had a 13-6 lead.

Wilson pitched 7 1/3 innings of relief and only allowed one run. The Tigers won the day's second game, 8-5, with four-run innings in the sixth inning and the ninth.

Boston Red Sox 5
Philadelphia Athletics 3

August 31, 1941 — Fenway Park
(first game of a doubleheader)

True, a hitter going for .400 doesn't like outs – but was this taking
things a little too far? Bob Dunbar of the *Boston Herald* let it be
known that the day before, Ted Williams had "bored a couple
of holes through the left-field fence with his new rifle...Teddy's
sharp-shooting ability was attested by the absence of one of the
'out' signs in the electric scoreboard."[73]

A hitter doing as well as Williams was also likes to hit. And the
Philadelphia Athletics were pitching around Williams; he drew
four bases on balls during the two games this Sunday afternoon
on the last day of August in 1941 – one in the first game and three
in the seven-inning second game.

Connie Mack's Athletics knew well what could happen when they
pitched to Ted Williams.

Jack Knott was his victim, again. Knott had given up a game-
winning homer to Williams on May 29. He did so in this game,
too.

Boston scored in the first. Manager/third baseman Joe Cronin
singled, then took second on a wild pitch. After Williams walked,
former Athletic Jimmie Foxx singled and Cronin scored. This was
a game with a Fox and a Foxx, and two unrelated Newsomes –
rookie starting pitcher Dick Newsome and shortstop Skeeter
Newsome.

The A's scored three runs in the top of the fourth on a walk, error
by Foxx, and Sam Chapman's three-run homer high up in the
netting atop Fenway's left-field wall. The score remained 3-1 until
the bottom of the sixth.

Right fielder Pete Fox led off and walked. Cronin singled to left. With runners on first and second, walking Williams was not really a palatable option – though in retrospect, it might have been the wiser move. One reporter speculated that "The wind was coming in so strongly from right field that we half suspect Knott figured he'd let Ted pull the ball to right and that it would go high and that [right fielder] Wally Moses unquestionably could pull it down."[74] Williams hit what proved instead a game-winning home run "into the right-field wing of the grandstand right into the teeth of a nasty east wind, and with two pals on base....It was lined eight rows deep and yards on the fair side of the yellow foul pole."[75] Burt Whitman offered the observation that "Ted the Kid stole the show...just the way Babe Ruth used to monopolize the spotlight when he was hitting them over the horizon for the old Sox and Yankees."[76]

Both pitchers worked complete games. Philadelphia won the seven-inning second game, 3-2.

Williams hit home runs on four game days in a row – there was no game on August 29, but he homered on August 28, August 30, August 31, and in both games of the September 1 doubleheader.[77]

Boston Red Sox 13
Washington Senators 9

September 1, 1941 — Fenway Park
(first game of a doubleheader)

———————————

Ted Williams entered the game batting .407, with an on-base percentage of .550. He'd walked 17 times in his previous 32 plate appearances, and at least once in every game over the prior eight.

Williams drew two more bases on balls against Washington Senators pitching in each game of the September 1 doubleheader, and also went 3-for-5 at the plate — with every one of the three hits a home run. After both games, his batting average rose from .407 to .410.

The game, though, looked like it was going to go the Senators' way.

Second-year lefty Mickey Harris started for the Red Sox, and first-year right-hander Alex Carrasquel for Washington.

Both teams scored one run in the first inning. The Red Sox took a 3-1 lead in the second inning on two singles, a walk, a productive out, and Joe Cronin's double. Ted Williams walked in the first and the third, but wasn't involved in any scoring.

Then the Senators scored five times in the top of the fourth, taking a 6-3 lead and driving Harris from the game. The big hit was a bases-loaded double by Doc Cramer that led to three runs.

The Red Sox clawed back one run in the fourth, but it was immediately matched by Washington.

Leading off the bottom of the fifth, Ted Williams homered. It wasn't the hardest-hit ball; it went "floating into the grandstand just beyond the foul line."[78]

Washington added two more runs in the sixth, taking a 9-5 lead.

Williams Paces Double Sox Win

Ted Poles Three Homers, Boosts Hit Mark to .410

Williams came up in the bottom of the sixth facing reliever Bill Zuber with the bases loaded and one out. He hit what was "possibly the longest ball he ever hit. It went out of Fenway Park completely over the right-field roof. The roof is around 60 feet high at that point and 400 feet from home plate. No one had ever hit a ball over the right-field roof before, and only one person has ever done so since (Carl Yastrzemski); the only problem is that both Ted's and Yaz's balls hit out were both foul balls."[79] Taking another swing, Williams flied out to Buddy Lewis in right. The *Boston Herald*'s Burt Whitman wrote that it was "caught so deep that it would have been a sure homer in every other A.L. ball yard."[80]

It was still 9-6, Senators in the bottom of the eighth. Lou Finney walked. Dom DiMaggio whiffed, but Pete Fox hit a "vicious double"[81] to center field. Cronin singled off the left-field wall, scoring both Finney and Fox. Washington's lead was down to 9-8.

Williams faced Zuber again. This time, he found his range. Williams homered on a 2-and-1 count, his second home run of the game, a two-run blast. He "drove in the tying and winning runs in the eighth frame, this wallop being a 420-foot drive in the bleacher ... just above the Red Sox bullpen roof in right field."[82] Boston had gone ahead, 10-9, and added three more runs before the inning was over.

POSTSCRIPT

By the end of the 1941 season, Williams had 37 home runs, leading both the American and National Leagues. He drove in 120 runs. Most notably, he hit for a .406 batting average, the last time any player from either of the leagues surpassed the .400 mark. He often reached base in other ways, too. His 147 bases on balls led both leagues. He drew 25 intentional walks. Williams had a .553 on-base percentage for the season. In the N.L. and A.L., there had been seven other hitters since 1901 who had hit over .400, but the last one before Williams had been Bill Terry of the New York Giants in 1930. He hit .401 in a year when the league average was .303. As Ben Bradlee Jr. pointed out, that was 32 percent higher than the norm, whereas in 1941 Williams's .406 was 53 percent higher than that year's .266 American League average.[83]

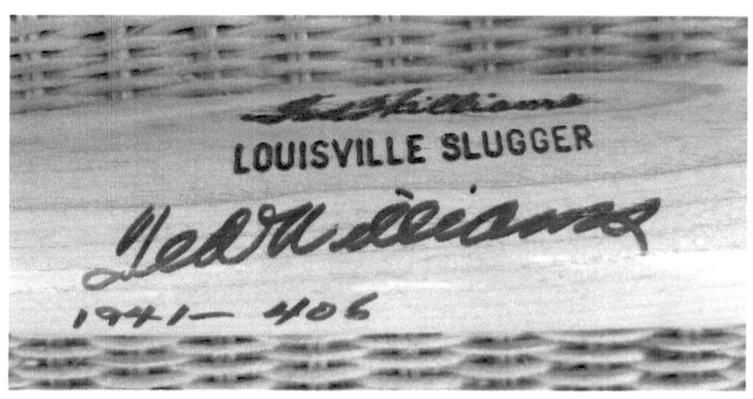

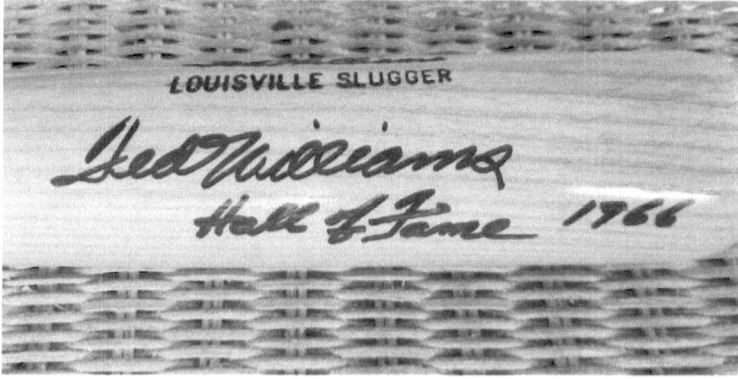

(Photographs by the author)

The 1941 All-Star Game

American League 7

National League 5

July 8, 1941 — Briggs Stadium, Detroit

Of all the home runs he hit, Ted Williams always maintained that the one in the 1941 All-Star Game was "the most thrilling hit in my life."[84]

It's not hard to understand why. First of all, it was a walkoff home run — always more exciting than a third-inning two-run homer that happens to win a game. The home run he hit that clinched the pennant in 1946 was a big home run, and it was an inside-the-park home run to boot, but that was in the first inning of a 1-0 game. No one could have known at the time how that game would unfold.

The home run he hit in his last at-bat in the major leagues was a satisfying one, but hit in the context of a seventh-place Red Sox team closing up a desultory season. His eighth-inning homer brought Boston within a run of the Orioles, but it wasn't a game-winning hit. The game was won on Willie Tasby's bases-loaded groundout on which two runs scored because of the second baseman's throwing error.

Certainly there had been game-winning homers which provided thrills. When he hit a home run to win a game on Ted Williams Day, just before departing to join the Marines during the Korean War, not knowing if he would ever play again, he said, "The home run I hit in the 1941 All-Star Game at Detroit had this one beat 10 to 1. I don't think anything will ever pass that."[85]

There were three regular-season walk-off home runs, but only three. All were against the Tigers, as it happened. Two were early in the season, in May, and one was in July. The July 19, 1958 one won the game in the 12th inning, so there was that – but the win still left the Red Sox 10 games behind the Yankees.

The All-Star Game has to be seen for what it was at the time. Other than the World Series, playing in the All-Star Game meant more than almost anything else in baseball. One was selected by one's peers, not through popular vote. In the days of the reserve clause, someone who was a true star tended to stick with one team (and thus one league) throughout one's career. There was no interleague play, other than the World Series and the All-Star Game. Suddenly, for one game, you were a teammate with the best in your league. Ted Williams was teammates with Joe DiMaggio and Bob Feller in the 1941 game. You were playing against the best players in the other league, and players truly cared which team won.

The Game Itself

The 1941 All-Star Game was played at Briggs Stadium in Detroit. It was, of course, midseason. The Red Sox were in third place, 7 ½ games behind the Yankees. Williams was hitting .405 before the break. Joe DiMaggio was 48 games into what became a 56-game hitting streak.

The American Leaguers scored first, one run in the fourth. Cecil Travis had doubled. Williams came up with two outs and Travis on third base, and doubled to right field.

The National League tied it on a sacrifice fly in the top of the sixth. The A.L. promptly re-established a one-run edge when Cleveland's Lou Boudreau singled in Joe DiMaggio in the bottom of the sixth.

The Pirates' Arky Vaughan hit a two-run homer with Enos Slaughter of St. Louis aboard and the N.L. took a 3-2 lead in the seventh. Then Vaughan did it again in the top of the eighth, another two-run homer, this time with Johnny Mize aboard. His first homer was off Sid Hudson, the second off Eddie Smith. Vaughan was poised to be anointed the star among the All-Stars.

With one out in the bottom of the eighth, Joe DiMaggio singled off the Chicago Cubs' Claude Passeau. Williams took a called third strike, but Ted's teammate Dom DiMaggio singled in his brother Joe. It was 5-3, N.L.

With one out in the bottom of the ninth, Ken Keltner pinch-hit for Smith and reached on an infield single. The Yankees' Joe Gordon singled to right field. Cecil Travis walked. That brought up Joe DiMaggio with one out and the bases loaded, his team down by two runs. He grounded out to the shortstop, a force play at second base. It was a one-run game, 5-4, but now there were two outs and runners on first and third.

Ted Williams was up. He had walked, hit that RBI double in the fourth inning, flied out to center, and struck out. Passeau could have intentionally walked Williams and pitched to Dom DiMaggio. They decided to pitch to Williams.

"You've got to be quicker," he says he told himself at the time, "you've got to get more in front."[86] Williams fired himself up. Regarding getting called out on strikes in the eighth, he told J. G. Taylor Spink of *The Sporting News*, "You'll never convince me that the third strike wasn't a low ball." Up to bat again, he said, "I stood back and sort of gave myself a fight talk. I said: 'Listen, you lug. He outguessed you last time and you got caught with your bat on your shoulder for a called third strike. You were swinging late when you fouled one off, too. Let's swing and swing a little earlier this time and see if we can connect.'"[87] He fouled off Passeau's first pitch, and then took two balls. He figured he was ahead in the count and the next pitch would be over the plate. He was cocked and ready. "It was a fast one, chest high and I got the fat of my bat on it and away it sailed." He knew it was gone the moment he connected. The only question was whether or not it would clear the roof. It struck off the front of the third deck. The three-run homer catapulted the A.L. to a 7-5 victory.[88]

Many have seen the film of Williams gleefully making his way around the bases. He "bounded down the first-base line...like the kid he was. He clapped his hands twice as he neared the bag then bounded over it with a joyful skip as he made his way around the bases."[89]

As he once put it himself, "I barely touched the ground."[90]

It was, he wrote in his autobiography, "the kind of thing that a kid dreams about and imagines himself doing when he's playing those little playground games we used to play in San Diego. Halfway down to first, seeing that ball going out, I stopped running and started leaping and jumping and clapping my hands, and I was just so happy I laughed out loud. I've never been so happy and I've never seen so many happy guys. They carried me off the field."[91]

Williams was mobbed by his delirious peers: "Brother, what a beating I took after I reached the plate!"[92] He was mobbed by the DiMaggios, Bob Feller, Eddie Collins, Herb Pennock, and more. He had to slip out of the ballpark, catch a ride with someone who actually didn't know to whom they were offering a ride, and then sneak his way into the hotel because of the crowd gathered there.[93]

It was, editorialized *The Sporting News*, "the greatest finish yet seen in inter-league competition."[94]

In his All-Star Game appearances, Williams hit .309 (13-for-42) with 10 RBIs and 10 walks. He homered four times, in 1941, twice in 1946, and once in 1956.

1942

The First Triple Crown

How does one follow up a season such as 1941? It would be a difficult task under any circumstances, but to make things even tougher the entire season was played while the United States was at war, declared in December 1941. As the country rallied together, there was tremendous pressure placed on all baseball players—fit young men—even stars like Ted Williams—to enlist.

What's more, as sole supporter of his mother, Williams was entitled to an exemption. At first, to make a point, he resisted joining, but on May 22nd he enlisted in the United States Navy and played out the season while also attending classes in preparation to become a Naval aviator.

Somehow, he retained his focus on being the best hitter in baseball. His .356 batting average led the league and his .499 on-base percentage led both leagues. He also led the league with 36 home runs, 137 RBIs, a slugging average of .648, and 141 runs scored—a Triple Crown and then some.

Meanwhile, the Red Sox finished in second place again, their 93 wins seven less than the Yankees. Williams hit six game-winning home runs.

All eyes are on the baseball after another graceful Williams follow-
through. (Leslie Jones photograph, Boston Public Library)

Boston Red Sox 4
St. Louis Browns 2

May 16, 1942 — Sportsman's Park, St. Louis

It was home run #99 in Ted Williams's career, and the third he had mashed off Bob Muncrief of the St. Louis Browns.[95] It was his 19th game-winning homer, hit in the ninth inning of a Saturday afternoon game. The win ended a five-game Red Sox losing streak.

Williams came into the game batting .297, down more than 100 points from the .406 batting average he had posted in 1941.

Muncrief was pitted against Tex Hughson, who was in his first start of his first full season.

Throughout the game, Muncrief saw a lot of Boston batters reach base, while Hughson allowed rather few St. Louis batters to reach.

First to score were the Red Sox with two runs in the top of the fourth. To that point, there had been a leadoff double by rookie shortstop Johnny Pesky, on his way to an impressive 205 base hits – which led both the American and National Leagues. There had been a two-out double by center fielder Dom DiMaggio in the second inning. And Ted Williams had drawn a base on balls in the third. Those were the only Red Sox to reach base over the first three innings.

The Browns were set down in order in the first and the second. Leading off the third, Vern Stephens drew a walk. They didn't get a hit until the fifth.

Come the top of the fourth, second baseman Bobby Doerr swung at the first pitch of the inning and led off with a home run "half way up into the left-field bleachers."[96] Boston scored a second run on a single, walk, single, and error.

Ted Williams led off the fifth with a single. Tony Lupien singled and Williams pulled up at second. Two outs followed, and when

DiMaggio singled and Williams tried to score, the Red Sox slugger was out at home plate.

Hughson got himself in trouble, walking the first two batters in the bottom of the fifth, seeing a successful sacrifice, and then a two-run single from Don Gutteridge.

Neither team scored in the sixth, seventh, or eighth, though there had been scoring opportunities. In the sixth, the bases were loaded for Ted Williams, but he hit to the first baseman, starting a 3-6-1 double play.

The score remained 2-2 through eight.

In the top of the ninth, Lou Finney doubled to left field. Ted Williams wasn't about to be asked to sacrifice. Instead he hit a home run. After fouling off the first pitch, he "shattered the two-all tie to wee bits by slamming a fast ball, away from him, onto the top of the right center field pavilion."[97] The ball left Sportsman's Park "over the roof in right-center over the 354-foot mark."[98] Five batters later, without further scoring, the game entered the bottom of the ninth with a 4-2 Boston lead.

Hughson threw a two-hitter, Gutteridge's two-run single in the fifth and a leadoff single by Vern Stephens in the seventh. He had walked five Browns batters, though. And the Red Sox only led by two runs, despite having 14 base hits and five walks. They had left 13 on base.

Hughson had his first win of the year. He won 21 more games in 1942, leading both leagues. He threw 22 complete games.

Ted Williams was on his way to a Triple Crown year, leading the league in home runs (36), RBIs (137), and batting average (.356.) His average was 50 points lower than the .406 he hit in 1941, but the success he had in all three categories led both the American and National leagues. The home run he hit in this game was the first of six game-winning homers he hit in 1942.

Boston Red Sox 14
Philadelphia Athletics 2

May 29, 1942 — Shibe Park, Philadelphia

Russ Christopher was the starting pitcher for Connie Mack's Athletics. It was the right-hander's first year in the majors. He'd only given up one home run to date – to Ted Williams back on May 10, a two-run homer in the ninth inning of a game that Christopher won.

This night each one of the first eight pitches Christopher threw was out of the strike zone.[99] He walked Dom DiMaggio and Johnny Pesky. Right fielder Pete Fox struck out.

Ted Williams was batting cleanup. He hit a three-run homer. "The ball landed on a roof behind the wall about 100 feet from the right-field foul line."[100]

Williams's home run was the only base hit Christopher gave up through the first five innings, but it made all the difference in the game.

The Red Sox starter was Tex Hughson. Through the first five innings, Hughson had allowed only two first-inning singles. And Christopher had allowed just one hit – Williams's three-run homer.

The Red Sox added two in the sixth. Pesky doubled to left field. On an error, the Sox had runners on second and third, so Williams was intentionally walked. Joe Cronin hit an infield single that scored Pesky. Doerr singled to center and the Sox booked their fifth run.

In the top of the seventh, the Red Sox added three more. After two outs, DiMaggio was hit in the back by a pitch. Pesky doubled to right-center field and DiMaggio scored. Pete Fox singled to third base, and Pesky scored all the way from second. Williams singled to right field and Fox reached third. Cronin scored Fox with a single to right.

After having retired 16 batters in succession, Hughson gave up a single and walk but no one scored in the bottom of the seventh.

The Red Sox added five more runs in the eighth off reliever Dick Fowler. Batterymates Bill Conroy and Tex Hughson both singled. Pesky collected his third hit of the game with a single, driving in Conroy.[101] Fox walked, loading the bases.

Ted Williams boosted the score to 13-0 with a grand slam to right field, "another prodigious homer onto a roof behind the right field."[102]

Doerr led off the top of the ninth with a home run into the left-field stands to make the score 14-0.

The Athletics broke up Hughson's shutout in the bottom of the ninth with a double and three singles.

The final score was 14-2. Ted Williams's seven runs batted in were half his team's total. Even though it had been way back in the top of the first inning, his three-run homer proved to be the game-winning hit.

Still May, Williams already had 52 runs batted in.

Boston Red Sox 1
Detroit Tigers 0

June 24, 1942 — Briggs Stadium, Detroit

Ted Williams hit 12 homers off Virgil Trucks, more than off any other pitcher. Needless to say, you have to be a good pitcher to even get into enough games to give up that many homers to one player. Trucks won 188 games in his career, but not this one. It was a 6:00 P.M. "twilight" game, and there was only one run scored in the game – Ted Williams driving himself in with his home run into the Briggs Stadium right-field stands.

For right-hander Trucks, 1942 was his first full year in the majors.

Sox Win on Williams Homer

Charlie Wagner was the pitcher for the Red Sox. This was his fifth season appearing for the Red Sox. Early in June, he had been 4-5 (despite a very good 2.80 ERA) but had won his last two decisions, a three-hitter against the White Sox at Fenway Park and a 1-0 shutout of the White Sox in Chicago on June 19.

After two outs in the top of the first inning, right fielder Lou Finney singled for Boston and left fielder Ted Williams did the same. After two outs in the bottom of the first, center fielder Doc Cramer for Detroit singled, too. No runs were scored by either team in any of the first six innings.

Williams doubled but was the only Red Sox to reach base in the fourth. Detroit's Rudy York almost hit one out, but center fielder Dom DiMaggio braced himself against the center-field wall and grabbed what would have been a home run. The *Detroit Times* called it a "superman leaping one-handed catch."[103]

Ted Williams was the first batter in the top of the seventh. He hit a 1-1 pitch and "met the ball so solidly that everybody in the park knew that it was ticketed for the circuit. It landed well up in the upper tier, out toward center."[104] It left the field of play "over the 370-foot mark into the lower deck of the right field stands."[105]

There was a walk, a passed ball, and another walk in the Red Sox eighth. Williams already had a single, double, and home run, so manager Joe Cronin yelled "Make it the cycle, Kid!"[106] Instead of tripling, he popped up to the middle infield and Bobby Doerr was called out on strikes.

No one reached base for either team in the ninth inning.

Charlie Wagner threw a three-hitter for the victory, only facing 28 Tigers (none of whom got past first base.) Wagner walked no one at all. The Red Sox left seven runners on base; the Tigers left one.

For Wagner, it was back-to-back 1-0 shutouts – the one in Chicago on the 19th and this one in Detroit.

Trucks finished the 1942 season with a 14-8 record and a 2.74 earned run average. Even though he'd given up this home run he only gave up two others all year long and led both leagues in home runs per nine innings with a 0.161 rate.[107]

Boston Red Sox 2
Washington Senators 1

August 15, 1942 — Fenway Park
(first game of a doubleheader)

Sox starter Tex Hughson (14-3) breezed through the top of the first inning, seeing fly balls distributed for outs to each of his outfielders: Dom DiMaggio in center, Ted Williams in left, and Lou Finney in right field. Boston was in second place, though 13 ½ games behind the Yankees.

Sid Hudson was the pitcher for Bucky Harris's seventh-place Senators, who were riding a five-game winning streak. He gave up a leadoff double to DiMaggio, but no runs.

Neither pitcher allowed a ball out of the infield in either the top or bottom of the second, each facing just three batters.

The Red Sox scored two runs – their only two runs of the game – in the bottom of the third. Hughson led off by flying out to center field. DiMaggio hit one back to Hudson, who threw to first. Johnny Pesky singled to right field. On a count of 0-and-1, Ted Williams "pulled an inside pitch powerfully into the right field bleachers, inside the foul pole."[108] A "solid swat," wrote Shirley Povich.[109] This was not what later became known as a "Pesky Pole" home run. Gerry Moore of the *Boston Globe* wrote that it "landed a dozen rows up in the right field extension."[110]

It was Williams's 25th home run of the season. The Red Sox had a 2-0 lead.

The Senators scored in the top of the fifth. With two outs, Hudson singled. So did left fielder George Case. Spence doubled off the wall in left-center. Hudson scored easily, but Case was tagged out on a throw from DiMaggio direct to Johnny Peacock at home plate.[111] The play was apparently something of beauty: The ball went over Williams's reach and struck the scoreboard in left-center. "Racing over from center, Dom not only played the carom perfectly, but his powerful peg cut down Case so clearly that the famed speedster did not even slide. ..."[112]

That ended the inning, the Red Sox lead cut to 2-1. There was no other scoring in the game. There were a number of threats; the Senators left nine men on base. One who was not left on was Roy Cullenbine, who had walked in the fourth inning but was struck by a batted ball and thus ruled out.

How one gets caught off first base on a popup to the second baseman is difficult to imagine, but it happened to Boston baserunners in both the fourth and sixth innings.

Rookie shortstop John Sullivan led off the Senators' seventh with a double. He was tagged out at third base when Hughson pounced on a bunt hit in front of the plate by Ellis Clary.[113] Another man was taken off the basepaths.

The Senators got 10 hits off Hughson, who won his ninth consecutive game. By the end of the year, his first full year in the majors, he was 22-6, the 22 wins leading both leagues.[114] The Red Sox won the second game, 7-6.

Ted Williams's two-run homer in the day's first game proved the game-winner – the 22nd game-winning home run of his career, of the 110 he ultimately amassed.

Boston Red Sox 8
Philadelphia Athletics 7

September 6, 1942 — Fenway Park

The Second World War was well underway and a number of the players either knew or suspected they might not be back in 1943. Some were having strong seasons. For the Red Sox, Ted Williams was on his way to a Triple Crown season, leading the American League in HR, RBIs, and batting average. Rookie shortstop Johnny Pesky was hitting the ball all over the field (he ended up leading the league with 205 base hits.) Both Williams and Pesky had already signed up for the United States Navy.

Pitching for the Red Sox this day was Charlie Wagner. He, too, spent the next three years in military service.

There was enough separation in the standings that neither team had more than an outside chance of changing their position; Boston was in second place and Philadelphia in last.

The Athletics scored first thanks to a leadoff triple by Dee Miles.

In the bottom of the third, Boston got to 19-year-old right-hander Bob Savage. Catcher Johnny Peacock singled. Wagner struck out. DiMaggio bunted to sacrifice Peacock to second. Pesky singled to left and drove him in. Williams walked. Lupien singled to first base, but Pesky was caught off third base and run down between third and home.

In the top of the fifth, the Athletics added one more run, to make it 3-1, on a leadoff double by Miles. Davis sacrificed to get him to third, and he scored on a groundout to second by Elmer Valo.

In the sixth, against reliever Yank Terry, another leadoff double led to another Athletics run, also scored on an out. It was 4-1.

Williams' 30th Homer Erases Athletics, 8-7

The Red Sox got one back on a fifth-inning two-out double by Jim Tabor and a single by Peacock.

With Dick Newsome pitching for Boston, the Athletics upped the ante, scoring two more runs in the top of the seventh, one on an error and the other on a sac fly. It was 6-2, in Philadelphia's favor and not one of their six runs had come in on a base hit.

In the bottom of the seventh, Boston scored five. There was a walk, two singles, two errors, a sacrifice fly, and a bases-loaded triple by Peacock into the right-field corner. It was his third hit of the game and gave him a total of four runs batted in.

In the top of the eighth, reliever Lum Harris helped put the Athletics back in the game, doubling off the left-field scoreboard and scoring Pete Suder. It was tied, 7-7.

In the bottom of the eighth, Pesky grounded out to first base unassisted. Ted Williams hit a home run "into the right-field grandstand, around the bend, a circuit drive in any big-league ballpark and a game-winner."[115] It was his 30th home run of the season.

Boston Red Sox 6
Chicago White Sox 1

September 13, 1942 — Comiskey Park, Chicago
(first game of a doubleheader)

The first game of the Sunday afternoon doubleheader in Chicago was a close, well-played, low-scoring affair until everything suddenly fell apart for the hosting White Sox. Starter Buck Ross had allowed Boston just one base hit through the first six.

The Red Sox starter was Bill Butland.[116]

The White Sox got a run in the third, Don Kolloway reaching on an error. After a walk and a force play at second, Kolloway was on third and easily scored when shortstop Luke Appling singled to left field.

That's where it stood after three more innings.

After six innings, the score remained White Sox 1, Red Sox 0. To this point, the White Sox had just three base hits while Ross had held the Red Sox to a single by Tony Lupien in the second.

Suddenly, everything changed. Johnny Pesky led off with a single to center. Ted Williams took two strikes, then a ball. When he was thrown the fourth pitch, he "spanked it wickedly to right, against an appreciable cross wind, into the fifth row of the lower grandstand."[117] Lupien collected another hit, a double to left-center. Singles followed from Lou Finney, Skeeter Newsome, and Johnny Peacock. One run came in on a groundout.

Joe Haynes relieved Ross. After a sacrifice bunt by Butland, Newsome scored on a wild pitch and then Peacock scored on another wild pitch. The score was 6-1. Over the final three innings, only one runner reached base for either team, Ted Williams on a walk in the eighth.

It was the Williams home run that had given the Red Sox the lead, and proved decisive. There had been a loud fan heckling

Williams over the first six innings, but the home run seemed to quiet him down.[118] The ball Williams had hit struck a fellow Navy man (Williams had already enlisted in the Navy) in the face, as Lt. Earl Newman had tried to catch it. The ball fell into the lower right-field stands.[119]

The Red Sox also won the second game, 5-0. Pesky added two more hits; he was now at 196 on the season. He ended with 205, leading both leagues. For Williams, it was his 32nd home run of the year. He hit four more before the season was over. This was his first Triple Crown year, leading both leagues in home runs (36), runs batted in (137), and batting average (.356).[120]

With the win, Butland had won his seventh game in his last seven starts, one win against each of the other American League ballclubs.

Williams prepares for another at-bat as two teammates look on. (Leslie Jones photograph, Boston Public Library)

1946

Postwar, the Pennant, and the First MVP

After three full years in military service and away from major-league baseball, naturally everyone wondered how Ted Williams—and other returning servicemen—would perform. Amazingly, he picked right up where he left off, and perhaps more amazingly, it was the year the Boston Red Sox finally overtook the Yankees, winning their first pennant since 1918.

Needless to say, Williams was a big part of that. For the fourth year in a row, he led the American League in runs scored. For the fourth year in a row, his .497 on-base percentage led as well. He hit 38 homers and drove in 123—both second to Hank Greenberg. Six of his home runs were game-winning homers, including his first one in a night game, at the end of July in Cleveland. He was voted Most Valuable Player in the American League.

Due to a serious elbow injury, Williams was subpar in the World Series against the Cardinals. He insisted on playing, but the pain was debilitating. His five singles and only one RBI in the 7-game series—his only World Series—was one of the few blemishes on his career.

Boston Red Sox 5
Detroit Tigers 4 (10 innings)

May 2, 1946 — Fenway Park

In his first at-bat after three years of military service during World War II, Ted Williams grounded out to first base unassisted on April 16. Not exactly the stuff of legend, but he did homer in his second postwar at-bat and the Red Sox beat the Washington Senators on the season's opening day. President Harry Truman was among those at the game. Williams drove in 10 runs in April but didn't have another home run. Having missed three seasons, the mental database he had built had to be refreshed and updated. There were a number of new pitchers. Even the height of the pitcher's mounds in some parks had been modified, something perhaps only Ted Williams would notice.[121]

On May 2, Williams hit his second home run of the year, and his first game-winning homer of the postwar years. The Tigers were in town and Virgil Trucks on the mound. Tex Hughson was pitching for Boston.

Ted Williams' Homer Beats Tigers in 10th

The Red Sox got three runs in the second on catcher Hal Wagner's home run into the right-field grandstand seats. The Red Sox led, 4-0, after adding one in the bottom of the sixth when Bobby Doerr doubled to left and Rudy York singled.

The Tigers scored four runs in the top of the eighth and tied the game on four singles and three walks, the fourth run after Hughson intentionally walked Pat Mullin, loading the bases, but then quite unintentionally walked pinch-hitter Roy Cullenbine.

Clem Dreisewerd relieved Hughson, and Tommy Bridges relieved Trucks in the bottom of the eighth. In the ninth inning, both pitchers retired the three batters they faced.

In the top of the 10th, Dreisewerd allowed two singles but no runs.

When the Red Sox came to bat, the first batter up was Ted Williams, 0-for-4 in the game and he'd appeared "listless and lacking his usual verve as a result of a heavy cold," according to the *Boston Globe*.[122]

Bridges' first pitch was a high and inside curveball which Williams fouled off. The second was a high slider and he missed it by inches. Burt Whitman wrote that Williams was probably angry at himself: "His head went up very soon after his swing." Bridges then threw a low one –another slider. "Where earlier swings had looked comparatively lazy and innocent, this one by Ted was his best cut. The ball went on a line, drilling right across the northwest wind and landed in the Tiger bullpen in far right-center."[123]

Bridges lamented, saying the pitch had been "A slider which broke below his knees. I don't know where you've got to throw the ball to keep that guy from lifting it out of the park. I certainly didn't give him any strike."[124]

The win was Boston's seventh win in a row.

Ted Williams hit homers on May 3 and May 4, too. He was voted American League MVP, finishing the 1946 season with 38 home runs and 123 RBIs. He hit .342 and had an on-base percentage of .497, leading all of baseball. His 146 bases on balls and 153 runs scored also led both leagues.

Boston Red Sox 7
Cleveland Indians 4
(12 innings)

May 22, 1946 — League Park, Cleveland
(first game of a doubleheader)

Williams's second game-winning homer of 1946 was also in extras, but on the road. The Red Sox had a six-game lead in the standings.

Mickey Harris was in a 3-0 hole after giving up a leadoff double to Lou Boudreau, seeing him advance to third, then score on a "topped roller single down the third-base line" by left fielder Buster Mills.[125]

Mel Harder, in his 19th year with Cleveland, kept Boston scoreless through the first six innings, allowing but two base hits. He'd helped his team add to their lead in the bottom of the fifth. Felix Mackiewicz hit a one-out triple off the right-field wall. He scored when the next batter, Harder himself, singled for the second run of the game, later scoring from second on a single by Mickey Rocco.

The Sox got three hits to start the seventh – a leadoff single by Bobby Doerr, a double off the right-field wall by Rudy York, and a single by Johnny Lazor. It was 3-2 and they tied the game with one in the ninth when Lazor hit a home run, just fair, down the right-field line.

The Indians failed to score in the ninth, and neither team scored in the 10th. In the 11th, Doerr led off with a triple. With one out, Rip Russell singled off Harder's pitching hand, driving in Doerr. Harder had to leave for x-rays, and Vic Johnson relieved.

Williams Belts Homer in 12th, Sox Win, 7-4

The Indians got a man on second with one out, and Boo Ferriss relieved Dreisewerd. The first batter he faced, Keltner, singled in the baserunner and the score was tied, 4-4.

Pete Center was Cleveland's new pitcher in the 12th. Johnny Pesky singled, his second hit of the game. That brought up Ted Williams, who had had a very frustrating day at the plate. He'd grounded out, grounded into a double play, flied out to the infield, flied out once more to the infield, and grounded out. In his first five at-bats, the *Plain Dealer* noted, Williams "hadn't even been able to get the ball out of the infield."[126]

Center "threw two pitches very close to The Kid's skull. Williams was raving mad. He stepped closer to the plate and took a tighter grip on his bat. Then Center tried to throw one by Williams. The Kid got a good cut at it and propelled it a good 400 feet off the roof of a house in back of the high fence in right-center."[127] The *Boston Herald* said it cleared the wall in right-center and the screen on top of the wall, and "landed in a vacant lot on the other side of Lexington Avenue."[128]

There was some minor drama that followed but Ferriss prevailed and got the win, improving his record to 6-0.

Boston Red Sox 11
Washington Senators 1

July 7, 1946 — Griffith Stadium, Washington
(first game of a doubleheader)

On the last day before the 1946 All-Star Game at Boston's Fenway Park, the Washington Senators hosted a doubleheader against the Red Sox. The Sunday afternoon game at Griffith Stadium drew very well, with 39,861 paid attendance. Boston had a reasonably comfortable 6½ game lead over the second-place New York Yankees. Washington was in fourth place.

The matchup in the first game was Sid Hudson (6-5) for the Senators against Tex Hughson (8-5).

The Red Sox left the bases loaded in the first and the Senators left two on base. Neither team scored in the first or second.

After Boston's Dom DiMaggio singled with one out in the top of the third, Ted Williams hit a two-run homer over Griffith Stadium's right-field fence. It was his 23rd home run of the season. After a second out, third baseman Rip Russell doubled, and Hal Wagner was walked intentionally. Hughson struck out. The Red Sox had a 2-0 lead. "The Kid gave them their start and the supporting cast took over," wrote the *Boston Herald*. "They made 18 hits for 28 bases in that opener."[129]

In the bottom of the inning, Mickey Vernon hit a ball into the right-field corner for a double, but was left stranded.

The only man from either team to reach in the fourth was Washington third baseman Billy Hitchcock, who got on because of an error by Williams in left field, his second of the game. He lost the ball in the sun.

The Red Sox blew the game open in the fifth, adding five more runs.

Washington got their only run of the game in the bottom of the fifth when Buddy Lewis bunted for a one-out single, scoring two batters later when Vernon doubled to right field.[130] The Senators never got a man past second base for the rest of the game.

Boston augmented their 7-1 lead with another run in the sixth, one in the seventh, and two more in the ninth.

The Senators amassed 10 base hits during the course of the game, but could never manage a second run.

Ted Williams built up his on-base percentage, reaching in nine out of 11 plate appearances. He was 4-for-6 on the day and walked five times, four of them on intentional walks – "and didn't like it," wrote the *Washington Post*'s Shirley Povich.[131]

Boston Red Sox 11
Cleveland Indians 10

July 14, 1946 — Fenway Park
(first game of a doubleheader)

The 1946 Red Sox only spent one day all season long during which they were not in first place – April 25. By the time this game got underway, they had a nine-game lead.

The first game was a close game but one in which a lot of runs were scored. Eight of Boston's 11 runs were driven in by one player - #9, Ted Williams, who hit three home runs. This came just five days after the 1946 All-Star Game, held at Fenway Park, in which Williams had homered twice and driven in five runs. This game's homers were #24, 25, and 26 of the regular season. He had 82 RBIs and it was still just mid-July.

Boston's starting pitcher Joe Dobson didn't make it out of the first inning. Cleveland scored four runs.

Williams' 3 Homers, 8 RBI's Rout Indians

Indians right-hander Steve Gromek didn't make it through the third. Two singles and a walk loaded the bases, with two outs. That brought up Ted Williams. It was one of those times a pitcher might have been better served to intentionally walk in a run. Williams hit a grand slam, the seventh of his career. It banged off the back wall of the visiting team's bullpen, and then bounced back onto the field of play.[132] Bobby Doerr singled, Rudy York doubled, and the score was tied, 5-5.

The Red Sox took a 6-5 lead in the fourth, but the score tilted the other way in the fifth. Lou Boudreau doubled with one out and Keltner homered over everything in left field. After Jimmy Wasdell lined out, catcher Jim Hegan doubled and Gromek's reliever, Don Black, doubled, making the score 8-6.

Williams led off the bottom of the fifth, swung at the first pitch he saw, and hit another home run, over the Boston bullpen and into the runway between the bleachers and grandstand.[133] It took a high bounce and went into the grandstand seats.[134] It was 8-7, Indians.

The Indians re-established the two-run lead in the sixth and added a 10th run in the seventh.

Williams singled and scored on a double-play ball in the bottom of the seventh. There were two on in the eighth when he came up to bat again, and hit his third home run of the game, off reliever Joe Berry, close to the right-field foul pole, giving Boston back the lead, 11-10.[135]

There were 34 hits in the game, 18 by Cleveland and 16 by Boston.

With his three home runs, Williams had – as noted – driven in eight of Boston's 11 runs. Each home run was off a different pitcher. He became the first Red Sox batter to hit three home runs in a game at Fenway Park.[136]

Boudreau himself had been no slouch. Left off the All-Star team in 1946, Boudreau went 5-for-5 with a home run and four consecutive doubles – 12 total bases to Williams's 13.

The Red Sox swept, winning the second game 6-4.

This was likely the game Bob Feller had in mind when, as Bob Feller told it, manager Boudreau had tried out what became known as the "Boudreau shift" or, soon, the "Williams shift." This involved moving three infielders to the right-field side of second base. Hitting over the shift was, of course, a very good way to foil it. Williams passed Boudreau as he trotted around the bases and supposedly said, "Lou, you forgot to put anybody up there in the bleachers."[137]

That said, the shift did have an effect. It has been calculated that he hit .354 before the shift in 1946 and .327 after it, and said that Williams himself believed his lifetime average would have been 15 points higher had it not been implemented as often as it was.[138]

Boston Red Sox 4
Cleveland Indians 0

July 30, 1946 — Cleveland Stadium

This game was yet another Boo Ferriss shutout.[139]

Starting for Lou Boudreau's Indians was Steve Gromek.

This Tuesday night game drew a huge crowd – 56,060.[140] Crowds were generally larger, with the Second World War over and the economy doing well. Night games were new to most ballparks.[141]

Many had their eyes on Ted Williams. Even in the parks of opposing fans, many confessed they were there hoping to see Ted Williams hit a home run.

In the top of the fourth, with one out, when Williams came to bat, Boudreau put on the shift again. Williams hit a home run into the first row of the lower deck of the right-field seats in the fourth. As *Cleveland Plain Dealer* put it, "willowy Ted Williams, incomparable slugger...defied Boudreau's unique defensive formations by pounding his 28th home run into the right field seats."[142] It was hit down the foul line, about 350 feet, and "not much fair," wrote the *Boston Herald*.[143] It just got in, Gerry Moore of the *Boston Globe* indicated. After pointing out that the Indians had not stationed an outfielder in the seats as White Sox pitcher Ted Lyons had also once suggested, Moore wrote, "Right fielder Hank Edwards gave a fan a fight for the Ted propelled poke, which landed in the first row of the right field lower deck."[144]

In the fifth, Boston's Rip Russell poled "a well-stroked smash deep into the lower left field seats and probably a little longer than Ted's thump to the opposite direction."[145]

Ferriss led off the eighth inning with a single to center field. Right fielder Wally Moses hit a "fiery triple to deep right center, a ball which went to the running track, 400 feet from home."[146] Pesky followed that with a single to center, scoring Moses. The score was now Boston 4, Cleveland 0.

Boo Ferriss shut out the Indians, allowing just three hits, all singles. He hadn't walked even one batter. He'd faced only 30 batters in the nine innings. Heinz Becker was the only Indian who got as far as second base. Ferriss even got credited for some fine fielding, covering first base twice and making commendable plays on Jim Hegan in the fifth and Gromek in the sixth.

When the year was done, Ferriss was 25-6 (3.26 ERA), leading both the American and National Leagues in winning percentage.

Boston Red Sox 1
Cleveland Indians 0

September 13, 1946 — League Park,
Cleveland

This one was not only a game-winner; it was also a pennant-clincher. And the only inside-the-park homer Ted Williams ever hit. The Red Sox held a 14-game lead over the second-place Tigers, but they still needed one win to clinch, and they lost six games in a row.

The champagne that had traveled with the Sox from Washington to Philadelphia and then to Detroit was again placed on a train and traveled on to Cleveland. One never would have guessed how the Red Sox would clinch the 1946 pennant, though that Ted Williams might be key wouldn't have been a bad guess. Ted Hughson won the game, a 1-0 victory.[147]

It was Friday the 13ᵗʰ and the Indians' Red Embree may have pitched the best game of his life – a two-hitter. Hughson only allowed three hits.

In the top of the first, Embree got Sox center fielder Dom DiMaggio to ground out to third base and struck out shortstop Johnny Pesky. Batting third was Ted Williams.

It was Cleveland's Lou Boudreau who'd developed the extreme shift to defend against Williams. The *Boston Globe*'s headline the next day: "Weird Indian Defense Finally Boomerangs to Give Sox Pennant."[148] On a 1-1 count, with two outs and no one on, Ted – perhaps still remembering advice he'd been given by Harry Heilmann – deliberately slashed a ball to left-center and he hit it hard. It would have been, the *Globe* wrote, "a routine out against an orthodox defense." But League Park had a very deep left-center field and the Tribe's defense had opened up huge holes on the left side of the field. The center fielder himself, Felix Mackiewicz, was to the right of center field, while left fielder Pat Seerey was "about 20 feet back of the grass behind third base, 15 or so feet from the foul line" – guarding against one down the line. Everyone else was shifted to the right side of the field. Ted's drive traveled about 375 feet before it hit the ground and then skittered up to 400 or 430 feet before it settled into a gutter at the base of the wall. By the time Mackiewicz got to it, Williams was almost to third base. He slid across home plate as Boudreau's relay home was a bit off the mark.[149]

Alex Zirin, writing in Cleveland's *Plain Dealer* said, "Ordinarily the drive might have been a double, but never a homer."[150]

The Red Sox had a 1-0 lead.

There wasn't another hit in the game – for either team – until the bottom of the sixth inning. And it was Embree who broke up Hughson's no-hitter by singling to Williams in left field.[151]

In the seventh, Cleveland's Ray Mack got a two-out double. In the eighth, Johnny Pesky got a single. That was it in the hitting department.

The game was over, 1-0 in favor of the Red Sox, and the well-traveled champagne could finally be uncorked.

Ted wanted to give Tex Hughson all the credit for the win. "He pitched a helluva game. My home run didn't mean a thing when I hit it."[152] Williams, years later: "Someone said, 'Is that the easiest homer you ever got?' And I said, 'Hell no, it was the hardest. I had to run!'"[153]

It was Ted's 38th home run of the year, a new season high. It was also his last of the year – and didn't hit one in the World Series, either.[154]

POSTSCRIPT

We won't dwell on it here, but Williams played injured throughout the entire 1946 World Series after being hit on the right elbow by a pitch in the days immediately beforehand during a simulated game meant to keep the players fresh as they awaited resolution of the National League pennant. The story is told in more detail in many other places.[155] Williams hit just .200 in the World Series, without a home run. The biggest headline he got came after Game Three, when he laid down a bunt to the left side just to get on base. The Red Sox won the game, 4-0. Rudy York homered. But Red Smith wrote a column that ran in the *Boston Globe* under the headline "Kid's Bunt Bigger Thrill for Spectators Than York's Wallop."[156]

Williams came within five RBIs of another Triple Crown in 1941, his .406 season, and within .00015 BA of another in 1949. (Photograph by the author)

1947

Another Triple Crown

His elbow was clearly healed. Williams won the Triple Crown once again. He led the league in batting average (.356, with a .499 on-base percentage), home runs (32), and RBIs (114). For the fifth year in a row, he led in runs scored, and for the fourth year in a row, in slugging percentage.

But as Williams knew as well as anyone, it takes a team to win the pennant. Despite Williams's second Triple Crown season, without a productive supporting cast on either offense or defense, the Red Sox slipped to third place in the standings, behind the Yankees and the Tigers.

It was evident in his home run hitting how much Williams carried the team. It was his biggest year for game-winning homers, belting an incredible 10 of them, for a team that was 83-71-3. In 12% of the team victories, it had been a Ted Williams a home run—not just a hit but a homer—that made the difference.

Boston Red Sox 9
Philadelphia Athletics 3

April 18, 1947 — Shibe Park, Philadelphia

It was just the third game of the 1947 season. The American League champions of 1946, the Boston Red Sox, faced Connie Mack's Athletics, who had finished in last place the year before, a whopping 55 games behind Boston. Coming off their pennant-winning season the year before, the Red Sox had every reason to expect to perform well again, but whereas their top four pitchers had combined for 75 wins in 1946, the top four only totaled 54 in 1947.[157]

Mack selected right-hander Bob Savage (3-15 in 1946) to pitch. Joe Cronin picked Boo Ferriss, whose 25-6 record had been tops.

Both teams scored once in the first inning, Boston on an error, walk, and single (the latter was a high fly ball that fell to the ground untouched in front of catcher Buddy Rosar, untouched by anyone, while Dom DiMaggio scored from second base.)

Philadelphia got their run on a single, walk, and single.

The Red Sox got another in the second when Sam Mele walked and then scored from first on Hal Wagner's double to right-center.

The game changed complexion quickly in the fifth inning. Shortstop Johnny Pesky hit a "tricky roller"[158] to Hank Majeski at third, for a single. DiMaggio singled to center and Pesky went first to third. Ted Williams hit a "high wind-blown fly, which sailed over the right-field fence."[159] The *Boston Globe* figured it would have been caught in front of the bullpen at Fenway Park – but this was Shibe Park and it was a home run.[160]

Boston scored one more run that inning.

The Red Sox were set down in order in the sixth, though the fly ball Williams hit to center for the third out was hit further than the one he had hit for a home run.

Doerr led off the seventh inning with a home run into the upper deck of the bleachers in left field, giving Boston a 7-1 lead.

With one out, Ferriss walked Eddie Joost. Elmer Valo singled, putting runners on first and second. This set up a Ferriss faces Ferris situation, Boo pitching to Philly first baseman Ferris Fain. Fain doubled "off the right-field wall"[161] and collected two RBIs as both runners scored. That reduced the Red Sox lead to 7-3. Neither Sam Chapman nor Barney McCosky could get Fain home, both making outs.

The Red Sox got two final runs on the ninth, after back-to-back walks, a groundout, and another walk. Mele grounded out to Joost, who threw to Pete Suder at second, forcing out York. Suder aimed for a double play but a "wild heave"[162] resulted in a throwing error – the third error of the game for Philadelphia – and both DiMaggio and Williams scored.

The Athletics failed to score any of the six runs they would have needed to tie the game.

Boston Red Sox 6
St. Louis Browns 5 (11 innings)

May 6, 1947 — Sportsman's Park, St. Louis

Before the May 6 game at Sportsman's Park began, St. Louis Browns starting pitcher Jack Kramer talked about Red Sox left fielder (and reigning American League MVP) Ted Williams. He "casually remarked that the only way to pitch to Ted if a run meant the ball game is to walk him."[163] The Browns might have benefitted by following his advice.[164]

Rookie lefty Mel Parnell was making just his fourth career start for the Red Sox. He gave up two runs in the bottom of the first.

With two outs and a 3-0 count in the first inning, Williams took a called strike and then singled hard off Kramer into right field – despite a defensive shift that saw three infielders on that side. Kramer then wheeled and picked him off second base. The Browns were no doubt pleased to take a 2-0 lead when they batted in the bottom of the first.

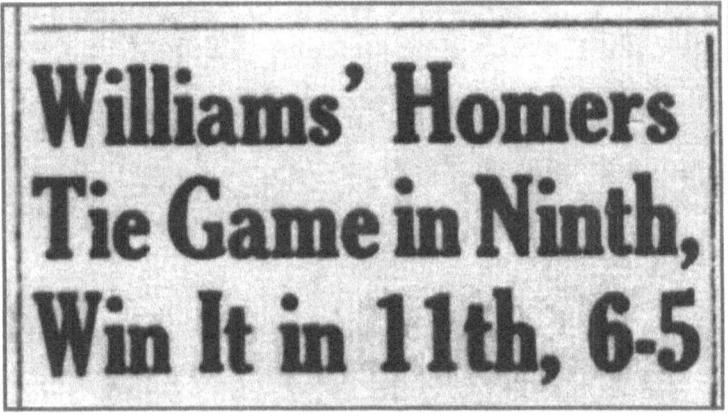

Williams' Homers Tie Game in Ninth, Win It in 11th, 6-5

The Red Sox responded right away with two of their own.

There were a few scattered singles – four by the Browns and two by the Red Sox – but it was still 2-2 entering the bottom of the seventh. The Browns edged ahead by one run, Kramer drawing a walk, seeing the bases get loaded, and tagging and scoring on a sacrifice fly by Vern Stephens, off Fritz Dorish, who relieved Parnell. With just two innings to go, the Browns held a 3-2 lead.

No one scored in the eighth. Top of the ninth, with the one-run lead and with one out, Ted Williams was up. The game was arguably not on the line, but Kramer pitched to him and threw a pitch that was "a bit too sweet...[He swung and the ball] sailed on a line, crashing against the metal of the light standards above the pavilion in right-center."[165] The 400-foot drive "caromed off a steel girder" and tied the game.[166]

Lehner tripled off Klinger with two outs in the bottom of the ninth but Stephens made the final out and the game went into the 10th.

Facing reliever Earl Johnson, the Browns got two singles and Johnson intentionally walked Les Moss. St. Louis didn't score.

Fred Sanford was Kramer's replacement as pitcher. Pellagrini doubled off the bleacher wall in left-center and Johnny Pesky walked. This brought up Ted Williams. Walk him to load the bases, with nobody out? No, Sanford pitched to him. Williams laid off the first pitch, a ball. Then he saw a pitch to his liking. Williams "unloaded. He gave it a terrific ride. It cleared the ten-foot high screen at the back of the right-field pavilion. It crossed Grand st. in back of the pavilion...a three-run smash."[167]

The score was suddenly 6-3, Red Sox.

Every run produced by Williams's three-run homer was needed. Johnson walked the leadoff batter in the bottom of the 11th, Bob Dillinger. He got two outs, but then gave up a two-run homer to Jeff Heath, a drive over the roof of the right-field pavilion. Only after he struck out Jerry Witte was the game complete. It was, wrote Stockton, "very much a Ted Williams victory, 6 to 5."[168]

Boston Red Sox 12
St. Louis Browns 7

May 16, 1947 — Fenway Park

This game-winning homer was hit "nearly as high as it was long."[169]

Boston pitcher Harry "Fritz" Dorish squared off against the Browns' Jack Kramer in front of 8,639 paying customers and another 3,719 women on "Ladies Day" at Fenway Park.[170]

The Red Sox starter was also 3-1, right-hander Harry "Fritz" Dorish. The 14-10 Red Sox were only two games behind league-leading Detroit, but the last-place Browns were only 7 ½ games behind Detroit. There was still plenty of time in a season only a month old.

Dorish gave up base hits to the first two batters he faced, but was bailed out by a double play and pop fly.

Kramer also gave up a leadoff single, to shortstop Eddie Pellagrini. Johnny Pesky lined out to left. Ted Williams walked. Rudy York singled to left, scoring Pellagrini; Williams took third. Second baseman Bobby Doerr flied out to right field, Williams tagged and scored and it was 2-0, Red Sox.

The Sox got three more in the third. Pesky bunted for a single, Williams singled. Rudy York walked. Pesky bunted for a hit. Williams singled. York walked. Bobby Doerr's sacrifice fly scored one.[171] Dom DiMaggio's single scored another, and Hal Wagner's sac fly scored the third.

The Red Sox upped it to 7-0 in the fourth on Pesky's single, Williams reaching on a throwing error that let Pesky score from first base, and York's double to center.

Walter Brown took over from Kramer. Right fielder Leon Culberson walked. After two outs, Pellagrini singled and Pesky walked. Ted Williams hit a grand slam to deep right field, "a 400 ft. wallop over the Sox bullpen and ten rows high in the right-field bleacher area."[172] It was also a ball hit "nearly as high as it was long."[173]

TED GRAND SLAMS AS SOX WIN

In the seventh, Paul Lehner took Dorish deep for a three-run homer. In the ninth, St. Louis scored four more times. Manager Joe Cronin left Dorish in so he could get a complete game, his first win in the big leagues.[174]

Though Williams's homer off Brown was the game-winner, providing runs 8 through 11 in a 12-7 game, the loss was given to starting pitcher Jack Kramer, who'd gotten the Browns in a 7-0 hole.

Boston Red Sox 5
Detroit Tigers 4

May 19, 1947 — Fenway Park
(second game of a doubleheader)

It was looking like a sad Monday for Red Sox fans at Fenway Park. The 1946 pennant winners played a daytime doubleheader, making up a game postponed due to rain from the previous day. They were hosting the 1945 world champion Detroit Tigers, who had finished second in 1946.

The first game was a heartbreaker of a loss. The Red Sox had nursed a 2-0 lead from the third inning, given up single runs in the sixth and eight and then losing it, 3-2, in the 12th. Boo Ferriss had gone the distance, but a walk and then a double by third baseman George Kell did him in. Al Benton won for the Tigers, a well-deserved win earned pitching seven innings of scoreless three-hit relief of Fred Hutchinson.

The second-game starters were Tex Hughson for the Red Sox and Hal White for the Tigers.

The Tigers put two runs on the board in the top of the third. After Hughson struck out the first two batters, Eddie Lake doubled and Kell singled, scoring Lake. Roy Cullenbine then singled, and Kell scored.

Detroit added a run in the fourth after Ted Williams lost a ball in the sun for an error, followed by a sacrifice and a single.

The Red Sox responded, scoring twice and pulling back to within a run. Sam Mele singled.[175] Roy Partee reached on an error. After Hughson made an out, Johnny Pesky walked, loading the bases. Wally Moses singled and drove in Mele. Williams picked up an RBI on a bases-loaded walk. The score was 3-2, Tigers.

The Red Sox tied it in the bottom of the eighth, thanks to a triple to left field by Eddie Pellagrini followed by a ball hit by Partee that nicked off George Kell's glove for a single.

The Tigers took a 4-3 lead in the top of the ninth after Eddie Mayo led off with a double off the left-field wall. Sacrificed to second, Doc Cramer pinch-hit for the pitcher and singled through the box.

The game was placed in the hands of Virgil Trucks, hoping to hold the lead.

He only got one out. Johnny Pesky grounded out. Moses got his second hit of the game, a single to center.

Trucks was wary of Ted Williams, the Boston batsman having previously hit three home runs off him. "Trucks was trying to avoid giving Williams a fastball to hit, but his first three pitches were off the plate. It was 3-0 and he either had to risk putting the winning run on base or throw one over. He fired a fastball, high and up by the letters, and Ted hit it and it went out – a walkoff, about five or six rows into the right-field grandstand."[176]

Boston Red Sox 5
St. Louis Browns 2

June 4, 1947 — Sportsman's Park, St. Louis

In 1947, Ted Williams hit 11 of his 32 home runs against St. Louis Browns pitchers, three of them against Bob Muncrief. This was the first.[177]

Jeff Heath played with the Browns in 1947 and the following March he talked about how some of the St. Louis pitchers lost the guessing game against Ted Williams. "He wore us out, and the reason was that our pitchers wanted to throw to him. They wouldn't walk him, like other sensible pitchers. They kept thinking they'd found his weakness. If he took a swing and missed, the pitcher would say, 'Ah, now I got it. I know how to pitch to him.' The next time Ted batted the pitcher would throw the same pitch, but this time Ted would hit it out of the park."[178]

Red Sox pitcher Tom Wright told Ben Bradlee Jr. that Williams told him, "I don't guess what they throw. I *figure* what they're going to throw."[179]

Williams struggled a bit in June. There were only three days during June when his batting average nudged above .300. He was hitting .292 before the June 4 game. This was the first twilight game of the year at Sportsman's Park.[180] It featured two right-handers as starters – Muncrief (4-4) for the home team and Joe Dobson (4-3) for the Red Sox.

Williams walked to lead off the second, though he had fouled the second pitch hard into his right instep and had to limp to first base. Center fielder Sam Mele walked, too. Bobby Doerr singled, Williams scoring. 1-0, Red Sox.

Boston added a run in the third. Dobson scored it. He singled to right field, was bunted to second, and scored when Wally Moses doubled over Jeff Heath's head in left field.

St. Louis got one back on a leadoff single, wild pitch, groundout, and a squeeze bunt by Muncrief. They tied it in the fifth on a two-out home run by Wally Judnich "on top of the pavilion roof in right."[181]

Leading off the sixth inning, Ted Williams swung at the first pitch, homering and breaking the 2-2 tie, with a liner "rifled to the top of the right-center field roof."[182]

The Red Sox added a pair of insurance runs in the eighth. Moses started with a single off first baseman Judnich's glove and into right field. He took second base when Williams grounded out to Judnich at first base. Sam Mele then saw a fastball to his liking and "gave it a long ride high up into the left field bleachers."[183] With the two-run homer, it was 5-2, Red Sox.

That score obtained through the end of play.

Dobson won the game; he had allowed only four base hits, and the Browns left not one man on base all game long. A pair of double plays erased two baserunners and a caught stealing another one.

Boston Red Sox 7
Chicago White Sox 2

July 16, 1947 — Comiskey Park, Chicago

Ted Williams hit a game-winning home run off a future Hall of Famer, 42-year-old Red Ruffing. He'd first homered off Ruffing eight years earlier, hitting the seventh home run of his career in just his second month in the majors. Ruffing was with the New York Yankees at the time and the Yankees were at Fenway Park. "The Kid" hit a two-run homer in the bottom of the first inning. Ruffing had 3,584 2/3 innings of major-league experience before throwing that first inning.[184]

Ruffing was facing a Red Sox team that hadn't been producing runs – over their prior six games, the Red Sox had scored a total of six runs. The reigning American League champions were 12 ½ games behind the first-place New York Yankees.

Ruffing had a rough first inning. Rookie third baseman Sam Dente led off with a single to right field. Johnny Pesky walked. Wally Moses hit a fly ball to deep right; Dente tagged and took third. Ted Williams singled to right, driving in Dente, with Pesky going to third. Bobby Doerr flied out to center, and Pesky tagged and scored.

Denny Galehouse was manager Joe Cronin's starter. The 35-year-old former St. Louis Brown had joined the Red Sox on June 20. He retired the side in the first, second, and third.

In the third, Boston scored another pair. Leading off, Pesky singled to left. Ruffing struck out Moses, but Ted Williams "thumped a 370-foot home run into the right-field stands."[185] He hit it "into the lower right field stands,"[186] giving Boston a 4-0 lead.

The White Sox got their first baserunner on a one-out double to left-center by shortstop Luke Appling in the top of the fourth. Nothing came of it. He remained camped on second.

With two outs, Moses doubled in the top of the fifth. Williams stepped in. He was given an intentional walk, his 101st base on balls of the 1947 season. Doerr fouled out.

Galehouse gave up two singles in the fifth, one in the sixth, and one in the seventh. The shutout held, Boston scoring a fifth run when DiMaggio doubled, leading off the sixth inning. Birdie Tebbetts singled off Ruffing's pitching hand into center field, and DiMaggio scored.

In inning number eight, Boston added two more off reliever Earl Harrist, on a walk, a couple of singles, a sacrifice, and an error, for a 7-0 lead.

Galehouse was working on a five-hit shutout but faltered in the bottom of the ninth. Taffy Wright singled to center. Rudy York doubled to left. Dave Philley singled, giving the Browns their first run of the game. York ran first to third, and tagged and scored on a fly ball from Thurman Tucker. Don Kolloway grounded into a game-ending double play.

Boston Red Sox 12
St. Louis Browns 1

July 26, 1947 — Fenway Park

July 26 must have been Ted Williams's favorite day. Over the course of his career, he hit 10 home runs on July 26 – more than on any other date. The first three times he did it, he doubled up – hitting two runs each time.[187]

The two home runs he hit on this date in 1947 were off different pitchers. The first of the two, hit in the very first inning, was the game-winning hit that day.

In the first inning, the Browns got a run off Joe Dobson that was dubbed "a little on the phony-baloney side" because the RBI triple that Paul Lehner hit had taken a "freak skid" and gotten away from him.[188]

Cliff Fannin started for last-place St. Louis, but he'd been pitching well, with a 2.70 ERA. Johnny Pesky walked and Williams hit a two-run homer, swinging on a 3-1 count and banging it "over the Red Sox bullpen and…eight rows up in the bleachers."[189] It was the third day in a row he had homered. He wasn't done yet.[190]

Boston first baseman Jake Jones hit another two-run homer in the second inning, into the screen atop the left-field wall, in the bottom of the second. Manager Muddy Ruel brought in a new pitcher, Bob Muncrief. In the third inning, Williams struck again. Sam Mele singled to center, leading off. Williams hit another homer to the same location, but a few rows higher.[191]

Ted caused Muncrief more grief with this one. He'd just hit a game-winner off Muncrief on June 29.[192] A seventh run scored when Bobby Doerr doubled off the left-field wall and Birdie Tebbetts singled him home.

Williams Belts Two More as Sox Picnic, 12-1

Dobson never gave up a run after the first inning, only allowing four scattered hits over the final eight innings.

The Red Sox, though, weren't finished. In the fourth, Pesky doubled and Mele singled him home. Williams almost hit a third home run. Right fielder Willard Brown "backed up and reached over a low fence between the grandstand and right field bleachers for a brilliant catch."[193]

The Red Sox scored four more times in the fifth – 12-1. Williams grounded out to short for the final out.

By game's end, every batter in the Red Sox starting lineup had two base hits except Dobson and Doerr; they each had to do with just one.

Ted Williams hit another home run on Sunday's game against the Browns, making it four games in a row he had homered, increasing his home run total for the year from 18 to 23.

In three weeks, he had added 39 points to his batting average and was hitting .331.

Boston Red Sox 2
Detroit Tigers 1

August 2, 1947 — Fenway Park

August 2 was celebrated as Bobby Doerr Day at Fenway Park. For the "silent captain" of the Red Sox, it was like Midsummer Christmas.[194] The *Boston Globe*'s Harold Kaese wrote that Doerr "had enough merchandise when the presentations were concluded to start a country store."[195]

The game was a Saturday night game, played in the first year that Fenway Park had lighting for night games.

All the runs in the ballgame that followed came in the first inning.

The visiting Detroit Tigers batted first, facing right-hander Tex Hughson. Alternating outs and singles initially, Roy Cullenbine singled over second base and into center field. George Kell singled to right field. Then Pat Mullin singled in Cullenbine.

Williams' Two-Run Homer Sets Back Tigers, 2 to 1

Pitching for Detroit was Virgil Trucks. On his very first pitch, he was greeted with a triple to the 379-foot marker in right-center field by Sam Mele.[196] Johnny Pesky and Dom DiMaggio both made outs and that brought up Ted Williams. On a 2-1 count, he clouted one "into the net, over the top of the deep left-center field wall, not far from the flag pole." It was a two-run homer, a "smack of genuine authority."[197] It was Williams's fifth home run off Trucks.[198] It gave Boston a 2-1 lead. Doerr ended the inning and was 0-for-4 in the game.[199]

No one reached base for either team in the second inning. Eddie Mayo singled for Detroit in the fourth, extending his hitting streak to 20 games. One player from each team got a base hit in the fifth, both with two outs. In the sixth inning, after two outs, both Evers and Mayo singled, but no runs scored. There were occasional hits by both teams (the Tigers even loaded the bases in the top of the eighth on a walk, an error, and an intentional walk), but pinch-hitter Vic Wertz, hit a "weak grounder to the box."[200] Hughson threw to first base for the third out.

Both pitchers went the distance. Hughson evened his record at 9-9. He'd given up seven base hits, all singles. He'd walked four. The loss incurred by Trucks left him with an even record as well: 7-7. Trucks had walked only one, but given up nine hits – including the leadoff triple by Sam Mele and the first-inning, game-winning home run to Ted Williams.

Boston Red Sox 9
Detroit Tigers 1

August 26, 1947 — Briggs Stadium
(second game of a doubleheader)

The Tigers and Red Sox were a half-game apart, jostling for second place.[201]

The second game's pitchers were Detroit's Hal White (4-4) and Boston's Tex Hughson (10-10).

First to score were the visitors. The Red Sox scored two runs in the top of the first. Between two strikeouts, Johnny Pesky walked. Ted Williams, batting cleanup, hit a two-run homer, "a line drive into the right field lower stands."[202]

A home run put the Tigers on the board, a one-out solo home run – "into the upper deck of the right-field stands" – by first baseman Roy Cullenbine.[203]

The second inning featured five strikeouts, two Tigers and three Red Sox.

The Red Sox added a run to their slim lead in the top of the third. After Hughson struck out, Wally Moses doubled. Pesky made an out, but Dom DiMaggio singled and drive in Moses. Ted Williams walked (his 136th of the season); there were 10 walks doled out during the game, five by each team.

The Red Sox scored three runs in the top of the fifth, taking a 6-1 lead. With one out, Moses singled and Pesky walked. DiMaggio singled, scoring Moses. White tried to pick off Pesky at second base, but threw the ball away and both runners moved up, to second and third base respectively. Ted Williams doubled, driving them both in. Johnny Gorsica relieved White, but it was already 6-1.

The Red Sox added a pair of runs in the sixth. Hughson walked and Moses hit a home run.

Two Tigers reached base in the sixth, and again in the seventh, but they couldn't cash in.

Perhaps just for good measure, the Red Sox added a ninth and final run in the top of the ninth inning on Ted Williams's sacrifice fly. It was his fifth RBI of the game. He'd also driven in the only Red Sox run in the first game. Williams was 3-for-7 on the day, with the six RBIs.

His two-run homer led the way and was the game-winner in game two. Compared to other homers he hit at Briggs Stadium, this was a more modest one – "into the lower deck in right field"[204] – but it was a home run all the same. Hughson threw a four-hitter.

The *Boston Globe*'s summary of the day: "Fans, your Red Sox couldn't do anything right in the first game of a double-header here today. In the second game, they couldn't do anything wrong."[205]

Boston Red Sox 8
Washington Senators 1

September 27, 1947 — Griffith Stadium, Washington

It was the next-to-last game of the 1947 season, played on a Saturday afternoon. The Senators were in seventh place and neither a win nor a loss would alter their place in the league standings, but the Red Sox were in third place and just one game behind the Detroit Tigers. They had a chance to move up and claim second-place money, but they also had the Cleveland Indians nipping at their heels, a game behind Boston.[206]

The game drew what the *Washington Post* termed "3148 shivering fans, the smallest crowd of the season and half of them ladies day 'freebies'."[207]

Walt Masterson (12-15) was Washington's starting pitcher; Joe Dobson (17-8) got the assignment for Boston.

The Red Sox jumped out to a quick 3-0 lead in the first inning. Merl Combs, playing in his 17th major-league game, led off and doubled. Johnny Pesky bunted, sacrificing so Combs could reach third base. Dom DiMaggio walked. On an 0-2 count, Ted Williams hit a ball that "hit the top of the right-field fence and dropped over on the far side."[208] The *Boston Herald* described the homer almost the same way: "With two strikes on him, Ted smote the ball into right center. It struck the top of the fence and dropped over for the three-run parade."[209] It was indeed a three-run home run.

Washington got a one-out solo home run in the second, hit just fair by Stan Spence, a liner over the fence in right field.

Boston mounted a threat in the top of the fifth, loading the bases, and did it again in the sixth. Neither time did they score.

The Red Sox blew open the gates in the top of the eighth. Jake Jones started with a single to left. He was dutifully sacrificed to second by Roy Partee. Dobson reached on an error by shortstop John Sullivan, Jones going to third base. Combs singled to center field; Jones scored. Pesky doubled to left field, driving in both Dobson and Combs and winding up on third base as Robertson incurred an error on his throw in. Masterson then threw a ball away, too – a wild pitch, letting Pesky scamper home.

DiMaggio singled to left. Williams walked. Moses singled to center and DiMaggio scored the fifth run on the inning, giving Boston an 8-1 lead.

Pesky doubled in the ninth, his third hit of the game and his 207th base hit of the year, the third time in his three seasons that he had hit safely more than 200 times.

Dobson faltered a bit in the bottom of the ninth, but the Senators left the bases loaded.[210]

With his 197th home run, Williams had given Dobson all the runs he needed with that three-run homer back in the top of the first inning.[211]

The 10 game-winning homers he hit in 1947 were the most in any given year. The Red Sox won 83 games in 1947.

Williams completes another head-down trip around the bases as
teammate Joe Cronin gets ready to step in. (Leslie Jones photograph,
Boston Public Library)

1948

Sox Miss Pennant on One-Game Playoff Loss

After something of an off year for the Red Sox as a team, they contended for the pennant down to the wire. In sixth place as late as mid-June, they began to accumulate victories and spent most of September in first place, though only by slim margins. The early-season leaders—the Cleveland Indians—recovered their form and overtook the Red Sox on September 26. On the final day of the 154-game schedule, Boston won and Cleveland lost, putting the two teams in a tie, necessitating a single-game playoff for the pennant. The Indians won the tiebreaker, 8-3 (and the World Series over the Boston Braves). An all-Boston World Series was not to be.

Williams hit four game-winning homers in 1948, and led the league in batting average (.369), on-base percentage (.497), and slugging (.615). He hit 25 homers (sixth in the league) and drove in 127 (third.)

Boston Red Sox 7
Cleveland Indians 4

June 16, 1948 — Cleveland Stadium

Cleveland was in first place. Boston was in fifth, 9 ½ games behind. Bob Feller was struggling a bit, having lost his last four decisions despite a 3.41 ERA.[212]

Feller gave up two runs in the top of the first inning. Dom DiMaggio singled to center field. Johnny Pesky walked. Williams reached on an infield single "to the right of [second baseman Joe] Gordon, who knocked the ball down, but was unable to make a play at any base."[213] DiMaggio scored on a double play. Vern Stephens singled and Pesky scored.

The Indians loaded the bases against Joe Dobson in the first inning, but did not score for the first four innings.

The Red Sox added a third run, in the third inning. Williams doubled to left, took third on a wild pitch, and scored when Stan Spence singled to center.

WILLIAMS' 4 HITS PUNCH HOLES IN 'BOUDREAU SHIFT'

Ken Keltner led off the fifth with a home run off Dobson into the lower left-field stands and it was 3-1, Boston. It was his 15th of the season, leading the American League.

The Red Sox leapt out further in front in the top of the seventh inning. After DiMaggio grounded out, second to first, Pesky worked a walk. Ted Williams hit a ball he "walloped over the 365-foot mark on the temporary fence in left field, on the second pitch."[214] The homer capped a 4-for-4 day off Feller.

Stan Spence singled to right field. Bobby Doerr hit a two-run home run over the left-field fence very close to the same spot where Williams had hit his. That made the score 7-1.

Steve Gromek took over from Feller in the eighth.

The Indians scored two runs in the bottom of the eighth. After back-to-back singles, an out, and a walk, the bases were loaded. Joe Gordon doubled over Williams's head in left field and drove in two.

Ahead by four runs as the bottom of the ninth began, Dobson got two outs but then began to play with fire, loading the bases on an infield single and two walks (his sixth and seventh of the game). He then walked Wally Judnich, forcing in a run.

Boston manager Joe McCarthy was so upset that he "picked up the resin bag and threw it the length of the dugout."[215] He summoned Boo Ferriss to relieve. The dangerous Joe Gordon hit a fly ball to DiMaggio in deep center field for the final out. It wasn't far from a grand slam, said the *Cleveland Plain Dealer*: "DiMaggio took the fly a few feet short of the fence."[216]

Among pitchers enshrined in the National Baseball Hall of Fame, Feller gave up the most home runs to Ted Williams. His 10 topped Jim Bunning and Early Wynn (8 apiece), Red Ruffing (4), Hal Newhouser (3), Lefty Gomez (2), and one each off Whitey Ford and Ted Lyons. So in all, 37 of his 521 home runs were hit off Hall of Famers.

Boston Red Sox 10
Chicago White Sox 5

August 27, 1948 — Fenway Park

The Red Sox were in first place by a half-game. The White Sox were in last, 31 1/3 games behind and in late August had only won 40 games all year.

Jack Kramer (14-4) started for the Red Sox. Chicago scored one in the first, which Boston matched. The Red Sox added two more off Chicago starter Marino Pieretti in the second.

The White Sox took a 4-3 lead in the top of the fourth. Two walks set the stage for a Cass Michaels triple to right-center. Denny Galehouse relieved Kramer. A sacrifice fly scored Michaels.

Ted's Three-Run Homer Features 10-5 Triumph

The score seesawed back the other way in the bottom of the fourth. Birdie Tebbetts doubled to center. With two out, Dom DiMaggio singled and Johnny Pesky tripled to right field.

In the bottom of the sixth, Pieretti retired the first two Red Sox. DiMaggio then singled to left. He stole second. Pesky walked. Family and friends back home in San Diego no doubt enjoyed seeing the *San Diego Union* headline: WILLIAMS CLOUTS HOMER TO HELP RED SOX WIN, 10-5. The pitch he hit "dropped into the right-field bleachers 400 feet from the plate," as the accompanying story explained.[217]

That three-run homer did the trick, giving the Red Sox an 8-4 lead.

Galehouse almost got burned in the seventh, with two singles, a double, and a walk, but no runs scored. On the second single, Williams had deftly thrown a ball he fielded to second baseman Bobby Doerr and caught the runner rounding second in a rundown.

DiMaggio singled in a ninth run in the seventh. He was 4-for-5 in the game, scored three runs, and drove in two.

Chicago got one more in the eighth, which Boston matched in the ninth. Williams led off with a double to left field. On a wild pitch, he ran to third base and then scored on a subsequent throwing error.

All told, the White Sox got 11 hits and were given a very generous eight bases on balls. The Red Sox only got two more hits (a total of 13) and six walks. Each team had five extra-base hits. Three White Sox errors hurt. The White Sox left 11 on base; the Red Sox left 8. The Red Sox, overall, however, were said to have just "had much too much power."[218]

Boston Red Sox 10
St. Louis Browns 2

August 29, 1948 — Fenway Park
(first game of a doubleheader)

In this day's game against the visiting St. Louis Browns, the Red Sox scored 10 runs, but it was the three-run homer that Williams hit in the first inning that carried the day and was another game-winner. Boston added four more runs in the first and three after that, but the Browns only scored twice. The homer was a come-from-behind home run, too. The Browns had scored once in the top of the first.

Joe Dobson pitched this first game of two. Dobson was 13-7 but he hadn't won since July 25.

The first two batters singled, and were bunted into scoring position. A sacrifice fly brought Bob Dillinger home.

Pitching for St. Louis was right-hander Karl Drews. He walked leadoff batter Dom DiMaggio on four pitches. Johnny Pesky also saw four balls go by. That brought up #9 – Ted Williams. Ball one. Ball two. Drews had thrown 10 pitches, every one a ball. Finally he put one over the plate – and Williams "hit it sky-high. The heavy wind caught the ball and sent it sailing into the concrete bleacher."[219] After Vern Stephens fouled out to the catcher, Bobby Doerr singled, to left, Stan Spence hit an infield single.

Browns manager Zack Taylor replaced Drews with Bryan Stephens, another righty. Stephens walked Billy Goodman. Catcher Birdie Tebbetts stepped into the batter's box. The bases were loaded "and 'Tarzan' Tebbetts promptly unloaded them with a drive into the netting, above the wall in left field."[220] Grand slam. Four more runs. The Red Sox took the field for the second inning with a 7-1 lead.

The first batter for the Browns, Hank Arft, homered to lead off the second inning.

The Red Sox reasserted their six-run lead in the third, when Spence walked and Goodman doubled to left.

Then they added two in the fifth. Doerr led off with a single. Spence singled and Doerr ran to third. Goodman flied out and Doerr tagged and scored. After a fly ball and a walk to Dobson, DiMaggio doubled to right field and Spence scored the 10th run.

After the third inning, Dobson only allowed two singles. He went the distance and booked the 10-2 win, raising his record on the season to 14-7.

There was a second game, which St. Louis won by a lopsided score, 12-4, similarly scoring enough runs (five) in the first inning to win the game and collecting 20 base hits to Boston's 10.

Boston Red Sox 5
New York Yankees 1

October 2, 1948 — Fenway Park

On the next-to-last day of the 1948 season, the Boston Red Sox and the New York Yankees both had identical 94-58 records, tied for second place, both teams only one game behind the league-leading Cleveland Indians. If the Indians were to win on October 2 – which they did, beating the Detroit Tigers, 8-0 – whichever team won this game in Boston still had a chance. The losing team would be eliminated.[221]

The Yankees weren't having the best year against Boston; they came into the game with a head-to-head record of 8-12. Boston's starter was Jack Kramer (17-5).[222] Left-hander Tommy Byrne (8-4) started for New York. He'd won six decisions in a row.

The first runs in the game came in the bottom of the first. With one out, Johnny Pesky drew a four-pitch walk. Ted Williams was walked three times in the game, but not his first time up. With a count of 2-2, Williams hit Byrne's next pitch into the "center-field end of the Yanks' bull pen. It was one of those old-time lordly and high affairs."[223] The Yankees had put on a shift, but as John Drebinger of the *New York Times* noted, "it would have made little difference where Harris placed his men."[224]

"It was one of the most important homers Ted has hit," wrote Hy Hurwitz in the *Boston Globe*.[225] It had, as it transpired, won the game and spared the Red Sox from elimination.

Jack Hand of the *Cleveland Plain Dealer* noted of Williams, "Of his 126 runs batted in, 28 have been against Yankee pitching, which he has also nicked for five homers."[226]

The only three Yankees to reach base over the first six innings were on singles in the first, second, and sixth. Kramer didn't walk a man or see one reach on an error.

The Red Sox added two more runs in their half of the third. Pesky walked again. Williams doubled to far right-center. Byrne struck out Vern Stephens, and then intentionally walked Doerr. Spence singled to right and everyone moved up a base, Pesky scoring. Joe Page relieved Byrne. Billy Goodman's sacrifice fly gave the Red Sox a 4-0 lead.

It bumped up a run in the fifth. Dom DiMaggio singled, Pesky doubled to left-center, and Williams was walked intentionally. Vern Stephens flied out to center, caught by Joe DiMaggio with his back pressed to the wall, allowing brother Dom to easily tag and score.

The only run the Yankees scored was in the seventh. Joe DiMaggio led off with a double off the wall in left-center. He took third on a ball Yogi Berra hit to Kramer. Two batters later, Joe D. scored on pinch-hitter Johnny Lindell's fly to right field.

Each team had five hits, but Yankees pitchers walked 11. Three of the walks were to Williams, two of them intentional. One is reminded of an anecdote Ned Garver once told about Yogi Berra complaining to an umpire for a ball four call on a pitch to Ted Williams. The umpire reportedly said, "Well, at least I held him to one base." Garver said, "If you walked him, he only got to first. If you pitched to him, you didn't know what the hell was going to happen."[227]

Williams had gone 6-for-8 in the last three games on the schedule. The October 2 loss knocked the Yankees out of the pennant race. The Red Sox won game #154, and the Indians lost, putting the two teams a tie for the pennant and necessitating a single-game playoff at Fenway Park.

POSTSCRIPT

In 1948, there was the homer that Ted Williams *didn't* hit. He was 1-for-4 in the playoff game and scored once, but the final was 8-3, in favor of the Indians. The Boston Braves had won the National League pennant, but there was to be no Boston/Boston World Series. Even if he had homered every time up, and hit four home runs, the Sox would have fallen short, since there was only once he came up with anyone on base – and that was with Pesky on second in the first inning.

The Red Sox had gotten to a poor start in 1948, already 11 1/2 games out of first place on the last day of May. They made up a lot of ground, but ultimately lacked that one final win that eluded them.

Williams ended 1948, having – as in 1946 – seen the Red Sox lose an elimination game. He'd hit 25 homers, the lowest since the 23 he hit in 1940. His 44 doubles led the league and he led in walks, with 126. Both helped him to his sixth season in a row leading in on-base percentage, this time .497. His .369 batting average led the league as did his .615 slugging percentage. He came in third in the MVP voting, with DiMaggio second, and Cleveland's player/manager Lou Boudreau deservedly coming in first. Boudreau had hit two homers in the playoff game and went on to lead his team to win the World Series.[228]

1949

Another MVP and Another Heartbreaking Pennant Loss

Ted Williams won the MVP award for the second time in 1949. For the seventh year in a row, he led the league in on-base percentage (.490). His 162 bases on balls led the A.L. for the sixth consecutive year. He led in home runs (43) and his runs batted in (159) led both leagues; both figures were career highs. He scored 150 runs, leading both leagues for the fifth time and the American League for the sixth time.

He played in all 155 games, one more than the 154-game schedule, the extra game being a 14-14, 13-inning tie on May 3 against Detroit. In that game, Williams went 3-for-7 with two doubles, a home run, and five RBIs. The end of the season was equally as bitter as 1948, maybe more so, due to who beat them. After winning won 12 of 13 games to close out September and take a one-game lead over the Yankees, the two met head-to-head in the final two games of the season, with New York prevailing 5-4 and 5-3 to take the pennant.

"The Kid" – in the year he turned 31 – hit eight game-winning homers, two of them in that September run, including a 1-0 game-winner on September 14.

Boston Red Sox 7
Chicago White Sox 4

May 18, 1949 — Fenway Park

It was a Wednesday afternoon in May. The Chicago White Sox were in Boston. The season was young. Chicago was in fourth place, 14-13. The Red Sox were 11-13, in seventh place, but were only five games behind the league-leading Yankees. The season was full of possibilities for both teams. The Red Sox had lost the 1948 pennant in a one-game playoff with the Cleveland Indians. The White Sox, though, had suffered a dismal 1948 season, finishing in last place, 44 ½ games behind. Perhaps unsurprisingly they had a new manager in 1949, Jack Onslow. Red Sox manager Joe McCarthy was back for a second season.

Fenway Park had been something of a "jinx" for the White Sox in 1948. They had won only once at Fenway, for a 1-10 record.

The starters were Ellis Kinder for Boston and Marino Pieretti for Chicago.[229]

Kinder retired the first three White Sox. Pieretti got tagged for three runs.

Center fielder Dom DiMaggio led off for Boston with a drive that "bounced past [center fielder] Gerry Scala for a triple."[230] Third baseman Johnny Pesky grounded out to first base; DiMaggio held at third. Ted Williams singled to right field and it was 1-0. Pieretti struck out shortstop Vern Stephens. Second baseman Bobby Doerr homered into the net above the left-field wall.

DiMaggio walked and Williams hit a two-run homer in the bottom of the third. It was "a tremendous belt about 10 rows up in the right field stands – a lordly poke with plenty of carry."[231] The homer was estimated by the *Chicago Tribune* at about 390 feet, hit "into the right field wing."[232]

In the fourth, Boston improved their lead to 6-0 when DiMaggio drew a two-out walk, driven in by a double to right-center by Johnny Pesky.

After Kinder got the first two outs in the top of the fifth, Gordon Goldsberry singled and Appling drew a base on balls. Left fielder Gus Zernial cut the lead in half with a three-run homer into the screen above the left-field wall, a drive that the *Boston Herald* said was still climbing when it hit near the top of the net.[233]

Pesky drove in Birdie Tebbetts for a seventh run, in the sixth.

In the top of the ninth, the White Sox scored once more – but only once. Zernial doubled in Goldsberry; Zernial had all four Chicago RBIs.[234] Williams had the game-winning base hit, his home run in the third inning.

Boston Red Sox 5
Washington Senators 4

May 28, 1949 — Fenway Park

The Red Sox were nearing the end of a homestand in which they won 10 of 13 games, including three extra-inning games and three games in which Ted Williams hit game-winning home runs.[235]

Neither starting pitcher made it through the fifth inning.

Jack Kramer started for the Red Sox. He saw three Senators get on base in the first, two in the second, and one in the third, but none of them cross home plate. In the first inning, the *Washington Post* wrote that the Senators had "performed the feat of accumulating a double, a single and a hit batsman without getting a man past second base."[236]

Ray Scarborough allowed one Sox batter on base in the first and the second, and then four runs in the third. Left fielder Gil Coan had to leave the game in the bottom of the first after crashing off the left-field wall trying to catch Johnny Pesky's double.[237]

Kramer kicked off the four-run rally by singling to left field. Dom DiMaggio doubled off the wall in left-center. Pesky shot a ball that "nearly decapitated" Scarborough, singling into center; both baserunners scored.[238] Williams singled, Pesky going to third base. Vern Stephens singled to left field and Pesky scored.

After five consecutive base hits and still no one out, Scarborough was relieved by 21-year-old Dick Welteroth, in his second season with Washington. Billy Goodman's sacrifice fly brought in the fourth run.

In the top of the fifth inning, Kramer got chased as the Senators tied it, 4-4, on three singles, a sacrifice fly, two walks, and a two-run single by catcher Al Evans.

Tex Hughson relieved Kramer and worked the final 4 2/3 innings, only allowing three hits and walking one.[239]

Welteroth worked five innings of relief and only allowed one run, but that was the one run that broke the 4-4 tie and made the difference.

In the bottom of the fifth inning, the first batter for Boston was Ted Williams. He swung at Welteroth's first pitch of the frame, and hit "a high drive which dropped into the bullpen reserved for visiting firemen."[240] In other words, he homered into the Washington bullpen in right field. The tie was broken.

Boston loaded the bases but scored no more. Over their last three innings, all they mustered was a walk in eighth.

The score remained 5-4 heading into the ninth inning. Hughson had held up, but he flirted with danger, giving up two doubles and a walk but not a run.[241]

Boston Red Sox 4
Philadelphia Athletics 3

May 30, 1949 — Fenway Park
(second game of doubleheader)

The Red Sox won both halves of the Memorial Day doubleheader against the visiting Philadelphia Athletics, 10-2 and 4-3.[242]

Ted Williams hadn't helped much until the eighth inning of the second game. In the first game, he had gone 0-for-3, hitting into two double plays, grounding out 3-1, and walking a couple of times.

The game was scoreless through the first six innings.

Left-hander Mel Parnell was pitching for the Red Sox and 22-year-old righty Carl Scheib was pitching for the Athletics.[243]

After Parnell struck out the first two batters he faced, Wally Moses "beat out an infield hit when Parnell failed to tag first in time after taking [Billy] Goodman's throw."[244] A's first baseman Ferris Fain walked. Chapman got his second hit off Parnell, singling to left field. Moses scored. Williams threw the ball in to shortstop Vern Stephens and Fain was out trying to go first to third on the play.

Boston didn't get a hit until Johnny Pesky singled in the fourth.

The Red Sox tied it up, 1-1, in the bottom of the fifth on a walk and singles by Al Zarilla and Dom DiMaggio.

In the seventh, they took a 2-1 lead on a wind-blown single by Goodman, a one-out single by Matt Batts, and an RBI single to right by Parnell.

The lead didn't hold. In fact, it tipped the other way. A walk off Parnell, and an RBI double from Moses tied it. Moses was sacrificed to third and scored on Ray Chapman's single.

Ted's Homer Gives Sox Sweep

The Red Sox came to bat in the bottom of the eighth. Johnny Pesky walked on five pitches. Ted Williams was up next. The *Boston Herald* set the stage: "He was due. He hadn't hit the ball out of the infield all day. He had walked twice in the first game but had slapped harsh drives into double plays twice in the opener and been thrown out by the over-shifted Philadelphia infield three times in the nightcap."[245] Bill Cunningham of the *Boston Herald* wrote that there was a lot of chatter during Williams's at-bats, with catcher Mike Guerra seeming to try to distract the Boston batter with conversation involving a woman. Perhaps it had worked some earlier on. This time Williams reportedly kept saying, "Yeah. Yeah," as Guerra appeared to intensify his tale. As Cunningham told it, Guerra came out with the climax line on a 3-2 count. Williams swung, connected, and sent the ball on its way. As he crossed the plate, having circled the bases, he's said to have asked Guerra, "Yeah, and what did she say?"[246]

The two-run homer tilted the scale back the other way. Now the score was 4-3, Red Sox.[247]

Will Cloney's next-day account quoted Red Sox catcher Birdie Tebbetts as saying that Williams had told him, "If he throws me a couple of curves, I'll knock one clear into the bullpen."[248]

The 4-3 score held. Parnell improved to 7-1. After the game, Parnell asked reporters: "But how about *my* hitting? That's eight games out of nine I've made one."[249]

Boston Red Sox 21
St. Louis Browns 2

June 24, 1949 — Fenway Park

Ted Williams would have had the game-winning homer had the score been tied 16-16 after 6 1/2 innings, since he also hit a leadoff home run in the seventh. It was his first-inning home run that made the difference in this one.

Who was the fortunate pitcher to be given so many runs in support? It was Ellis Kinder, who worked a complete game.[250]

Ted Belts Two Homers, Goodman Gets Five Hits in Mayhem at Fenway

Williams drove in seven runs – two on a single and one on a bases-loaded walk. Dom DiMaggio drove in three and so did Billy Goodman. Even Kinder drove in one. The only player in the lineup who did not was Johnny Pesky, but he was 3-for-4 at the plate and scored three times.

The Browns actually held an early lead, when Whitey Platt hit a two-out solo home run in the top of the first inning. The lead didn't last long.

When the Red Sox came to bat in the bottom of the first, they faced Joe Ostrowski.[251]

DiMaggio singled to center. Pesky got his first hit, a double to right, and then Ted Williams hit "a tremendous wallop into the dead centerfield seats about 15 rows up."[252]

Andy Anderson hit a leadoff home run for St. Louis in the third. The score was thus 3-2. The Red Sox upped the ante a bit with four consecutive singles – Goodman, Al Zarilla, Birdie Tebbetts, and Kinder – resulting in two more runs.

They added five more runs in the fourth and four in the fifth. In the fourth, Williams walked but later struck out for the third out. In the fifth, he picked up another RBI on a bases-loaded walk.[253]

A one-out Goodman double (his fifth consecutive hit of the afternoon), and then singles by Zarilla, Tebbetts, and DiMaggio scored two more, boosting Boston to 16-2.

Ted Williams led off the bottom of the seventh, a solo home run off reliever Ray Shore, "a line drive which went into the right-field end of the grandstand."[254]

This was the only run the Sox scored in the seventh, but they took advantage of one more opportunity in the eighth. With the bases loaded, Ted singled to right field and drove in two. The Red Sox pulled off a double steal, with Williams stealing second and Johnny Pesky stealing home. Bobby Doerr singled to left field and Williams scored the 21st Red Sox run.[255]

The only innings in which the Red Sox did not score were the second and the ninth, in the latter case because with a 21-2 lead, there was no batting in the bottom of the ninth.

A third of the runs – seven of the 21 – were batted in by Williams.

POSTSCRIPT

This was the year in which Williams set career highs in home runs for a season (43) and runs batted in (159). Remarkably, he shared the RBI crown with teammate Vern Stephens – 318 runs batted in between the two of them.

Williams was well aware of the value of having Stephens hit behind him in the order, later writing. "Your opportunities...depend a lot on who is batting behind you...If you're Babe Ruth you had Lou Gehrig behind you, so you got your share of opportunities. When I had Junior Stephens hitting behind me and he was at the top of his game, we had a great thing going."[256] One might speculate how many more RBIs Stephens could have accumulated had Williams not cleared the bases 43 times with a home run before Stephens came to bat.

Boston Red Sox 11
Detroit Tigers 1

July 16, 1949 — Briggs Stadium

The Red Sox won this Sunday ballgame in the top of the first inning.

They were emerging from a streaky stretch, where they lost eight games in a row, then won eight games in a row. They lost 8-7 on July 15 when the Tigers rallied for four runs in the bottom of the ninth.[257]

Virgil Trucks was 10-5 with a 2.91 ERA. He hadn't worked for 10 days, though.

After first baseman Billy Goodman inauspiciously grounded the ball right back to Virgil Trucks for the first out of the game, Johnny Pesky reached on an error and Ted Williams hit a Trucks fastball "about 12 rows back in the upper right-center tier."[258] It was, wrote the *Detroit Times*, "a mighty drive high up into the second deck of the right field stands."[259]

Two runs, but enough to win the game as things played out.

Left-hander Mel Parnell started the game for the Red Sox. He finished it, too, throwing a complete game, his 15th complete game of the season.[260]

Pesky drove in another Red Sox run in the second.

Doerr and center fielder Tommy O'Brien both singled in the Boston third and Tebbetts hit a two-out three-run homer into the lower deck in left field. 6-0, Red Sox.

Trucks was pulled for a pinch-hitter, relieved by Marv Grissom.

The Red Sox made it 10-0, adding four more runs in the top of the fourth. Ted Williams surprised everyone with a bunt to the left side of the infield. With the "Williams Shift" deployed, it was just too easy. He "bunted the first pitch down toward the third base and didn't even have to hurry to get himself a base hit."[261] Vern Stephens walked. Doerr doubled, scoring Williams. Al Zarilla hit a three-run homer into the lower deck in right field.

In the sixth, with Grissom still pitching, Doerr hit a solo home run that made the score 11-0. It landed about six rows deep in the left-field stands.

The Tigers broke their string of zeroes on the scoreboard with a run in the bottom of the sixth. Neil Barry doubled down the left-field line. Groundouts by Paul Campbell and George Kell pushed Barry across. When the run scored, many of the 20,520 at the ballpark cheered derisively.[262]

"Marvelous Mel" Parnell got the win, of course. He only allowed four hits, though he did walk three.[263]

Tebbetts, Zarilla, and Doerr all homered for the Red Sox, too, accounting for nine of Boston's 11 runs. It was Ted Williams's third homer of the year off Trucks and his seventh of the year (of the 21 he had hit) against Tigers pitching.

POSTSCRIPT

Trucks may have been getting a little tired of this, it being the fourth time Williams had hit what proved a game-winning home run off him. "I liked to pitch against him because he was such a great hitter," Trucks said. "I just loved to watch him hit, except when it was against me. He sure got a lot of glares from me when he would get a home run...I also called him a few choice names as he rounded the bases. He ignored my remarks."[264]

This was the year that George Kell beat out Ted Williams for the American League batting title, by less than one percentage point (Kell was .3429 and Williams was .3427). Kell was 0-for-4 in this game, and Williams was 2-for-5. Had Williams had one more base hit, or made one less out, he would have won the title, but that is maybe something more for another day. Homering twice and winning another game with one of them was no doubt good enough for the moment. At game's end, it was actually Dom DiMaggio who ranked higher in batting average, .343 to Kell's .341. Williams was hitting .330.

Boston Red Sox 6
New York Yankees 3

August 9, 1949 — Fenway Park

The Red Sox and Yankees ended the season tied and, for the second year in a row, the Red Sox had to play a one-game tiebreaker to determine the pennant. At this point in the season, however, New York had a six-game lead over third-place Boston, who were a half-game behind the Cleveland Indians.

Ellis Kinder (12-5) was the Boston starter and Vic Raschi (15-6) started for Casey Stengel's Yankees.

The first runs scored were three, by Boston, in the bottom of the second. Vern Stephens walked, followed by two outs, a throwing error leaving Billy Goodman on second. Al Zarilla doubled him home. Birdie Tebbetts then hit a "rising line drive into the left field screen."[265]

Once more, Kinder got outs from the three Yankees who batted. He struck out Raschi.

Center fielder Dom DiMaggio led off the bottom of the third inning with a fly ball to his brother Joe DiMaggio in center field. Johnny Pesky doubled to left field. Ted Williams hit a two-run homer to right field – "a direct line into the Red Sox bullpen"[266] giving the Red Sox a 5-0 lead.

It was the 250th home run of his major-league career.[267]

Brother Joe DiMaggio singled in the Yankees fourth but he was the only Yankee to get on base. Joe D.'s hit struck high off the left-field wall, missing a home run by maybe a foot, "bouncing back so quickly he had to settle for a single."[268]

New York got one run in the fifth, when Raschi doubled and drove in Jerry Coleman. Hank Bauer led off the Yankees' sixth with a solo home run over the left-field wall and into the screen, just inside the foul pole.

In the top of the eighth inning, Bauer did the very same thing he did leading off the sixth. He hit a solo home run, but this one was over everything in left-center field. Kinder retired the next three, but the Yankees had shaved down what had once been a 5-0 lead to one that was 5-3.

The Sox loaded the bases in the bottom of the eighth. Kinder hit a ball, "a freak hit off Raschi's glove, the ball rolling almost back to the plate while Goodman streaked home" with the sixth Red Sox run.[269] Dom hit another fly ball to Joe. With that out, brother Dom was 0-for-5 in the game and his 34-game hitting streak had come to an end.[270]

With this win, the Red Sox had won 26 of their last 34 games. On the Fourth of July, they had been 12 games behind the Yankees. Now the gap had closed to 5 ½.

Boston Red Sox 1
Detroit Tigers 0

September 14, 1949 — Fenway Park

The race for the American League pennant had tightened considerably. The Red Sox came into the game just 2 ½ games behind the New York Yankees. It had truly become a race. The Red Sox had been 12 games behind on the Fourth of July, seven back at the end of July, and as close as just one game back on September 10.

They didn't know it yet, but this win was the second in a stretch of 11 consecutive wins that ran from September 13 through the 27th, and saw them either in first place or tied for first from September 24 to the final game on October 1.[271] Suffice it to say that every game was crucial at this point.

Ellis Kinder was pitching for the Red Sox, going for his 20th win.[272]

It was a day game, on a Wednesday afternoon. Given the import of the game, one might have thought Fenway Park would have drawn more patrons but it wasn't quite half-full.[273]

The Tigers got leadoff singles in both the first inning and the second, but both times the second batter grounded into a double play.

Veteran left-hander Hal Newhouser was 16-9 coming into the game, with a 3.31 ERA. His last start had been a shutout of the Cleveland Indians on September 8. The Tigers were in third place, 3 1/2 games behind the Red Sox with this game and 12 others to play. The first hit he gave up was in the third, when catcher Birdie Tebbetts led off with a single to center. He stole second base, and took third on Dom DiMaggio's groundout. Johnny Pesky walked, giving Boston runners on first and third and Ted Williams at bat, but Williams flied out to right.

Kinder of Red Sox Takes 20th, 1-0, On Williams' Blow Against Tigers

Ted Hits No. 38 Into Left-Field Screen in Sixth to Beat Newhouser—Sharp Support Helps Boston Hurler Win 10th in Row

The Sox loaded the bases with one out in the fourth, but Tebbetts hit into a 4-6-3 double play.

There was still no score at the halfway point. It was a game with seven double plays.[274] Through five innings, Newhouser had completed a string of 18 consecutive scoreless innings.

The first Boston batter in the bottom of the sixth was Ted Williams. On a 2-2 count, he hit a home run – "a high fly to the right of the scoreboard in left."[275] It was "a 370-foot homer against the portside screen," wrote the *New York Times*.[276] With the home run, he tied two career marks. It was his 38th home run of the season, matching the 38 he'd hit in 1946. It was also his 145th run batted in of the year, tying his personal best (the official 145 he was credited with in 1939).[277]

There was a dispute; the Tigers argued that the ball had hit the top of the left-field wall and bounced back onto the field. The umpires huddled and all "agreed that it had hit a girder, bounced into the screen and then out on the diamond."[278]

Kinder threw a six-hit shutout.[279]

Newhouser had thrown a four-hitter but one of the hits was Ted's home run.

Boston Red Sox 9
Cleveland Indians 6

September 21, 1949 — Fenway Park

There were 27 hits in this game, 10 bases on balls, and 10 pitchers used, but the score was only 1-1 after the first four innings. Neither starter made it through the fifth, the Indians scoring three runs and the Red Sox scoring four.

A Wednesday afternoon game at Fenway Park saw the Red Sox in second place, only three games behind the first-place Yankees. They'd won six games in a row and not gained any ground, but there remained eight games to play. The Yankees lost five of their next six games and just four days later – on September 25 – the Red Sox and Yankees were tied for first place.

Starting for Boston was 5-8 Jack Kramer. It was far from his best season.[280]

Right-hander Mike Garcia, 13-5, was having a very good year – his first full season in the big leagues. By year's end, his 2.36 ERA was the best in the two major leagues.

Each team scored once in the second inning, Garcia's single to center producing Cleveland's run and a sacrifice fly and then a groundout scoring Bobby Doerr, who had doubled.

With two on, Ted Williams hit into an inning-ending double play in the third.

The Indians sent Kramer to the showers in the fifth. Garcia started things off with a single to left field. A single, a sacrifice bunt, an RBI single by Mickey Vernon, an RBI sac fly by Larry Doby, and a double by Luke Easter gave them a 4-1 lead.

Garcia had already beaten the Red Sox three times in 1949.

The Red Sox responded right away, though. and one-upped the Indians. With one out, catcher Birdie Tebbetts singled to left field.

Tom Wright pinch-hit for Masterson and he doubled down the line in left field. DiMaggio walked, which loaded the bases. When the count got to 3-0, Garcia pitching to Johnny Pesky, Boudreau called on Bob Feller to pitch in relief. This wasn't as rare an occurrence as one might expect; Feller relieved in 86 games over the course of his career. Feller threw one pitch and walked Pesky, forcing in a run. Ted Williams flied out to right field and Wright tagged and scored. Vern Stephens singled to left field and both DiMaggio and Pesky scored, giving Boston a 5-4 edge.[281]

Al Benton relieved Feller. Al Zarilla greeted him with a homer over the Red Sox bullpen and into the right-center-field bleachers.

Boston reliever Chuck Stobbs walked both Vernon and Doby and then Easter doubled, driving in Vernon for his second RBI of the game. Ellis Kinder relieved Stobbs. A sacrifice fly tied the game, 6-6.

Ted Williams led off against new reliever Steve Gromek. The count on Williams went to 2-1. He swung at the next pitch and "lifted the ball loftily toward right center. Easter gave chase and made a leap for the ball as it dropped into the Red Sox bullpen, a homer by inches."[282] With his 41st home run of the season, the Red Sox took a 7-6 lead.[283] They added another run and a ninth run in the eighth.[284]

Red Sox Defeat Indians 9-6 on Ted's Homer; Yanks Lose

Kinder won his 22nd. It was the 19th consecutive win for the Red Sox at Fenway Park, and the seventh win in an 11-game winning streak that brought Boston into contention. Williams hit six homers in those 11 games, two of them game-winning homers and the other four clearly helping. They won the next two home games as well, the last two home games of the year, beating the Yankees both times and tying them for first place. But then lost back-to-back games against the Yankees, in New York, and lost the pennant on the final game of the year – for the second year in a row.

Williams later said, "We just had to win one game, just one lousy, flippin' game…We lose again. Lose the game. Lose the pennant. And I lost the batting race – and another Triple Crown. Boy, that was one tough series. One tough series."[285]

"I had no idea at the time," he later wrote, "but I would never be that close to a pennant again. The whole team was heartbroken. Sick. To come that close twice in a row was an awful cross to bear."[286]

Willams led the AL in intentional walks nine times, including as a 20-year-old rookie. His career high of 33 came 18 years later when he compiled a slash line of .388/.526/.731. (Leslie Jones photograph, Boston Public Library)

1950

97 RBIs and Seven Game-Winning Homers in 89 Games

This year could have been Ted Williams's greatest year. At the All-Star Break, he was off to the most productive start of his career. Halfway into the season (after 77), he had 25 home runs, 83 RBIs, and 75 RS. He was on a pace for 50 homers and 166 RBIs, not to mention 150 runs scored.

Unfortunately, he broke his elbow in the 1950 All-Star Game, banging into the wall while catching a long drive by Ralph Kiner. He missed 55 games, not returning until September 7. Williams ended up hitting three more homers (for a total of 28), drove in 14 more runs (finishing with 97 in 89 games!), and 82 runs scored, also nearly one per game.

Williams always said he never regained the full power he had had before the injury. He hit seven game-winning homers, all of them before the end of June.

Despite the Red Sox scoring an incredible 1,027 runs on the season (6.67 per game), mediocre pitching kept their win total down to 94, four less than the Yankees collected and one less than the Tigers.

Boston Red Sox 6
New York Yankees 3

April 19, 1950 — Fenway Park
(first game of a doubleheader)

The Patriots Day dual admission doubleheader at Fenway Park constituted just the second and third games of the 1950 season for the Boston Red Sox. They had lost a 15-10 slugfest against the visiting New York Yankees the day before, despite starting the game with a 9-0 lead and having won 22 consecutive home games as they closed out the 1949 season. Scoring 10 runs and losing might in some ways have hinted at a couple of things in the season before them; when it was all over, the Red Sox had set a franchise record by scoring 1,027 runs (in a 154-game season) but despite all the runs, they finished in third place, four games behind the Yankees.

Joe Dobson was Joe McCarthy's starter for Boston in the 10:00 A.M. first game. Casey Stengel started Vic Raschi.[287]

The Red Sox pounced on Raschi for two quick runs. With one out, Johnny Pesky singled and Ted Williams walked. Vern Stephens drove in his third run of the 1950 season with a single that scored Pesky. Bobby Doerr singled and drove in Williams.

The Red Sox got two more runs in the bottom of the third. Pesky walked, leading off. It was a chilly morning game (the Red Sox typically play their Patriots Day games in the morning) and Williams hit his first home run of the year, one that was "well stroked because it had to soar through a stiff east wind before it dropped into the Yankees bullpen."[288] It was 4-0.

Boston added their fifth and sixth runs in the fourth inning on singles by Billy Goodman and Matt Batts, Dobson reaching on an intended sacrifice bunt, and then a double play Dom DiMaggio hit into that scored one, and successive walks to Pesky, Williams, and Stephens.[289]

The Yankees had been held hitless for the first four innings but scored in the top of the fifth, twice, on singles by Cliff Mapes and pinch-hitter Dick Wakefield, batting for Raschi. They added a third run in the sixth and Gene Woodling's single, an error by Williams, and Yogi Berra's double.

Boston mounted a couple of threats, but scored no more.

After allowing the New Yorkers the three runs he had, "Dobson deftly regained his grip"[290] and allowed just one lone single in the final three innings.

After the Yankees went down in order in the eighth, Pesky walked and Stephens singled for the Red Sox, but neither scored. It was Pesky's third walk. With a pair of singles as well, he had reached base five times in five plate appearances.

Dobson also set down the Yankees in order in the ninth.

Raschi recovered well and led the American League in winning percentage in 1950, going 21-8 despite an earned run average that was on the nose at 4.00.

The Yankees won the 3:00 P.M. afternoon game, 16-7.

Boston Red Sox 5
Chicago White Sox 2

May 5, 1950 — Fenway Park

The two starting pitchers were Joe Dobson for the Red Sox and Billy Pierce for the White Sox.[291]

"You see, it's like this. You get the guy out a couple of times and the law of averages is bound to catch up with you." – White Sox starter Billy Pierce.[292]

Dobson retired the three White Sox he faced in the top of the first, each out being made by an infielder.

Williams' Homer Gives Red Sox Victory Over White Sox, 5-2

Pierce struggled at the start, walking each one of the first three Boston batters he faced – Dom DiMaggio, Johnny Pesky, and Ted Williams. He was lucky to escape with only one run scored, on a bloop single by Vern "Junior" Stephens.[293]

Stephens picked up another RBI with a solo home run in the third inning, a line drive into the left-field screen.

The White Sox scored twice, tying the game 2-2, in the top of the fifth inning on rookie shortstop Chico Carrasquel's homer into the screen atop the left-field wall, just about three feet inside the foul line.[294] It was his first major-league home run.

The score remained 2-2 through the sixth.

In the bottom of the seventh, Johnny Pesky walked. Pierce had already struck out Ted Williams once and got him to pop up to third base with the bases loaded. This time Williams swung at the first pitch and homered to right field, hitting a ball about a dozen rows deep into the lower seats in Section 1 in right field. It was the hit that won the game, making it 4-2, Red Sox.

After the game, Pierce said, "It was supposed to be a sweeping curve but it didn't break very much and he hit it perfectly. This is no alibi, but I had trouble getting a grip on the mound out there. It's clay and you don't get any traction."[295]

The Red Sox added one more run in their half of the eighth. With Birdie Tebbetts on third and Dom DiMaggio on first, reliever Howie Judson tried to pick off DiMaggio, but threw the ball some 15 feet wide of first baseman Luke Appling.[296]

Dobson increased his lifetime record against the White Sox to 15-4.[297]

Chicago batters had actually out-hit the Red Sox in this game, eight to six, but White Sox pitchers doled out 13 walks while Dobson walked no one.[298]

It was a nice win for the Red Sox, but it was played on a chilly day and before what the *Providence Journal* said was the smallest Fenway crowd in two years: 3,415 paying customers and 588 women.[299]

Boston Red Sox 11
Chicago White Sox 1

May 6, 1950 — Fenway Park

Ted Williams went on a bit of a homer-hitting spree over a 2 ½ week stretch early in the 1950 season – he homered twice on April 30 (both of them three-run homers), then again on May 2, 5, 6, 7, 11, 13, and then another two-home run game on May 16.[300]

The Red Sox team homered six times in the May 6 game at Fenway Park. His home run over the left-center-field wall was the first of the six, as they battered the White Sox, 11-1. Every one of the 12 runs scored in the game was produced by a home run.[301]

For the Red Sox, Birdie Tebbetts hit two homers, and Vern Stephens, Dom DiMaggio, and Bobby Doerr each hit one. The Williams home run was a three-run homer that was the game-winner, giving them all the runs they needed to win. For the White Sox, the lone run came courtesy of a solo home run by Gus Zernial halfway up in the net in left, near the center-field light tower.

The 20-year-old Boston starter Chuck Stobbs more or less cruised to victory, only allowing four hits. It was Ken Holcombe's first start for Chicago.

It was three up/three down for Chicago. For Boston it was three up/three runs. Dom DiMaggio led off with a single to center. Johnny Pesky walked. Ted Williams hit a three-run homer – to left field. It "disappeared over the wall high above the 379 foot mark in left-center."[302]

Zernial's homer came as leadoff batter for the White Sox in the second inning.

Boston catcher Birdie Tebbetts led off the bottom of the second and he mimicked Zernial, also hitting a leadoff home run to deep left field. After a walk and a Pesky single, Luis Aloma relieved Holcombe. Aloma had only two innings of major-league experience. He got the two outs he needed, getting Ted Williams to ground into a 3-6-3 double play.

When Tebbetts came up to bat again in the third, there were runners on base, Tom Wright on an error and Walt Dropo on a walk. Tebbetts hit a three-run homer, to the "same spot" as his first one.[303] Stobbs had a 7-1 lead.

John Perkovich was the new pitcher for Chicago starting in the fourth. He worked the rest of the game – but it was his only major-league game. Bobby Doerr hit the third leadoff homer of the game in the fifth, into the Boston bullpen.

With an 8-1 lead, Stobbs singled as first up in the Boston eighth. Every Boston batter thus had at least one hit. Every Boston batter scored at least one run. DiMaggio hit a two-run homer over everything in left. Vern Stephens hit a solo homer to make it 11-1.[304]

On May 5 and May 6, he had hit game-winning homers on two successive days.

Boston Red Sox 6
Detroit Tigers 1

May 16, 1950 — Briggs Stadium, Detroit

It was a Tuesday afternoon at Ted Williams's favorite homer haven – Briggs Stadium in Detroit. His first nine home runs of 1950 had all come at home, at Fenway Park. This game became something of a "Ted and Junior" show. Ted Williams hit two home runs in the game and so did Vern "Junior" Stephens. Both of Stephens's homers were solo home runs. Both of Williams's were two-run homers. Between them, they accounted for all the Red Sox runs in a 6-1 win over the Tigers.

The first runs weren't scored until the third. Art Houtteman, named an All-Star at midseason, started for the Tigers. Dom DiMaggio led off for Boston and reached on an error. Al Zarilla singled to center. DiMaggio was thrown out trying to go first to third. Williams homered into the upper deck in right field, to give Boston a 2-0 lead. Stephens followed up Williams's home run with one of his own, this one to left.

Joe Dobson pitched for Boston and only allowed a couple of singles and three walks through the sixth inning.

In the top of the seventh, Stephens hit his second homer off Houtteman, again to left field. The score stood, 4-0, at the midway point of the seventh inning. Johnny Groth drew a one-out walk. With two outs, Aaron Robinson singled to center field, a play on which second baseman Bobby Doerr was charged with an error, allowing Groth to score.[305]

Reliever Hal White set down the Red Sox in order in the top of the eighth.

Detroit loaded the bases in the bottom of the inning on a single, wild pitch, one-out infield single by George Kell, and a walk.[306] With one out and Johnny Lipon on third, Vic Wertz flied out to Williams in left. It wasn't deep enough for Lipon to tag; Williams was known to have a decent arm. Groth had two hits and a walk, but hit to ball right to Dobson, who threw to first base.

With two outs in the top of the ninth, Zarilla walked. Williams homered again, extending the Red Sox lead to 6-1. Both his homers were hit into a "stiff wind blowing against him."[307] It was a carbon copy of his earlier home run. "Both Williams's drives ended far up in the upper deck of the right field stands."[308]

Williams and Stephens Homer Twice as Sox, Dobson Defeat Tigers, 6-1

The Williams home runs were his 10th and 11th of the year. He was hitting them at a faster clip than any other year, and at a faster pace than Babe Ruth had in 1927.[309] His four RBIs edged him ahead of Stephens, 32 to 31.

The game was Joe Dobson's 100th career win, a six-hitter (all singles) with no earned runs.

Boston Red Sox 11
Cleveland Indians 9

June 3, 1950 — Fenway Park

Twenty runs, 21 base hits, 41 total bases, 13 walks, three errors, seven pitchers, three pinch-hitters. There was a lot of action in this game.

The scoring started pretty quickly when Luke Easter hit a two-run homer off Mel Parnell in the top of the first.[310]

Cleveland starter Mike Garcia had led both the American and National Leagues in ERA in 1949 with a 2.35 mark over 41 appearances, half of them starts. He had been 14-5. On June 3, he only lasted five batters before being replaced. Dom DiMaggio singled to left. Johnny Pesky walked. So did Ted Williams. Vern Stephens singled, and two runs scored. Walt Dropo doubled "high off the left-field wall" and another run scored.[311] Manager/shortstop Lou Boudreau concluded that Garcia didn't have it and summoned reliever Gene Bearden.[312]

Bearden walked Al Zarilla, reloading the bases, and then gave up a triple to Bobby Doerr, a ball which "did some tricks bouncing around the flagpole."[313] The Sox had six runs.[314]

It was the second game in a row the Red Sox had scored six runs in the first inning against the Indians; they had won on June 2, 11-5. All six of those runs had scored off Bob Feller, who'd started the game by walking the first three batters.

The Red Sox added two more in the second. DiMaggio reached on a fielding error by Bearden. Pesky singled to right field. Williams walked again, and, for the second inning in a row, Boston had the bases loaded with nobody out. One scored on an infield single and the second on a groundout.

The Indians scored five in the fourth, shaving the Red Sox lead to 8-7. In the process, Al Papai relieved Parnell. The Indians loaded the bases in the top of the fifth but did not score.

Boston added three in the bottom of the fifth, off reliever Jesse Flores. Birdie Tebbetts led off with a home run, "a drive to left that barely scaled the fence and landed in the net."[315] Papai walked. After two outs, Williams homered "a dozen or so rows up in the right-field bleachers above the visiting bullpen."[316] That made it Boston 11, Cleveland 7.

Suddenly the scoring ceased. Neither team scored in the sixth, seventh, or eighth.

With one out in the ninth, Bob Kennedy tripled off the top of the center-field fence and Larry Doby hit a two-run homer, hit to "almost the identical place" as Kennedy's but "Doby's was a little higher and went into the screen for a home run."[317] The *Cleveland Plain Dealer* said Doby's two-run homer "merely made the final outcome less humiliating."[318]

Papai got the win. The Williams home run that produced the 10th and 11th runs in the 11-9 victory was the hit that made the difference.

Boston Red Sox 29
St. Louis Brown 4

June 8, 1950 — Fenway Park

It was quite a homestand for the Boston Red Sox. From June 2 through June 11, they played 11 games and scored 127 runs, an average of more than 11½ runs per game.[319] They had just come off the road, beaten the Indians 11-5 and 11-9, and then the White

Sox, 17-7 and 12-0. After an 8-4 loss, to Chicago, Boston crushed the St. Louis Browns 20-4, on June 7.[320]

The starting pitchers for this game were Chuck Stobbs (Red Sox) and Cliff Fannin (Browns). Neither team scored until the bottom of the second when the Red Sox scored eight.

Al Zarilla doubled. Bobby Doerr walked. Matt Batts doubled off the wall, driving in Zarilla. A walk to Stobbs loaded the bases. A sacrifice fly made it 2-0. With two outs, Ted Williams slammed Fannin's pitch 10-12 rows up in the right-field bleachers over the Red Sox bullpen.[321] Vern Stephens walked. Walt Dropo hit a two-run homer into the netting above the left-field wall. Zarilla hit his second double of the inning; Doerr singled in Zarilla.

Stobbs let St. Louis score three in the top of the third.

Browns reliever Cuddles Marshall walked five batters in the bottom of the third inning – including Stobbs, whom he walked twice. He gave up only three hits, but they included a two-run double by Vern Stephens and a two-run single by Dropo. Doerr's sacrifice fly drove in the fifth run of the inning.

In the fourth Stobbs set down the Browns 1-2-3. And the Sox scored seven more runs, on six hits, a walk, and an error, even though Williams made two of the three outs in the inning.[322]

Both Doerr and Batts picked up an RBI in the fifth. Doerr had driven in one or more runs in four consecutive innings.

The sixth inning passed with no scoring by either team, but Doerr hit a two-run homer in the bottom of the seventh, making it 24-3.

With the Red Sox unlikely to need to bat in the ninth, they poured across five more runs in the bottom of the eighth. Pesky doubled and Williams hit his second homer of the game (over the left-field wall). Vern Stephens singled and then Dropo hit his second homer of the game. Zarilla flied out to "the foot of the center field wall," which the *Boston Herald* said came "within inches" of going for a fifth double for himself.[323] Bobby Doerr came up next and hit his third homer of the game; all three went over the left-field wall. 29-3. Doerr's third homer was Boston's seventh of the day and the 12th homer in the two games against the Browns.

The Browns scored another run in the top of the ninth, but fell 25 runs short of tying the game.

The final score was 29-4. The Red Sox had set a record for runs scored (29) in a major-league game, and they did it all in eight innings. The record lasted 57 years until the Texas Rangers beat Baltimore 30-3 on August 22, 2007. Six of those Rangers runs scored in the top of the ninth.

The total of 17 extra-base hits in one game by the Red Sox remains through 2020 a major-league record.[324]

Everyone in the lineup had one or more runs batted in except Zarilla (though he was 5-for-7, with four doubles and a single, and scored four times) and Stobbs, who scored three times.

Doerr drove in eight runs, Dropo drove in seven, and Williams drove in five.

Even with all the scoring – a combined 33 runs, 36 hits, and 18 walks, the game lasted only 2:42.

Boston Red Sox 6
Philadelphia Athletics 2

June 28, 1950 — Shibe Park, Philadelphia

In a three-game stretch, Ted Williams homered at Philadelphia's Shibe Park on June 27, 28, and 29. On the 29th, he drove in six of Boston's 22 runs. His homer on this Wednesday night game on the 28th broke a 2-2 tie in the top of the eighth inning and won the game for the visiting Boston Red Sox.

The Red Sox were just coming off a stretch where they had lost 11 of 13 games, from June 9 through June 22. They then won seven in a row; this was the sixth of the seven wins and the sixth win in a row under new manager Steve O'Neill.

Connie Mack's choice to start was Lou Brissie.[325]

Starting for the Red Sox was Ellis Kinder (5-7).

Williams Homer Beats Athletics, 6-2; Red Sox Win Sixth Straight on Road

Philadelphia scored one in the first inning.

In the top of the third inning, the Red Sox took a 2-1 lead. Al Zarilla walked and Dom DiMaggio hit a two-out two-run homer onto the roof of the second deck in left field.[326]

The Athletics tied the game in the sixth. Ferris Fain singled to center field and Eddie Joost hit a double down the left-field line.

After seven innings complete, the Red Sox had but four hits off Brissie while the Athletics had nine off Kinder, but the game was still tied, 2-2.

In the top of the eighth, "Ted Williams belted one of the longest home runs of his life...a twisting smash just inside the foul line," wrote the *Boston Globe*.[327] It, like his homer the day before, landed on the roof of a house outside the park on 20th Street. It was fair by about five feet.[328]

It was a two-run homer, with Goodman on first base after he had hit a one-out single to center field. The next batter after Williams, Vern Stephens, homered, too, the ball striking the front of the left-field upper deck.

The Red Sox manufactured one more run in the top of the ninth.

Both pitchers had thrown complete games. They had each walked three. Brissie had given up eight base hits, and Kinder given up 11, but the Red Sox had gotten more out of their eight than had the Athletics out of their 11. The A's had one extra-base hit, Joost's game-tying double in the sixth. The Red Sox had three home runs.

POSTSCRIPT

This was the year when Ted Williams broke his elbow during the July 11 All-Star Game at Comiskey Park. The 43 home runs that Williams had hit in 1949 were his all-time high. He had hit his 23rd homer on July 22 that year. This home run was #23 of 1950 – and it was still June. He added #24 the next day, giving him 13 home runs in June. He hit #25 on July 7.

Had he not suffered the broken elbow, and been out of action until September 7, he might well have hit at least 50 in '50.

1951

Six Game-Winners Out of 30 Long Blasts

In 1951, Williams played in almost every game (148 of 154) and led both leagues in walks (144) and on-base percentage (.464). He led the American League in slugging percentage with .556. He hit for a .318 average and collected 30 homers and 126 RBIs. He ranked fourth in average and second in the league to Gus Zernial in home runs and RBIs. It was far from a disappointing season—rather incredible in fact for nearly anyone not named Ted Williams—but one does wonder if the elbow problem did indeed hamper him in some ways.

The Red Sox finished third again, but this time it wasn't close. They had started slowly, worked their way up to first place for most of a couple of weeks in mid-June, but then dropped off again and wound up 11 games behind the first-place Yankees.

Boston Red Sox 5
St. Louis Browns 4
(10 innings)

May 6, 1951 — Sportsman's Park, St. Louis
(first game of doubleheader)

The Red Sox left 16 men on base (two shy of the American League record at the time for a nine-inning game.) They had held a 4-3 lead over the St. Louis Browns (who had a record of 4-13 coming into the game), and they had two outs and two strikes on third baseman Johnny Berardino, who could have been the final batter of the game. Berardino singled, though, and so did left fielder Ray Coleman, which tied the game, setting the stage for extra innings.

Ted Williams was the first man up in the top of the 10th, and it was no small homer he hit (his only hit of the day's doubleheader). It was "a towering drive that sailed far over the roof of the right-field pavilion at Sportsman's Park."[329] Boston took a 5-4 lead.

Williams Homer Clinches

The Browns had taken an early lead, scoring once in the first inning and once again in the second. The Red Sox had put two on in the top of the first, Williams walking and shortstop Lou Boudreau being hit by Lou Sleater's pitch. No damage was done; Boston had left its first two men on base. Sleater was in his rookie year. He'd pitched a total of one inning in 1950.

Bill Wight was Boston's pitcher. The first batter he faced, second baseman Bobby Young, tripled to center field. Berardino grounded out to Boudreau, Young scoring. The Browns got their second run on a leadoff home run by Roy Sievers.

The Sox scored two and tied it when Boudreau reached on an error by shortstop Tom Upton and Red Sox shortstop Vern Stephens followed with a two-run homer to deep left field, "a long drive into the left-field stands."[330]

St. Louis reclaimed the lead in the bottom of the fourth on a walk and Hank Arft's double.

The Red Sox tied it again, 3-3, in the sixth on a single, a walk, an error, and a productive groundout. They took a one-run lead in the top of the eighth. Billy Goodman singled and walks were doled out to Williams, Stephens, and – with two outs – Doerr, on Sleater's ninth base on balls.

As noted, the Browns tied it up again at the very last minute.

And then Ted Williams won it with his "clear-the-works" home run.[331]

Reliever Ellis Kinder alternated strikeouts and walks in the bottom of the 10th, for the win.[332]

Four years earlier, on May 6 of 1947, Williams had won the game at Sportsman's Park in the 11th inning.

Boston Red Sox 9
Detroit Tigers 7

May 21, 1951 — Fenway Park

Ted Williams was in a slump. He had been struggling badly in 1951. Over the course of his first 27 games, he was batting just .226, though he did have seven home runs. Asked about it before the game, Tigers manager Red Rolfe said, "Williams will get started, don't worry. He'll make somebody suffer."[333] Days earlier, Tigers great Ty Cobb had said, "Williams has fine ability but he cannot be classed as a great hitter. No player can be called a truly great hitter unless he can hit to all fields."[334]

Starting for Boston was Willard Nixon, 1-0 in his second major-league season.

Dizzy Trout (2-2) had started his career the same year as Williams, back in 1939. He was 36 years old and already had 153 wins to his credit.[335]

In the second inning, Nixon walked leadoff batter Vic Wertz. A single and a sacrifice got Wertz to third base, and he scored on a ground ball to second base by Joe Ginsberg.

In the bottom of the third, the Red Sox exploded for seven runs, but that didn't prove enough to win the game. Moss drew a walk. With a couple of outs mixed in, Dom DiMaggio tripled, Johnny Pesky doubled, Williams doubled high off the wall in deep left-center field, and Lou Boudreau singled. Hank Borowy relieved Trout.

Borowy walked Walt Dropo. Bobby Doerr doubled. Moss was walked intentionally. Nixon himself got in on the action, shooting a single into center field and collecting two runs batted in – driving in Dropo and Doerr.

Left fielder Pat Mullin got one run back for the Tigers with a solo home run into the Tigers bullpen in the top of the fourth.

> **Williams Gets 3 Hits to Left as Sox Beat Tigers 9-7**
> 2-Run Homer in 7th Win Margin; 10 Pitchers Used

Marlin Stuart took over pitching to the Red Sox in the bottom the fourth. He gave up only one base hit in the fourth or the fifth, a Williams single to left "past George Kell, third baseman who was playing shortstop in Detroit's overshifted defense."[336]

Nixon was touched for one more run in the top of the sixth on Kell's single, Wertz's double, and Pat Mullin's sacrifice fly.

In the seventh, Dick Kryhoski homered into the left-field net and it was a two-run game, 7-5.

Gene Bearden was Detroit's new pitcher. He walked eighth-inning leadoff batter Tom Wright. Ted Williams followed with a home run to deep left-center field. That made it 9-5.

In the top of the eighth, the Tigers continued to show life and the Red Sox used three pitchers, allowing two runs but no more. In all, Boston used four pitchers and Detroit used six.[337]

Williams had lashed three hits to left – to spite Ty Cobb? His homer in the seventh was the game-winner. His three base hits bumped his average up from .226 to .247.

Boston Red Sox 7
Washington Senators 1

May 27, 1951 — Fenway Park
(second game of a doubleheader)

It was a Sunday afternoon doubleheader at Fenway Park. The Red Sox beat the visiting Washington Senators, 9-3, in the first game, thanks to a six-run bottom of the seventh. Vern Stephens's three-run homer featured in that frame. Lou Boudreau and Ted Williams had each driven in a pair during the game.

The second game was marked by another big inning, the bottom of the third. It was also marked by another big hit, this time a grand slam by Ted Williams.

Harry Taylor pitched the second game for Boston.[338] Bucky Harris had Julio Moreno start for the Senators.[339]

Williams' Slam Highlights Double Win by Sox, 9-3, 7-1

A third-inning walk to Les Moss, a single by Dom DiMaggio, and infield single by Billy Goodman loaded the bases with one out.[340] That brought up Ted Williams. He'd been slumping; as late as May 15, he was hitting just .216. He'd brought his average up and was batting .288 through May 26. He went 3-for-3 in the first game and climbed over .300. Moreno's first two pitches were in tight on him, but Ted unloaded on the third pitch. "Williams pulled and sent the pitch high and far to the [Senators] bull pen, where Mickey Harris made a back-hand stab of the four-run clout."[341]

Boudreau singled. Walt Dropo walked. Bobby Doerr cleared the bases again, hitting a three-run home run over the fence in left field, where it struck a stanchion and bounced back on to the field.[342] The Red Sox took a 7-0 lead.

Only one more run scored the rest of the day. Taylor was still working on a one-hitter going into the seventh. Jack Barry's account in the *Boston Globe* detailed a number of fielding plays made by Red Sox fielders.[343] He gave up a couple of singles, a wild pitch, and a groundout.

With a six-run lead, there wasn't any significant tension. The Senators did get three singles off Taylor in the ninth and loaded the bases, but all three were left on base.

In the four games against Washington, Williams had gone 9-for-14, and four of the hits were, very uncharacteristically, doubles to left field.[344] He drove in 13 runs. Williams's first grand slam of 1951, as part of a 6-RBI day, gave him the league lead in runs batted in.

Boston Red Sox 3
St. Louis Browns 0

June 17, 1951 — Fenway Park
(second game of doubleheader)

On July 17, the Red Sox hosted the St. Louis Browns for a Sunday doubleheader at Fenway Park. The 1951 Red Sox might have wished they played all their games as doubleheaders. After winning both games on June 17, they had swept five doubleheaders and only been in swept in one. There were two which they split.[345]

The Red Sox won the first game, 5-4. Ray Scarborough got the win.[346]

The second game pitted Mel Parnell (6-4) against Al Widmar (3-4).

Parnell walked the first batter, but got a double play and a groundout.

With one out, Johnny Pesky singled to right field. Billy Goodman grounded to short, forcing out Pesky. On a 3-2 count, left fielder Ted Williams homered; he "belted the ball into the left-field screen, to the right of the light tower."[347] The Red Sox had taken a quick 2-0 lead. Vern Stephens singled. Bobby Doerr singled. Clyde Vollmer struck out.

The Browns had their opportunities. Ken Wood's double in the second went to waste. Widmar himself singled in the third. Parnell allowed a two-out double to catcher Matt Batts in the top of the fourth. He walked Wood, but Hank Arft grounded out unassisted to Goodman at first base.

The first two St. Louis batters both singled off Parnell, starting off the fifth inning, but a fly ball to Doerr at second base and a 4-6-3 double play ended that potential threat.

Parnell retired the side with no one reaching the base in the sixth, the first time in the game he had done so.

In Boston's sixth, Williams hit a one-out single to left. Vern Stephens singled to short and, as Upton misplayed the ball, Williams was able to get all the way to third base. Doerr flied out to left, but Vollmer cashed in with a single to left field, scoring Williams. He might have been tagged out, but Batts "dropped the ball as Williams crossed the plate."[348] The score became 3-0.

Williams Clinches 1st With Single, 2d by Homer—Shutout for Parnell

Parnell gave up two singles in the eighth, but back-to-back groundouts bailed him out.

After a 40-minute rain delay, the Browns had Bobby Hogue take over pitching. Wanting to play it safe on the now-wet grounds, Sox manager Steve O'Neill pinch-hit for both Goodman and Williams.

Parnell gave up a single and a walk in the ninth, but that's all. He had shut out the Browns on May 23, a four-hitter. Now he had done it again. This time he gave up eight hits and also walked four, "but was pulled out of harm's way by three double plays."[349] Widmar hadn't walked anyone.

Williams's bat had produced the winning hit in both games. The Red Sox win was their 10th consecutive win at Fenway Park over the Browns. The last time the Browns had won a game at Fenway was a little over a year earlier, on June 9, 1950.

Boston Red Sox 4
New York Yankees 2

September 5, 1951 — Yankee Stadium, New York

There was a pennant race. This Wednesday night game drew 58,462. Only percentage points separated the Yankees (82-48, .631) and Cleveland Indians (84-50, .627), with Boston just four games behind (77-51, .602) and still 20-some games to play.

Casey Stengel started Vic Raschi (17-8, 3.63). Boston got two quick runs. After two outs, Ted Williams walked, Bobby Doerr singled, and Billy Goodman hit a ball over first baseman Johnny Mize and down into the right-field corner for a two-base hit. Both Williams and Doerr scored.

Rookie left-hander Leo Kiely, 21, from nearby Hoboken, started for the Red Sox. He was awaiting induction into the Army but allowed to finish the season. He didn't allow a run for the first seven innings, and only five scattered singles.

With two outs in the top of the third, and on a 1-1 pitch, Ted Williams "got a toehold...and it was a jackpot wallop. The ball bounced off a railing fronting the top deck of the three-tiered stand in right field."[350] It had been hit right down the line and struck a girder supporting the second tier of the grandstand.[351] "He powdered the ball deep into the right-field stand," wrote the *New York Times*.[352] It was 3-0, Red Sox.

Williams had been out for a few days with the grippe. He was still weak, but asked into the game and said that manager Steve O'Neill could take him out if he wasn't handling it well.[353] "My legs are wobbly, but I'll try to go four or five innings," he said before the game.[354] Williams walked twice, singled, and hit the game-winning homer, and got extra credit for his outfield play. He took one ball from Hank Bauer right up against the fence in left field.

The Red Sox added a fourth run in the fifth. Again it began after two outs. Johnny Pesky walked – and wound up on third base, after a wild pitch and Berra's errant throw past second base and into center field. Williams walked. Doerr singled to deep left-center, scoring Pesky. Stengel replaced Raschi with Joe Ostrowski, who struck out Goodman.

The Yankees finally scored in the bottom of the eighth. It started with an error by Kiely, who couldn't grip a topper Mize sent his way. Mickey Mantle, playing in his rookie year, pinch-hit for Ostrowski. Mantle was batting .259. He drew a walk (the only one Kiely granted). Bauer singled. The Yankees had their first run. Phil Rizzuto singled and they had their second. With runners on first and second, still just one out, and Gene Woodling up, Mickey McDermott relieved Kiely. McDermott got two outs on his first pitch – a "hot liner" to Pesky, who turned an unassisted double play.

The Ted Williams homer won the game for Boston, but the team's September played out poorly.[355]

Boston Red Sox 9
St. Louis Browns 6

September 14, 1951 — Fenway Park

The Red Sox were just 3 1/2 games out of first place. The Browns were deep in the cellar, 43 ½ games back.

Ted Williams had the game-winning hit, a two-run homer off Al Widmar in the second inning that gave the Red Sox a 7-2 lead. The Sox held on and won, 9-6.

The biggest home run story of this game, though, was when "a sportswriter hit two home runs in his first two major-league at-bats. Bob Nieman was a 24-year-old journalism student at Kent State who homered in the second and homered in the third, both off Maury McDermott."[356] Nieman drove in four of St. Louis's six runs.

McDermott, 22, was Boston's starter, in his second full season in the majors. The Red Sox scored five runs for him in the bottom of the inning. Al Widmar replaced Browns starter Fred Sanford.[357]

Widmar hit the first batter he faced, Fred Hatfield, but closed out the inning without further incident.

Nieman was the second batter up in the top of the second. He hit a solo home run off McDermott, "a long clout high into the left-field net."[358] A second run followed.

Dom DiMaggio singled in the second, and Williams hit a two-run homer some 12 rows up in the bleachers over the visitors' bullpen, to give the Red Sox their sixth and seventh runs. The home run gave him his 119th and 120th runs batted in of 1951.[359]

With two outs in the top of the third, St. Louis center fielder Ken Wood singled. Nieman came up again. He hit another home run, this one clear over the left-field netting. The score became 7-4.[360]

In the bottom of the third, Dom DiMaggio hit a two-run homer into the left-field net to make it 9-4.

Ted Williams's final at-bat came in the bottom of the eighth, facing reliever Satchel Paige, a pitcher the 33-year-old Williams had first seen pitch in San Diego when "The Kid" was still a teenager. Williams struck out. He was far from pleased with himself.

POSTSCRIPT

"Paige was 44 at the time, and he fooled Ted, who'd swung at a pitch outside the strike zone. Angry at himself, Williams 'smashed his bat into pieces. He first whacked it against the railing of the runway leading to the dressing room. When that didn't suffice, Williams flung the bat towards the rack. He still wasn't satisfied, so he smashed it on the floor of the dugout. That ended the bat's worth for good. All the while Williams was doing his rail-splitting act, ol' Satchimo [sic] was laughing his head off on the mound.'"[361]

After the game, Paige said, "I've never seen anything like it in the big leagues. He was sore because I crossed him up."[362] Williams had anticipated Paige's patented slowball but got a fastball instead. "I don't throw to any hitter's strength," Paige said. "If Ted's going to hit home runs off me, he's going to hit them over the left field fence."[363] Williams only faced Paige 11 times. He was 2-for-9, both singles, with two walks, one intentional.

"I wasn't mad at Paige or anyone else but myself for striking out," Williams said after the game. "I have said before Paige must be one of the greatest pitchers of all time. I still think that. But I was mad at myself for striking out."[364]

On his own initiative, Nieman bunted for a single in the top of the ninth.[365] Nothing came of it.

Ellis Kinder, who had worked the end of the game, was awarded the win, his record improving to 11-2. Sanford bore the loss. The Red Sox season record against the Browns improved to 15-6.

The Yankees overtook the Indians and won the pennant by five games. The Red Sox finished third, 11 behind, and the Browns finished in last place, 46 games behind the Yankees.

After his playing days were done, Nieman – with a lifetime .295 batting average – went on to more than 20 years as a scout.

Ted Williams notably devoted a portion of his 1966 acceptance speech on his induction into the National Baseball Hall of Fame expressing his hope that some of the great Negro Leagues players such as Satchel Paige and Josh Gibson would one day also be recognized in Cooperstown.[366]

1952

An Unforgettable Farewell on "Ted Williams Day"

Ted Williams hit just one game-winning homer in 1952, and it was in the last game he played that year. He ended the season 4-for-10, having appeared in only six games. It was on April 30, announced and promoted as "Ted Williams Day." He was 33 years old, but with the Korean War well underway, the U. S. Marine Corps recalled a number of pilots to action. Williams had not seen combat in World War II, but he was about to.

For a team that was already in decline, Williams's departure was more than the Red Sox could overcome. They plummeted to sixth place, 19 games behind New York. They were entering a decade of doldrums. With a 76-78 record, they had lost more games than they won for the first time with Williams on the team.

Ted's homer won that game, but he had every reason to wonder if he would ever hit another one. In February 1953, on just his second combat mission, his aircraft was hit by groundfire over North Korea. With some of his instrumentation knocked out and his landing gear not functioning, he limped back to an American base, crash-landing his plane and scrambling out of it just before it burst into flames and was incinerated.

Boston Red Sox 5
Detroit Tigers 3

April 30, 1952 — Fenway Park

The day before he left to join the Marine Corps, Ted Williams homered to win a game.

Over the course of his career, he homered six times off Dizzy Trout. The last one of them won a ballgame.[367] It was his first – and last – home run of 1952. It came on "Ted Williams Day."[368]

He had time to get into only six games in 1952 before having to report for duty. In 10 at-bats, he had four base hits – a .400 batting average. He also walked twice, for a .500 on-base percentage.

His final line for the '52 season had two singles, a triple, and this home run, which won the game, a two-run homer with one out in the seventh to break a 3-3 tie. More than 45 years later, Williams remembered, "Dominic DiMaggio was on first and I launched, just launched, one into the right-field bleachers, against Dizzy Trout. Final score: Sox 5, Tigers 3."[369]

¡Ted's Farewell Homer Wins for Red Sox, 5-3

The *Boston Globe* reported that "Williams clipped a curve ball into the [right-field] grandstand section near the runway, about eight rows deep."[370] The *Boston Daily Record* said, "[T]he sphere sailed majestically over [Vic] Wertz's head and landed among a group of sailors seated in the right-field bend of the grandstand."[371] It was caught by Mike Lopilato, a 36-year-old fruit vendor from Boston, and Ted swapped him a new signed ball for it after the game.[372]

"How did it feel? How would you feel? It felt great, great! It was a curve ball, and I hit it pretty good. I figured he would curve me."[373] Was it his greatest thrill, to win a game with a home run his last time up before going off to war, perhaps never to play again? No, he answered honestly. "The home run I hit in the 1941 All-Star Game at Detroit had this one beat 10 to 1. I don't think anything will ever pass that."[374]

Neither team scored in the first four innings. Williams singled off Tigers starter Virgil Trucks in the first inning but struck out for the final out in the third. One of the strikes had been a foul ball that went over the right-field roof at the park, one of the only balls to ever leave the ballpark over the roof.[375]

Detroit scored first, one run in the top of the fifth off Mel Parnell. The Red Sox scored three times, the first two when Parnell bunted with two aboard and the throw to first base hit him on the shoulder and caromed into right field.[376] Both runners scored, Parnell made it to third base, and Dom DiMaggio singled him home.

The Tigers tied it in the top of the seventh. Ike Delock replaced Parnell to get the final out.

In the bottom of the seventh, DiMaggio reached on an error. After Jimmy Piersall flied out to right, Ted Williams stepped into the batter's box. He launched the home run that won the game.

On May 2, Williams drove out of Boston with two friends to report for duty at Willow Grove, Pennsylvania.

POSTSCRIPT

"Ted Williams Day" hadn't been a day of unalloyed praise for Williams before the game. On the field, though he had assented to the occasion asking that no gifts be given him, he wound up with a blue Cadillac and a "memory book" signed by 400,000 well-wishers. One who hadn't signed was a sportswriter antagonist, Dave Egan, who criticized Williams bitterly, writing that he should be horsewhipped instead of honored.[377] He said that Williams set the "poorest possible example" for American youth. That sour note aside, the governor of Massachusetts, the mayor of Boston, and many others wished Williams well.

As it happens, Williams won the game with his home run, in what could have been his last at-bat in baseball. Afterward, manager Boudreau proclaimed, "A scriptwriter couldn't have provided a more perfect setting. What a grand way for the big guy to bow out."[378]

Williams later wrote, "That night I threw a party at the Hotel Kenmore. I invited bellhops, cab drivers, bartenders, bat boys, cops – guys I knew. I had to think at the time that it was my last home run in big league baseball. I was thirty-three years old. I would be thirty-five when I got back. Chances were I wouldn't play again."[379]

Less than a year in the future, Williams's F9F Panther jet was shot down over North Korea. He limped back south and crash-landed it on an airstrip, him escaping from the aircraft just before it burst into flames. He flew 39 combat missions into North Korea, serving in the same squadron as John Glenn.

1953

13 Homers (and Three Game-Winners) in 94 At-Bats

Williams recovered, but after 39 combat missions in the Korean War, another incident occurred that affected his ability to pilot a plane, and the Marine Corps mustered him out. Williams returned stateside in time to take in the 1953 All-Star Game.

He then rejoined the Red Sox, again wondering what the time away from baseball would do to his game, especially now that he was nearly 34. Williams started his season on August 6 and ended up getting into 37 games, the first seven of them as a pinch-hitter, before getting back to regular play. In his second time up, he homered in a losing effort.

Despite everything, Williams's production was incredible—again. He did hit three game-winning home runs for the Red Sox. He homered 13 times in all in only 91 at-bats (one per seven ABs), with 34 RBIs. Three long balls were game-winners. He had a career-best slugging percentage of .901. And to top it off, he hit for a .407 batting average, with nowhere close to enough at-bats to qualify for the record books, but a nice touch nevertheless.

Boston Red Sox 6
Philadelphia Athletics 4

August 19, 1953 — Fenway Park

Capt. T. S. Williams, USMC, had completed his combat duty in Korea, missing most of the 1952 and 1953 seasons. He had been back less than a month. This was his third four-bagger since returning. He almost didn't play in the game; he was reported as being rather sore and stiff before the game.

Ben Flowers started the game for Boston. He had appeared in 22 games as a reliever in 1953, setting a major-league record at the time by appearing in eight consecutive games from July 25 through August 1.[380] He got his first start on August 5.[381]

The Red Sox scored once in the first off Charlie Bishop. He had lost his last eight decisions. Leading off, Billy Goodman doubled. George Kell singled him home.

Williams walked in the first and again in the third.

The Athletics took a 2-1 lead in the top of the fourth on a two-run home from Gus Zernial. The Sox responded with a pair of their own.

In the sixth, back-to-back Philadelphia homers from Eddie Robinson and another from Zernial gave them a 4-3 edge. Ellis Kinder relieved Flowers.

In the Red Sox seventh, Al Zarilla, who had replaced Piersall back in the fifth inning, singled to right field.[382] On a 3-and-1 count, Ted Williams homered to right, a "410-foot smash far into the right-field stands" – maybe as far as 28 rows up into the Section 3 seats.[383] Afterwards, he said, "I guess I hit that one as well as anything I've hit for a long time."[384]

A double by Kell and a single by Sammy White gave Boston a 6-4 lead.

In the top of the ninth, Athletics manager Jimmy Dykes used four different pinch-hitters but they couldn't manufacture a run.

Seven times before, Ted Williams had hit home runs on August 19. It was apparently a date on which he liked to hit home runs. The one he hit this Wednesday afternoon at Boston's Fenway Park was his 327th career home run. He had previously hit homers #18, 49, 78, 79, 80, 117, and 319 on August 19. His home run provided the run that won this game against the visiting Athletics.

Paid attendance for the game had been 12,084. It was also Ladies Day, and there were 1,987 ladies, too. Enlivening Fenway Park were 4,000-5,000 Little Leaguers there as guests of the Red Sox, and they got to see Ted Williams hit a game-winning homer.

Boston Red Sox 6
Cleveland Indians 4

August 31, 1953 — Cleveland Stadium

After returning Stateside from military service, Ted Williams wasn't fully back in shape, but he entered the August 31 game batting .447.[385]

The eight-column headline in the next day's *Cleveland Plain Dealer* read, "Williams's Homer Sinks Indians, 6-4."[386] Back in Boston, the *Boston Globe* headline said: "3-Run Homer by Williams Wins for Sox."[387] Friends and family following back in his native San Diego would have read, "Williams's Homer Tops Tribe, 6-4."[388]

WILLIAMS' HOMER SINKS INDIANS, 6-4

Before the home run, the Red Sox left fielder had been having a rough day. He took a called third strike in the first inning, grounded into a double play in the third, and grounded out short to first in the fifth.

Starting for Cleveland was Mike Garcia (16-7).

The Red Sox scored once in the top of the second. Billy Goodman doubled to left-center, and came around to score on an error and a groundout. With two outs in the third, after two singles, Boston starter Maury McDermott, a good-hitting pitcher batting sixth in Lou Boudreau's batting order, singled in a second run.

In the bottom of the sixth, the Indians reclaimed one run. Boston 2, Cleveland 1.

With one out in the top of the seventh, both Johnny Lipon and Billy Consolo singled for the Red Sox. Lipon was cut down at the plate on a ball Jimmy Piersall hit back to Garcia.

On a 1-and-1 count, Ted Williams followed with "a colossal three-run homer" that gave the Red Sox a 5-1 lead.[389] The home run went into the second tier in right field.[390] The *Plain Dealer* had noted the day before that Williams's first-inning home run off Bob Feller on August 30 was the first hit into the upper deck all year and with this home run he'd done it two days in a row. It was only a few rows short of the previous day's homer. There were only 12,228 fans and "only a teen-aged youngster was within sections of the ball and he didn't even have to hurry to recover it as a souvenir."[391]

Hoot Evers replaced Williams in left field for the rest of the game.

McDermott got in trouble in the bottom of the eighth and departed with the bases loaded; Ellis Kinder relieved him. Bobby Avila singled to Lipon at shortstop and two runs scored when Lipon threw the ball into the Cleveland dugout. Both teams scored one run in the ninth, Boston's on Evers' sacrifice fly and Cleveland's on a two-out homer from Larry Doby.

Williams was clearly not yet in condition and was unable to start the next day's game. He said, "I'll be available to pinch hit, but I just can't start the game."[392] He had, however, at least one base hit in every one of the 11 games he had started. The streak ran four more games. He finished the season batting .407.

Boston Red Sox 2
Detroit Tigers 1

September 17, 1953 — Fenway Park

There were only six games left to play in the season and the standings were pretty well fixed. There weren't that many at this Thursday afternoon game. The official attendance was a season low of 2,272.[393]

Red Sox manager Lou Boudreau started 5-9 Sid Hudson. Fred Hutchinson's choice to pitch for the Tigers was Ned Garver, 11-10.

Detroit got a run off Hudson in the top of the second. That 1-0 score stood until the eighth inning. Hudson only allowed two more hits and walked two.

In the fifth, the first two Red Sox batters singled and Garver threw a wild pitch, but with one out, Hudson hit a shot to left field – a ball that looked like a home run "until a strong breeze got hold of the ball."[394]

Hudson kept the ball in the infield in the eighth, retiring all three batters. The Tigers carried their 1-0 lead to the bottom of the eighth.

Garver got the first two Red Sox batters to fly out, but then Jimmy Piersall singled to center field.

Ted Williams was bothered by a stiff neck. He had flied out to left, fouled out to third base, and fouled out behind the plate to the catcher. This time he slammed Garver's pitch "far and high into the eighteenth row of the right-field stands."[395] A man in a brown suit caught the ball. It was a two-run homer that put the Red Sox in the lead for the first time in the game.

Williams said, "It was a slider, but I don't think that Ned got it where he wanted to. This one was over the plate. The two he got me out on were almost on my fists."[396] He added, "The home run was just lucky."[397]

Remarkably, Garver was trying to walk Williams at the time. He talked about it afterward. The count was 3-1 and he didn't want to come in with anything good, figuring he'd take his chances. "I'm going to put him on base and pitch to George Kell...I just threw it in there plenty bad [very high and inside, and not a strike] and Williams stepped back and hit that sucker for a home run...I'm trying to walk him and he hits a home run to make it 2-1 and win the ball game."[398]

Ted's 13th Gives Hudson Decision Over Garver, 2-1

Ellis Kinder relieved Hudson. It was his 67th relief appearance of the 1953 season, breaking Ed Walsh's 45-year-old American League record set in 1908.[399]

Williams had 13 home runs on the season, one more or less every seven at-bats since he'd returned from Korea.[400]

1954

Passing DiMaggio With a Game-Winner

Injury struck early, with Williams breaking his collarbone on the very first day of spring training, and as a result he was slow to get going, appeared in just 117 games, finishing just shy of the 400 at-bats required to win the batting title. not getting into enough games to qualify for the batting title. (By today's rules, his 526 plate appearances would have been enough and his .345 average would have outpaced actual league leader Bobby Avila by four points.)

Williams made the most of his times to the plate, homering 29 times and driving in 89 runs. He drew 136 walks and his .513 on-base percentage led both leagues. His .635 slugging percentage led the American League. He got on the game-winning homer board late, belting two in August and two in September.

The Red Sox finished with a losing record of 69-85, which somehow earned them a spot in the first division, but they finished in fourth place, an astonishing 42 games behind the 111-43 Cleveland Indians, as they and the Yankees (103 wins) feasted off the rest of the league.

Boston Red Sox 3
Baltimore Orioles 1
(10 innings)

August 6, 1954 — Memorial Stadium, Baltimore

In their first season in Baltimore, the last-place Orioles were struggling. Boston was in sixth place, themselves already 30 games behind first-place Cleveland.

Right-hander (and Massachusetts native) Joe Coleman pitched an excellent game for the O's, allowing just three base hits and one unearned run in seven innings. That run came in the fifth, when Harry Agganis walked and Grady Hatton singled. Billy Consolo hit one back to Coleman, "a harmless roller which Coleman booted."[401] Agganis scored from second base, but a double play ended things.

Matching Coleman with an equally good start was Willard Nixon, who worked eight innings, giving up a total of one run and four hits.

In the bottom of the sixth, the Orioles evened the score. All of a sudden, Nixon couldn't find the plate, walking the first three Baltimore batters. Bob Kennedy hit into a double play, as the tying run scored without benefit of a base hit.

Williams' Homer in 10th Gives Red Sox 3-1 Victory

In the eighth, Bob Chakales relieved Coleman.[402] With a runner on second and two outs, he intentionally walked Ted Williams, the slugger's second walk of the game.[403]

The Red Sox loaded the bases with one out in the top of the ninth, but failed to score.

For the bottom of the ninth, the Red Sox reliever was Ellis Kinder. He got three flyball outs, interrupted only by a two-out single to right field by Young.

The first batter up in the 10th inning was Jimmy Piersall and, on the first pitch he saw, he singled to left field. Ted Williams left the on-deck circle for the batter's box.

It was maybe not a good idea to taunt Ted Williams. He'd had five official at-bats in Baltimore in 1954 and failed to get a hit. The Orioles dugout was giving him a hard time in the top of the 10th in a 1-1 game. Williams glared at the dugout, and dug in. What was the percentage in heckling Ted Williams in a situation like this? He hit a 1-1 pitch "with jet-like force"[404] and "lashed a line drive about eight rows deep into the stands, two sections over from the foul line about 330 feet out."[405] Both papers agreed that Ted had twice paused and looked directly at the Orioles dugout, and then "as Ted crossed home plate, he looked over at the Orioles bench, wearing a big grin."[406] At this point, the *Globe*'s Bob Holbrook wrote, "You just don't rib the big guy...Most of the players were looking at their shoe tops."[407]

Suddenly, it was 3-1, Boston.

Kinder retired the Orioles in order and got the win, Chakales got the loss. One unfortunate pitch (and maybe some dugout mouthing-off) had meant all the difference.

Boston Red Sox 10
Washington Senators 1

August 11, 1954 — Fenway Park
(first game of a doubleheader)

In a Wednesday dual admission doubleheader, Tom Brewer pitched the first game for the hosting Red Sox. The first batter he faced swung at his first pitch and hit a home run. Third baseman Eddie Yost hit it into the left-field screen.[408] It was the only run the Senators got.

Pitching for Washington was Connie Marrero, finishing up his fifth major-league season. He gave up base hits to the first two batters he faced. On the third pitch, right fielder Jimmy Piersall hit a ball that landed behind the in-ground flagpole in center field, a double. Batting second in the lineup was left fielder Ted Williams. Marrero's pitch was sent into the right-field stands, into the lower seats of Section 2. The *Herald* said it landed about 10 rows up.[409] It was 2-1, Red Sox.

Come the third inning, the Red Sox somewhat replayed their first — Piersall singled (to left in this case) and Ted Williams hit a two-run homer (this time into the center-field bleachers into the triangular section behind the Red Sox bullpen.) It was the 359th home run of Williams's career, tying him with "The Big Cat" — Johnny Mize — for sixth place all-time. The score was 4-1, Boston.

Brewer gave up a single in the second and a walk in the fourth. In the fifth, though, perhaps surprised by pitcher Mickey McDermott pinch-hitting for Marrero, Brewer walked him and the next two Senators. There had been two outs, though, and Mickey Vernon lined out to Harry Agganis at first base.

Bunky Stewart was the next Washington pitcher. The first batter he faced was Piersall who homered to deep center field, into the screen to the left of the flagpole. Williams singled to left field, the ball striking his bat as he was ducking from a pitch.[410]

There was no further scoring in the fifth, but the Red Sox added four more runs in the sixth. After two singles and a walk loaded the bases with nobody out, Brewer singled to right, driving in one. Piersall hit a fly ball that produced another run. With first base open, Williams was walked intentionally. The Red Sox picked up two more runs on a pair of errors by Washington's second baseman in 1954, Johnny Pesky. It was Boston 9, Washington 1.

Billy Consolo hit a leadoff home run off new pitcher Gus Keriazakos in the eighth, "about eight rows up in the distant center field seats."[411]

Washington's *Evening Star* commented, "Washington's first-game run production started and ended with the first pitch, which Eddie Yost belted for a home run."[412]

There was another game to play, that evening. The Senators won, 5-4.

Boston Red Sox 11
Philadelphia Athletics 1

September 3, 1954 — Connie Mack Stadium, Philadelphia

As the number of his homers built, Ted Williams knew where he stood on the career list of home-run hitters. Joe DiMaggio had retired with 361 home runs. On August 26, Williams tied DiMaggio for fifth place. His next home run – his 25th of the 1954 season – would see him pass Joe D.[413]

Starting for manager Eddie Joost's Athletics was righty Arnie Portocarrero (7-15); the 44-87 Athletics were already 50 games out of first place. Williams flied out to center field in the first inning.

Boston's Frank Sullivan (11-11) walked Philadelphia's leadoff man, Spook Jacobs. While Lou Limmer was batting, Jacobs stole second but made it to third base on a throwing error by Boston catcher Sammy White. Limmer singled to center and Jacobs scored.

In the third, Milt Bolling walked, then took second on a wild pitch. Sullivan struck out. Billy Goodman doubled, driving in Bolling and tying the score, 1-1. Williams then hit the ball that eclipsed Joe DiMaggio's record. Clif Keane of the *Boston Globe* described the trajectory: "The ball carried over a 40-foot wall and landed on one of the chimneys that loom up like gravestones on the apartment houses on No. 20th Street. After hitting the chimney, it caromed off the roof of the home and bounced into the backyard of Bill Gillard, a middle-aged man who lives at No. 2743."[414] Gillard said he'd heard the ball bounce off his roof and went out to retrieve it.[415]

WILLIAMS GETS EPIC HOME RUN BALL

Ted Surpasses Joe DiMag in Circuit Clouts

The score was 3-1, Red Sox. The Athletics never scored again, but the Red Sox scored five more runs in the fourth on six singles and two errors.

There was no more scoring until the eighth. Williams got up once more, in the sixth, and grounded out, second to first. After the half-inning, Karl Olson took his place in left field.

In the top of the eighth, Frank Sullivan drew a one-out walk. Goodman bunted for a single. Olson grounded into a force play at second, but the second baseman threw the ball away trying to hold up Sullivan, and Sullivan was able to score. It was the fifth error of the game for Philadelphia.

The Red Sox added two final runs in the ninth. With one out, Sam Mele walked. Grady Hatton tripled. Sammy White singled. It was 11-1.

Sullivan threw a four-hitter.

"The pitch was a fastball, up high," Ted said, and he was indeed aware of the significance of the moment. He had atypically stopped halfway to first base to watch the baseball leave the stadium.[416]

Williams said of achieving sole possession of fifth place, "Everyone has a goal. This was one of mine."[417] He added, "Records were made to be broken. In two years either Musial or Kiner will beat me. But in ten years Eddie Mathews will beat us all."[418]

Boston Red Sox 5
Philadelphia Athletics 2

September 20, 1954 — Fenway Park

It was a Monday afternoon game in late September between two teams that were far from first place. The Red Sox were 43 ½ games behind the league-leading Cleveland Indians and the Athletics were 59 games behind. John Gillooly of the *Boston Daily Record* dubbed them the "Philadelphia Pathetics."[419]

Only 1,555 fans turned out at Fenway Park for the game; those who were Red Sox fans enjoyed the game.

Rookie right-hander Tom Brewer was 9-9, hoping to break into double digits and finish with a winning record. Johnny Gray pitched for Philadelphia. He was a rookie, too, but came into the game with a record of 3-11.

Neither side scored in the first three innings.

Brewer retired the three A's he faced in the top of the fourth, striking out two of them.

Boston's Grady Hatton led off with a walk. Jimmy Piersall reached on an error. Sammy White bunted, a successful sacrifice. Milt Bolling singled to center field and both runners scored. The Red Sox had a 2-0 lead.

That score held until the bottom of the seventh when Ted Williams led off with his 28th home run of 1954, "a high drive which was escorted into the visiting bullpen by the wind."[420] Jackie Jensen singled to left. So did Sam Mele. After one out, Piersall "poked a double down the right field line"[421] and drove in two more runs – Jensen and Mele – but was himself thrown out at third base, trying to grab an extra base, because of a strong relay by Pete Suder. Sammy White hit a foul popup to end the inning. Williams had missed 37 games due to a broken collarbone, but was second in home runs only to Larry Doby's 30.

It was 5-0, Red Sox, with two innings left to play.

In the top of the ninth, Elmer Valo pinch-hit for the Philadelphia pitcher and walked. Two outs followed. Down to their last out, Jim Finigan hit a two-run homer over the left-field fence. Gus Zernial flied out to Ted Williams in left field and the game was over.

Brewer got his win, though the homer spoiled his shot at his first major-league shutout. He'd thrown a four-hitter, at one point retiring 15 batters in a row.[422]

"Did I think I'd win 10 games in the American League this season?" Brewer asked rhetorically after the game. "I didn't think I'd even be in the American League this season."[423]

POSTSCRIPT

It wasn't until August that Ted Williams had a game-winning homer in 1954. This was the year he broke his collarbone on the first day of spring training. It took him a long time to get right, and some things didn't quite go his way. He hit two homers in the second game of the May 16 doubleheader in Detroit, but the Red Sox still lost, 9-8, in 14 innings. This was the year he hit .345 and led both leagues in walks with 136 and in on-base percentage with .513, but he had only 386 plate appearances – below the threshold necessary to win the baiting title, which went to Bobby Avila instead.

Ted Williams 1954 Bowman baseball card.

1955

Favorite Foe Detroit Victimized Five Times

In 1955, Williams didn't play his first game until May 28, and this time the reason was not an injury. Instead, he was in the midst of a divorce, and in order to minimize his apparent earning potential, before the season he announced that he was retiring from baseball.

Williams missed the first 41 games of the season, appeared in 98 of the remaining schedule, in which he drove in 83 runs, homered 28 times (six of them game-winners – and four of those against the Tigers), and hit for a .356 average. Again, he didn't collect enough at-bats to qualify for the batting title. Young Al Kaline took the honors with a .340. mark. He did lead the league with 17 intentional walks, the sixth time he had topped the AL in that category. And he did finish fourth in MVP voting despite collecting only 320 at-bats, ahead of none other than Mickey Mantle, who hit 37 home runs and led the league in on-base and slugging average. At age 36 he was named to the All-Star team for the 12th time.

Boston Red Sox 5
Detroit Tigers 2

June 10, 1955 — Briggs Stadium, Detroit

The Associated Press observed, "The friendly, dark green outfield walls of Briggs stadium, home of the Detroit Tigers, cures all ills for Williams, makes him as frisky as a young colt."[424]

"The closer we got to Briggs stadium, the better I felt," said the Red Sox left fielder.[425]

Rookie Duke Maas got groundouts from the first two Boston batters. Ted Williams hit a line drive into the lower right-field seats at Briggs Stadium, "like a golf shot into the lower deck, about 345 feet out. It hit a chair and bounced back on the field."[426]

Sixth-year Red Sox pitcher Willard Nixon walked two in the second, but didn't give up a hit until the third.

Frisky Williams Bombs Tigers

Boston only had the one hit until shortstop Billy Klaus singled in the third, a hard-hit ball down the right-field line, but Klaus deliberately held up at first base.[427]

Ted Williams hit another one hard, this one deep into the upper deck in right field, another two-out homer, but this time a two-run homer. The Red Sox took a 3-0 lead.[428]

The *Boston Herald*'s Henry McKenna wrote, "If Yankee Stadium is the House that Ruth built, then Briggs Stadium should be tabbed 'the House that Williams owns.'"[429]

It didn't take long for the Tigers to get a couple of runs back in the bottom of the third.[430]

A couple of errors in the top of the fourth inning enabled Boston to add two more, for a 5-2 lead. Norm Zauchin hit a ball to third base, and Fred Hatfield muffed it. Zauchin ended up on second. Catcher Sammy White hit a ball to Harvey Kuenn, whose throw was off, enabling Zauchin to come home. Grady Hatton doubled to right-center and White scored. There was still nobody out, but Maas worked his way of the inning without any more runs.

Williams took a called third strike from reliever Al Aber in the seventh, and singled to second base in the top of the ninth. Gene Stephens replaced him as a pinch-runner, but Jackie Jensen hit into a routine double play. Williams said he still felt lousy after the game, very ill.

Nixon went to 5-4 with the complete-game win. The fifth win had been a long time coming. Since winning his fourth, Nixon had lost three games and been involved in three no-decisions.

Williams hit a total of 28 home runs in 1955, drove in 83 runs, and hit for a .356 batting average.

Boston Red Sox 5
Detroit Tigers 4

June 21, 1955 — Fenway Park

Until the seventh-inning stretch, this game was a pitcher's duel between right-handers Willard Nixon of the Red Sox and Ned

Garver of the Tigers. Detroit led for most of the game, but only by one run, which they scored in the second inning when first baseman Earl Torgeson drew a base on balls and left fielder Jim Delsing hit a long double to right field, Torgeson scoring all the way from first base.

After 10 zeroes were hung in the scoreboard, the Red Sox finally broke through in the bottom of the seventh and took the lead, but it was a narrow lead at that. They scored two runs. Williams was up first. He walked. Jackie Jensen singled to left field, Williams stopping at second. Norm Zauchin singled to short left field. The bases were loaded with nobody out. After Sammy White lined to Delsing, Grady Hatton doubled to right field and both Williams and Jensen scored, the Red Sox taking a 2-1 lead.

Williams 3-Run Homer in Eighth Wins for Sox, 5-4

The momentary excitement among Fenway's faithful didn't last long. Nixon saw the first four batters he faced reach base safely, two scoring, and saw Tom Hurd come on in relief. With the bases loaded, pinch-hitter Harvey Kuenn hit a sac fly to right field. It was 4-2, Detroit.

Gene Stephens batted for Hurd and blooped a single to center. Billy Goodman lined a single over second base. After one out, Ted Williams was up. Garver was being cautious; Williams already had five home runs off him. And Williams had hit two homers in the previous game, against Cleveland on June 19.

The count ran to 3-0. Williams swung and connected on a 3-0 pitch. He hit an arcing three-run home run into the right-field grandstand and, just like that, the Red Sox were back in the lead, 5-4. The hone run became the game-winner. It was hit into "the extreme edge of the right-field grandstand."[431] It wasn't hit deep. Right fielder Al Kaline leapt for it but couldn't corral it. It landed in the second or third row of seats in Section 1, just to the right of the Tigers bullpen. It proved the game-winner.[432]

"The moral of this story is," wrote Bob Holbrook of the *Boston Globe,* "never take a chance on Ted Williams, regardless of the count."[433]

Williams, who had only begun the season on May 28, had hit nine home runs and seven in his last 10 games. Ever the perfectionist, Williams mostly complained after the game that he hadn't hit the pitch well, not like the two he'd hit on the 19th. Hitting a ball *well* was important to Ted Williams. "I didn't get a good pitch to hit all night," he grumbled. "I think it was supposed to be some kind of a breaking pitch. But it didn't do much."[434]

The home run, however, proved the game-winner.

Boston Red Sox 5
Detroit Tigers 0

July 29, 1955 — Fenway Park

Not often does a solo home run in the first inning turn out to the game-winning hit in a ballgame. Ted Williams's 383rd career homer won this game.

The pitcher for the Detroit Tigers was Jim Bunning, pitching in his third major-league game. The future Hall of Famer (and United States Senator) was 1-1 at this point in his rookie year; his debut had been just nine days earlier.

The Red Sox were in contention for a possible pennant. They came into this game having gone 23-8 over the previous month and – while in fourth place – they were only three games out of first place. The Tigers were in fifth place, only 2 ½ games behind the Red Sox.

Willard Nixon was the Red Sox starter. Harvey Kuenn led off with a single to his counterpart at short, Billy Klaus, the ball taking an unexpected hop and glancing off Klaus's arm. Bill Tuttle then grounded into a double play. Al Kaline struck out.

Bunning got groundouts from the first two batters he faced, Billy Goodman and Klaus. Ted Williams came to bat, facing Bunning for the first time. Williams hit a home run, "tight up the right-field line and well back into the stands."[435] It was 1-0, Red Sox.

Nixon gave up a single in the third inning, but not another hit until the seventh. In the meantime, the Red Sox added three runs in the bottom of the fifth. Grady Hatton singled to right-center, and Jimmy Piersall bunted for a single, Hatton reaching third on a throwing error. Nixon singled in Hatton. Billy Goodman bunted, reaching on Bunning's error. A wild pitch let another run in. Williams was walked intentionally. A ball glanced off Jackie Jensen's bat as he was avoiding a pitch and Nixon scored.

In the bottom of the eighth inning, after two singles and a walk, reliever Paul Foytack walked Goodman, forcing in a fifth run.

Nixon threw a complete-game four-hit shutout. He walked no one. No Tiger reached third base. Most of the outs were infield outs; only five outs were recorded by Red Sox outfielders.[436] Nixon's career record against Detroit improved to 12-4.

Over the five years that followed, Williams hit seven more home runs off Jim Bunning. His solo home run in the first inning had won this game.

Boston Red Sox 8
Detroit Tigers 3

July 31, 1955 — Fenway Park
(first game of a doubleheader)

The battle between pitcher and batter was one Ted Williams enjoyed. And Hank Aaron appreciated what Ted brought to it. "What made Ted so great was that he refused to think that a pitcher could get him out. I mean he just refused to buckle, and that's what it takes to be great. Somehow you've got to feel that you are the best. That's how he played the game, and that's how he left the game, as the best."[437]

Sox Win on Williams Slam, 8-3

Ned Garver was a pitcher Williams hit well, batting .417 against him over the years and connecting for 10 home runs. A little over a month earlier, on June 21, his three-run homer off Garver had won a game for the Red Sox. On this last day of July, his fourth-inning grand slam was another game-winner.[438]

Starting for Boston was right-hander Frank Sullivan, whose 18 wins in 1955 led the American League. He came into this game with a 2.98 ERA and 13-8, but the Tigers didn't take long to pounce. They grabbed two runs in the top of the first.

The Red Sox got one run on Billy Klaus's solo homer in the bottom of the third.

Three Sox singles in the fourth loaded the bases with one out. Sullivan then singled past shortstop Harvey Kuenn's glove and two runs scored. With two outs, Klaus walked, reloading the bases.

That brought Ted Williams to the plate. He'd walked his first time up and grounded out to shortstop the next.

In this at-bat, the first pitch he hit was a hard-hit long drive to right field, but foul. Then he hit one out, a grand slam on a 2-2 pitch that "went into the visitors bull pen, eluding [Tigers right-fielder Charlie] Maxwell's desperate attempt to grab it."[439]

Maxwell hit a solo home run for Detroit, leading off the sixth.

Gene Stephens replaced Williams in left field after the sixth inning.

The Red Sox loaded the bases in the eighth on a double, a walk, and – after a second out – an intentional walk. Norm Zauchin drew a base on balls, which forced in a ninth run.

It was Sullivan's 14th win, a four-hitter.

"Williams is never better than when he's playing against the Tigers," wrote the Associated Press.[440]

In the second game, the teams were tied 2-2 in the bottom of the ninth and Piersall hit a leadoff home run, helping reliever Frank Baumann win in his debut.[441]

Writing about pitchers who were stubborn in their approach, Williams said, "Ned Garver was another one. Sliders all the time, and you could anticipate when and where they'd be, usually inside. A guy who can swing a bat is going to hurt a pitcher who throws him inside – from the middle of the plate in. In a jam, I could always figure on a slider from Garver. I got to Garver pretty good."[442]

Boston Red Sox 8
Washington Senators 4

August 15, 1955 — Fenway Park

In his book *We Played the Game*, Danny Peary quotes Washington Senators pitcher Pedro Ramos regarding his 1955 rookie teammate Ted Abernathy:

"Ted Williams was the best hitter I ever faced. He didn't swing at bad pitches so you had to throw him strikes. I struck him out only once in my life. I remember when Ted Abernathy, who threw underhanded, struck out Williams twice in a game in Boston. He went by me to drink some water and he said, 'Pete, I got the Big Man twice.' I said, 'You better shut up because the Big Man has to come up at least one more time.' Oh, man, in the eighth inning the bases were loaded and the Big Man came up. Abernathy got two quick strikes, but then I could hear Williams christen his bat: he rapped the ball all the way into the bleachers. [Cookie] Lavagetto took Abernathy out and I reminded him of what I said. I can't repeat what Abernathy said."[443]

It didn't happen quite that way, but it's still a great story. It was in the second inning the Big Man hit his game-winning grand slam.[444]

Williams' Slam Leads Sox 8-4 Win

Starting for Boston was Mel Parnell. He gave up a couple of singles, but no runs, in the top of the first.

The first two Boston batters got on base against Abernathy – Billy Goodman walked and Billy Klaus blooped a single into center field, Goodman stopping at second base. That brought up Ted Williams. Two on, nobody out, no place to put him. Abernathy struck him out on three pitches.[445] He then struck out Jackie Jensen, too. Jensen was no slouch; he'd driven 117 runs in 1954 and in 1955 was on his way to leading the American League in RBIs with 116. To strike out both Williams and Jensen back-to-back was something in which any pitcher could take pride.[446]

Looking at some of the strikeout numbers posted by some of the sluggers of the 21st century, it is remarkable to note that only three times did Williams strike out as many as 50 times in a season, and those three times were all in his first four years.

In the bottom of the second, Abernathy had trouble finding the plate and walked the first two Red Sox batters, Grady Hatton and Jimmy Piersall. Parnell bunted for a hit. Abernathy walked Goodman, forcing in Hatton, and Klaus, forcing in Piersall. He found himself facing Ted Williams, again with nobody out but this time with the bases loaded.

He had faced Williams twice before, earlier in the season. The first time, Williams tripled. The second time, he walked. But in this game he had struck out the Big Man.

Not this time. On a 2-1 count, Williams hit a grand slam, and he drove the ball about 440-450 feet, "a king-sized homer" 10 rows up in the center-field bleachers.[447] The *Boston Herald* put it "to the left of the 420-foot sign and landing some six seats deep among the customers."[448]

The score was 6-0.[449]

The Senators came right back with four runs in the top of the fourth (including a three-run homer by Roy Sievers), driving Parnell from the game. Leo Kiely threw 6 2/3 innings of one-hit relief. Piersall hit a two-run homer in the seventh for the Red Sox.[450]

Boston Red Sox 4
Detroit Tigers 3

August 27, 1955 — Briggs Stadium, Detroit

Frank Lary shut out the Red Sox for 8 2/3 innings. The last time he had faced them was on July 14, and he'd shut them out then on six hits, 6-0.

The Red Sox gave Frank Baumann his second major-league start.[451]

Boston got two on in the first inning, but did not score. Detroit scored once.

The 1-0 score lasted until the third, when the Tigers added two more. Harvey Kuenn led off with a walk and Bill Tuttle homered off the façade of the upper left-field deck. Baumann retired the next three batters but he and his team were in a 3-0 hole.

Red Sox catcher Sammy White singled in the fourth. Baumann himself singled in the fifth. Both singles came with one out. Neither batter advanced even as far as second base.

In the sixth, the Sox succeeded in getting a man to second. With two outs, White walked and third baseman Grady Hatton singled to right, but White could get no further than second base.

Baumann, for his part, never gave up another hit in the game. After retiring the side in order in the sixth, pinch-hitter Gene Stephens took his place in the Red Sox seventh. Nothing came of it. Stephens struck out.

Tom Hurd relieved Baumann and retired the three Tigers who came to bat in the seventh. No one got the ball out of the infield.

The Red Sox finally got a runner to third base in the top of the eighth. It was Ted Williams, who had drawn a one-out walk. Jackie Jensen doubled to left field, Williams stopping at third base. But Lary buckled down, striking out White and getting Hatton to ground out.

Hurd retired the Tigers in order once again in the eighth.

In the ninth, Piersall popped up, foul, to the catcher. Eddie Joost singled. So did pinch-hitter Throneberry, who singled off Lary's foot. Billy Goodman matched Piersall's at-bat, popping up foul.[452] Two outs. Klaus singled to right field, and Joost held at third base. The Red Sox, after all, needed three runs to tie the game, not just one. And Ted Williams was on deck. Lary had allowed three singles, but not a run had crossed the plate. It was still a shutout.

With Williams, who batted left-handed, coming up, Bucky Harris decided to go with a lefty specialist, Al Aber.[453]

Just the day before, Williams had come up in the ninth inning with Boston trailing the Tigers by just one run. He took three called strikes and was out.[454]

Aber's fourth pitch was over the plate. "Ted didn't take this one. He measured it. He ducked a little to make certain he got under the ball. With his quick wrists, he lifted it high into the upper deck of the right-field stands."[455]

It was his third grand slam of the 1955 season.[456]

AFTERTHOUGHT

Had Williams been watching Aber warm up and picked up any cues? We'll never know, but he did say that one the advantage he had in Detroit was that he had a good view of Tigers pitchers as they warmed up. "I used to watch all these opposing pitchers in the bullpen. They were always playing around and experimenting. They show you what they've got in the bullpen because they want to throw everything they've got and work on certain pitches and all the rest. I was well aware of those pitches a lot of times. I can think distinctly of Detroit, where I was in left field and they'd be warming up out there, and I could see them and see everything that was going on. So I had a pretty good insight as to the type of pitcher a guy was. That's what good hitters have to do if they want to stay ahead of the game."[457]

1956

Nine Game-Winners in a Three-Month Span

Williams got into 136 games and led both leagues in on-base percentage for the ninth time, with a mark of .479. He hit .345 and was walked 102 times, the 10th time in his career he reached the century mark. Williams homered 24 times, with an amazing 9 of the 24 being game-winning homers by the definition we use in this book. It was his second-highest total of game-winners, just one less than the 10 in 1947. It was another excellent year for a player who turned 38 in August.

The Red Sox managed another fourth-place finish, again going 84-70, and again finishing behind New York, Cleveland, and Chicago—in that order—this time 13 games out.

Boston Red Sox 9
Baltimore Orioles 0

July 8, 1956 — Fenway Park
(first game of a doubleheader)

Ted Williams didn't start the 1956 season in earnest until May 29. Most of his appearances before then had been in pinch-hitting roles. He had suffered a "shower-sandal foot injury" that had badly hampered him.[458]

Ted Williams's first-inning home run was the game-winner in this Sunday's first game. It was his 399th home run – he was on the brink of 400. This was his first game-winning hit of the 1956 season.[459] The home run was only his fifth one of the 1956 season, an uncharacteristically slow start. His first home run of the year had not come until June 22.

Starting for Boston was Frank Sullivan. For the Orioles, it was Ray Moore.

Sullivan breezed through the first inning.

Moore walked leadoff batter Billy Goodman. After Billy Klaus popped up foul to the catcher, Ted Williams homered, a two-run drive into Fenway Park's "right field bleachers just above the Red Sox bull-pen."[460]

The Red Sox scored again in the second. Jimmy Piersall led off with a double to left-center, and scored when Don Buddin doubled to left. Sullivan walked. At this point, Bill Wight relieved Moore. Klaus singled, driving in Buddin. Ted Williams "dropped a pop single in the midst of three fielders in left."[461] Goodman scored. It was 5-0, Red Sox.

With two outs in the bottom of the fourth, Ted Williams doubled to left. Vernon singled to left, driving in Williams.

The Red Sox continued to add runs, pushing two more across the plate in the bottom of the fifth. The first came on Buddin's sacrifice fly, and the second – four batters later – on a bases-loaded walk taken by Ted Williams, then leaving for a pinch-runner.

Sullivan faced the minimum in the sixth inning and in the seventh. He walked Willy Miranda leading off the eighth, the first walk he issued. With one out, Dick Williams singled, the sixth hit off Sullivan. A strikeout and groundout followed, ending any threat. His shutout remained intact.

Williams was 1-for-5 with an RBI in the second game, an 8-4 win for the Red Sox, a win that overcame the Orioles' early 4-0 lead. His third-inning single drove in the 1,500[th] run of his career.[462]

Two days after this July 8 home run at Fenway Park, Williams hit another home run – in the 1956 All-Star Game. He hit a two-run homer off Warren Spahn, into the right-field bullpen at Washington's Griffith Stadium. It was his fourth All-Star Game home run. Also homering in the 1956 All-Star Game were Willie Mays and Mickey Mantle.

Williams's 400th home run was hit on July 17 at Fenway Park. It was another game-winner.

Boston Red Sox 1
Kansas City Athletics 0

July 17, 1956 — Fenway Park
(second game of a doubleheader)

The Sox won the first game of a twi-night doubleheader, 10-0.[463]

The second pitted a pair of right-handers, Bob Porterfield for the Mike Higgins-led Red Sox and Tom Gorman for Lou Boudreau's Athletics.[464] Both pitchers threw excellent games, though both ran into trouble in the first inning. Porterfield gave up back-to-back singles to the first two batters. With one out, he walked Harry Simpson, but he escaped damage.

With one out, Gorman walked Billy Klaus. Ted Williams singled and Klaus scooted to second, but a double play followed.

Both pitchers were helped by double plays in the second inning. There was no scoring through the first five, until Ted Williams came to the plate, leading off the bottom of the sixth. He swung at Gorman's first pitch. He connected. At the moment of impact, there was "no doubt about the destination of his smash."[465] The ball "streaked on a line toward the bullpens, unlike typical Williams homers of the well-remembered sky-scraping variety. It carried over almost the middle of the two bullpens, landed at least half a dozen rows into the stands and the crowd came to its feet as one."[466]

There was "quite a scramble" for the ball in the bleachers.[467]

It was 1-0, Red Sox. Neither team scored any other runs.

400th Blast His First '56 Game-Winning Hit

There had been opportunities. Eddie Robinson doubled with one out for Kansas City in the top of the seventh. The Red Sox loaded the bases in the bottom of the seventh. The Athletics put two runners on base in the eighth, but an unassisted double play shut that down.[468]

But the day ended as a double shutout day for the Red Sox, 10-0 and then 1-0.[469]

"MOVE OVER BABE, JIM, MEL, LOU!" read a headline in the next day's *Boston Globe*.

Hitting homer #400 put Ted Williams into a very exclusive club. At the time, he was only the fifth man to hit 400 or more home runs. Babe Ruth (714), Jimmie Foxx (534), Mel Ott (511), and Lou Gehrig (493) were the ones who preceded him.[470]

After the game, Williams said of hitting homer #400, "I didn't think I'd ever get it. It was a long time coming. But it sure felt good."[471]

For Williams, it was mid-July and just his sixth home run of the year. He'd been under some criticism from Boston sportswriters for his lack of power. As he completed his home run trot, he had made a spitting gesture toward some members of the press as he crossed home plate, and admitted it afterward. "Sure, I spit in the direction. I didn't actually spit, but the only reason was I might have hit Mickey Vernon. And you guys know why I did it. I don't have to tell you."[472]

The "surprisingly large crowd of 24,441 gave Williams a roaring ovation as he reached home plate but he made no effort to acknowledge it."[473] Mickey Vernon said that Williams "was so intent that 'as I put out my hand to congratulate him he didn't even see me'."[474]

Boston Red Sox 5
Kansas City Athletics 3
(10 innings)

July 26, 1956 — Municipal Stadium, Kansas City

Troy Herriage was the starter for Kansas City, a right-hander working in what proved to be his only season in major-league baseball. He was 1-9 with a 6.45 ERA of 6.45.

The Red Sox starter was Frank Sullivan (9-4, 3.31 ERA).

Both were pitching in near 100-degree heat.

Herriage was staked to a 2-0 lead in the first inning with Al Pilarcik's one-out double, a two-out single, and two more singles. On the third one, Vic Power was thrown out at third base after the run scored.

In the bottom of the third, Kansas City took a 3-0 lead, with Pilarcik hitting a leadoff home run over the fence in right field.

The Red Sox scored their first run in the top of the fifth. Sullivan made the first out, Billy Goodman walked and Billy Klaus singled, sending Goodman to second. Williams singled and drove in Goodman. The next two batters flied out.

Ike Delock took over pitching for Boston in the bottom of the seventh.

Ted Williams led off the top of the eighth inning and lined out to Power at first base. Mickey Vernon walked and Jackie Jensen singled. To pitch to Jimmy Piersall, who was 0-for-11 in the series to this point, manager Lou Boudreau called on Bobby Shantz to relieve Herriage. Piersall swung at Shantz's first pitch which he "slammed off the center-field fence for a double,"[475] driving in both baserunners and tying the game, 3-3. He was thrown out trying to stretch the double into a triple. Catcher Pete Daley fouled out to first base.

Though the Athletics threatened in the bottom of the eighth, that was squelched.

Neither team got a runner on base in the ninth inning, and the game went into extra innings.

Ted Lepcio pinch-hit for Klaus, leading off the top of the 10th. He drew a base on balls. Ted Williams also saw the count run to 3-2. Shantz's pitch came in. A "flick of Williams's wrists...clipped the next pitch right on the button" produced "a lofty smash that cleared the center-field wall better than 400 feet from the point of origin."[476] The ball "soared so far over the regular fence a little bit to the right of dead center that it landed at the base of the huge electric scoreboard that was transported from Braves Field."[477]

The home run was the ninth homer Williams hit on the date July 26. It was also his ninth home run of the 1956 season. Five of the nine were against Kansas City.

The Red Sox led 5-3 and Delock – working his fourth full inning in relief – put down the A's 1-2-3 for the win, two flyball outs sandwiched around a strikeout.

Boston Red Sox 2
Cleveland Indians 1

August 5, 1956 — Cleveland Stadium

Ted Williams hit home runs in successive weekend days off two future Hall of Famers. On Saturday afternoon August 4, he hit a two-run homer in the top of the first inning off Early Wynn, one of eight home runs he hit off Wynn. The Red Sox won that game, in 10 innings, 6-5.

On Sunday afternoon, the starting pitcher for Al Lopez's Indians was Bob Lemon. Lemon was inducted into the Hall of Fame in 1976, four years after Wynn.

The game – intended as a Sunday doubleheader – turned into a pitcher's duel with Dave Sisler, who allowed four base hits to the five Lemon allowed.[478] It was the third hit off Lemon which made the difference – a sixth-inning solo home run by Ted Williams.

Cleveland scored first. Sisler walked Bobby Avila. With one out, Al Smith tripled off the fence in left field. Al Rosen then hit a shot to Don Buddin at shortstop, which he backhanded, throwing off-balance to Mickey Vernon at first base for the third out, "nipping him at first base by a whisker"[479] and preventing Smith from scoring.

Cleveland's leadoff batter walked again – Rocky Colavito. After a flyball out, advanced on a one-out sacrifice bunt to Sisler, despite it being the pitcher who was up next. Lemon singled, as Goodman "slipped on the soggy turf,"[480] an infield single to second base. Colavito had to hold at third base. Avila grounded into a force play at second base.

Right fielder Jackie Jensen led off the top of the fifth with a solo home run over the fence in left-center. That tied the score, 1-1.

The two Billys (Goodman and Klaus) both hit the ball to Vic Wertz, resulting in back-to-back unassisted outs at first base in the sixth. Ted Williams gave the Red Sox a 2-1 lead with a home run to right field. It was well-struck. The *Boston Globe* said, "He didn't leave much doubt about his homer he drove deep in the right-field lower stands."[481]

Weather was threatening.

Lemon had pulled a muscle in his right thigh during the fourth inning. Cal McLish took over the pitching duties for the Indians in the seventh. He kept the ball in the infield for three outs.

In the bottom of the seventh, Gene Woodling pinch-hit for catcher Jim Hegan. He hit a fly ball to Williams in left. Carrasquel grounded out, Klaus to Vernon. Hal Naragon pinch-hit for McLish. He grounded out to Vernon, who flipped to Sisler covering first base.

A violent storm ended the game, called by plate umpire John Stevens after an hour and 40 minutes, statistics reverting to seven full innings. The drenched playing field completely washed out the planned second game, too.

Boston Red Sox 7
Baltimore Orioles 2

August 8, 1956 — Fenway Park

Did Ted Williams hit better when he was angry? Biographer Michael Seidel said he once asked Williams why more pitchers didn't brush him back from the plate. The succinct response: "They knew I hit better mad."[482] Ben Bradlee Jr. has quoted Roger Kahn as writing that Williams "nurtured his rage."[483]

This Wednesday night game was "Family Night" at Fenway Park. There had been some controversy coming into the game. Red Sox owner Tom Yawkey had reportedly fined Ted Williams $5,000 for spitting toward the fans and the press on August 7, but some fans were said to be raising money to help him pay the fine (despite his being one of the most highly-paid people in America.)[484]

The "Splendid Spigot" hadn't exactly been contrite. (The nickname was Gillooly's in the *Record*.)[485] Before the game, Williams said, "I'd do the same thing again if I get mad enough. I was right."[486]

Mel Parnell (5-2) was the Red Sox starter. Connie Johnson (4-6) started for Baltimore.

In the bottom of the third, Don Buddin doubled to left. After Parnell struck out, Billy Goodman tripled off the center-field wall for the first run and then Billy Klaus singled and drove in Goodman. Parnell returned to the mound with a 2-0 lead.

Baltimore tied it in the top of the fourth on singles by Hal Smith and Tito Francona. Dick Williams reached, loading the bases, on an error by Goodman at second base – on a play that should have ended the inning. Billy Gardner singled to center field and drove in two.

First up in the bottom of the sixth was Ted Williams. He hit a "long, tie-breaking homer into the wings of the right-field grandstand" and – after shaking hands with third-base coach Jack Burns, on-deck Mickey Vernon, and the batboy – clamped his right hand over his mouth in a gesture to indicate his mouth was tightly closed. A smile had been seen, though, by those close enough to see. "Everybody in the park was watching intently and this action produced a park-rocking roar of laughter."[487]

The home run, Bob Holbrook asserted, was "his mightiest of the season at Fenway Park. It carried well into the distant right field pavilion and looked for a moment as if it might land on the roof."[488]

Parnell was working with a one-run lead, 3-2. He survived a bases-loaded situation in the seventh, and benefitted from Mickey Vernon's eighth-inning three-run homer into the Baltimore bullpen. Jimmy Piersall tripled and scored Boston's seventh run on Sammy White's sacrifice fly to right field.

Parnell closed out the game with relative ease.

As to the fine, Ted Williams later said, "Actually, Mr. Yawkey never did take it out of my pay. He kept me hanging for a while, then he said, 'Aw, Ted, we don't want your money.'"[489]

Boston Red Sox 4
Baltimore Orioles 2

September 1, 1956 — Fenway Park

Frank Sullivan hadn't won a game since August 9. The tall Red Sox right-hander had led the league the year before with 18 wins. He was 10-6 with a month to go.

The Red Sox faced Baltimore starter Hal "Skinny" Brown, a former teammate. He was 8-4 coming into this game for manager Paul Richards.

Williams had been in something of a forbidding mood of late. John Gilooly wrote in the *Boston American*, "Apparently, he intends to keep it that way, keep his fancied or real tormentors at a safe distance and keep himself totally quixotic."[490]

The Orioles put a run on the board in the top of the fourth with a one-out solo home run "high into the left-field wiring" by Gus Triandos.[491] The Red Sox went down in order, as did Baltimore in the top of the fifth. Red Sox right fielder Jackie Jensen evened the score with a leadoff homer in the bottom of the fifth, hit into the left-field screen, his 18th of the season. It was just the second hit of the game for the Red Sox.

In the bottom of the sixth, Boston took a 2-1 lead. With one out, third baseman Billy Klaus walked. He went first to third on a two-out single by Mickey Vernon and easily scored on Jensen's "sizzling single" to left.[492]

The Orioles tied the game, 2-2, in the top of the eighth. Dick Williams led off with a single. Bob Boyd singled, too. George Kell hit a fly ball, deep enough to left field that Williams tagged up and took third base. He scored on a groundout.[493]

Sox Win, 4-2, on Ted's 2-Run Homer

In the bottom of the eighth, Klaus led off with a single off Billy Gardner's glove and into left field. Left-hander Morrie Martin was brought in from the bullpen to pitch to Ted Williams. "At the time I thought it was the right move," Richards said after the game. "[Reliever George Zuverink] has had trouble with left-handers. But it didn't work out."[494] On a 1-1 pitch, Williams hit "a low line drive into the right-field grandstand."[495] It was "pasted into the right-field grandstand for 4211 gleeful children guests to scramble after."[496] It was "hit into the near pews of the right-field pavilion... just inside the foul pole."[497] It was also his first home run in two weeks.

Tito Francona led off the top of the ninth with a double to right field, but no more offense was in the offing.

Sullivan got the win. Zuverink bore the loss. For Ted Williams, it was home run #412, another game-winner.

After he'd been replaced by Stephens before the top of the ninth, Williams took a quick shower and departed the park. Reporters hoping for a quote were "left phraseless," as Gillooly wrote.[498]

Boston Red Sox 6
Baltimore Orioles 1

September 8, 1956 — Memorial Stadium, Baltimore

Top of the first inning. Single. Single. Three-run homer. Game over. Not quite – the rest of the game still had to be played, but the hit that proved the game-winner was indeed the Ted Williams home run hit before the first out of the game.

There was a bit of a backstory that preceded the game. Baltimore starter Billy Loes had been heckling Williams and Jimmy Piersall since a game on June 30.[499]

In his SABR biography of Loes, Gregory H. Wolf quotes Jimmy Breslin as dubbing Loes "a Dizzy Dean from the sidewalks of New York" and noted that Loes "cultivated his zany personality" while saying he "made headlines for his wacky statements and bizarre, typically candid pronouncements that left many wondering whether he was cocky, stupid, or a combination of both."[500]

Loes could perhaps talk a good game, but his record was 2-7 coming into the September 8 Saturday night game at Memorial Stadium.[501]

With Billys Goodman and Klaus singling in the top of the first, Williams came up, and "Ted jumped on a one-ball, two-strike pitch and lashed it into the right-field bleachers."[502]

Boston scored three more runs off Loes in the third, on singles by Jackie Jensen and Piersall. After an out, catcher Pete Daley hit a long single to center for the fourth Red Sox run. Brewer was up next and he "measured his shot" hitting a "pop fly just over second baseman Billy Gardner's head for a two-run single."[503] The *Herald* called it a "broken bat looper to right with the infield drawn in."[504] Both Piersall and Daley scored. It was 6-0.

Through six, Brewer had only allowed one base hit, a leadoff single to left-center field by Gardner in the second inning.

The O's got one run off him in the seventh on a walk, single, and sacrifice fly.

The game-winner had been hit by Ted Williams back in the first inning. It was his third game-winning homer against the Orioles in a one-month span.[505]

Brewer only allowed four hits, but walked four. There were three errors in the game, all three by the Red Sox, one of those being Brewer's. He struck out seven. The Red Sox got 14 hits in all, with at least one by each member of the starting lineup. Brewer got two. Jensen and Piersall had three apiece.

Under manager Pinky Higgins, the Red Sox finished the season in fourth place, 13 games behind the New York Yankees but only one behind the Chicago White Sox. Paul Richards's Orioles finished sixth, 28 games out of first place.

Boston Red Sox 5
Chicago White Sox 3

September 11, 1956 — Comiskey Park, Chicago

The White Sox and Red Sox, and the Indians, were all in contention for second place.

Bob Keegan started for the White Sox.[506]

Willard Nixon started for Boston. Three Chicago first-inning singles gave them an early 1-0 lead.

The lead didn't hold long. Minutes later, Boston went on top, 2-1. Jimmy Piersall singled. Pete Daley walked, and Nixon himself "singled sharply into center field,"[507] tying the game. Billy Goodman followed with another single, scoring Daley.

The White Sox tipped the scoring see-saw the other way, putting two runs across in the bottom of the third, and making it 3-2, Chicago. Nixon created the problem all by himself, walking the first three batters he faced. One run scored on a forceout at second base and the other on Sherm Lollar's sacrifice fly.

In the top of the fourth, Boston's Ted Lepcio singled, and so did Daley, Lepcio going first to third. Nixon grounded to short, and into a force play at second, but in the process picked up his second RBI. It was 3-3.

Ted Williams led off the fifth inning. On a 2-1 count, he clobbered "a vicious line drive that carried 430 feet and bounced off the Red Sox bullpen roof in center field."[508] Other newspapers say the ball came to rest in the White Sox bullpen.[509]

The Red Sox went on top, 4-3.[510]

After shortstop Billy Klaus doubled to right-center field, leading off the Boston seventh, Paul LaPalme replaced Keegan to pitch to Ted Williams. LaPalme walked him on four pitches, and then saw Vernon bunt the ball right back to him. LaPalme slipped and fell and Vernon had an unexpected single. The bases were loaded with nobody out. Klaus tagged and scored on a line-drive out to left-center.

Chicago loaded the bases in the seventh after Nixon let the first two batters reach and reliever Ike Delock hit Larry Doby with a pitch. He recovered, striking out Minnie Miñoso. They had the tying run at the plate in the ninth, but Delock got Nellie Fox to fly out to right field.

Nixon and Delock had combined on a five-hitter, all singles. The loss, coupled with a Cleveland win over the Orioles, dropped the White Sox to third place, just a half-game ahead of the Red Sox.

With his two RBIs, Nixon drove in twice as many runs as the Red Sox starting left fielder, Mr. Williams, but the Ted Williams home run had been the difference-maker, a solo home run yet still a game-winner.

Boston Red Sox 10
Washington Senators 4

September 25, 1956 — Fenway Park

With only five games to play in the season, the Red Sox were in fourth place but just two games ahead of the fifth-place Tigers. Finishing fourth in the eight-team American League placed a team in the "first division" and thus earned a share of postseason money, but finishing fifth left a team out of the money. Aside from individual statistics, and pride in one's work, this was a meaningful game for the team. It was less so for the seventh-place Senators, playing for manager Chuck Dressen, but Washington had lost nine in a row and were working for a win.

Dave Sisler started for Boston.

On Mickey Vernon's two-run homer, the Red Sox got two runs in the bottom of the first inning off starting pitcher Pedro Ramos, in his second year and hailing from Cuba. The 21-year-old Ramos entered the game 12-9, with a 4.99 earned run average, but he had been particularly effective against Boston. His record against the Red Sox was 6-0 on the season.[511]

Catcher Sammy White was the first out in the bottom of the second, grounding to second base. Sisler hit an infield single, to shortstop Lyle Luttrell. Mauch singled to right field, Sisler going to second base. Klaus doubled to center, Sisler scoring. Mauch stopped at third base but simply trotted home when Ted Williams hit a 2-2 pitch for a three-run home run over the visitors' bullpen in right field. Boston had a 6-0 lead.

Sisler held the Senators hitless through three. He walked center fielder Whitey Herzog. First baseman Pete Runnels, in his sixth year with the Senators, hit a home run – the first hit of the game off Sisler.

In the fifth inning, reliever Bob Wiesler walked five Boston batters. Piersall doubled in the first two of them. Mauch singled and scored Piersall. Billy Klaus walked and loaded the bases. Ted Williams walked, too, forcing in the 10th Red Sox run.

Sisler gave up two more runs to the Senators in the top of the sixth, but the scoring was done.

Ted Williams had driven in four runs, but with a 1-for-4 game had lost ground in his battle against Mickey Mantle for the American League batting title.[512]

The Nats loss was their 10th in a row. They lost the next day as well. Their record over the final 20 games of the 1956 season was 2-18. Against the Red Sox for the full season, however, they were 13-9.

The Ted Williams home run proved the game-winner. In all, Williams hit six home runs off Ramos. Each one of the last four home runs were game-winners, #430 in 1957, #482 in 1958, and, in September 1960, the last one of his career, number 520.

A Ted Williams
Game-Winning Walk

"I got a walk with the bases loaded to win the game. But I wanted to *hit*, dammit! I was so mad I flung my bat straight up in the air."[513]

Needless to say, there were also games in which Williams provided the ultimate winning run with a single, a double, maybe a triple (he did have 71 career triples) – even with a sacrifice fly or a groundout on which a baserunner was able to score from third base. There was one time in 1956 that galled him no end – even though the Red Sox won the game. It took place against the New York Yankees before a standing-room only crowd at Fenway Park on August 7, 1956. He didn't have a good game, 0-for-3 at the plate with a walk as the scoreless game headed into extra innings. Willard Nixon was pitching for the Red Sox and Don Larsen for the Yankees and neither allowed a run through 10 innings.

Williams had hit into an inning-ending double play, grounded out to second base, and flied out to left field. He'd walked in the bottom of the ninth. In the top of the 11th, he dropped a fly ball hit by Mickey Mantle. "The fans were booing like hell," he wrote. "I hate front-runners, people who are with you when you're up and against you when you're down." He was livid, loudly cursing at the fans. He offered some hyperbole: "If I'd had a knife I probably would have stuck it in somebody." But he was angry, and he "spat toward right field and spat toward left field. Then, after I got inside the dugout, I leaped back out and spat again. And boy, that *really* got them going."[514]

Nixon was first up, batting for himself in the bottom of the 11th. He reached on an error by the third baseman. Billy Goodman reached on an error by the first baseman. Larsen walked Billy Klaus. With the bases loaded, nobody out, the score 0-0 in the 11th, with Ted Williams coming to bat, Stengel called in Tommy Byrne to relieve Larsen.

"I stood pretty close to the plate, watching him warm up, and he practically dusted me off just warming up. But after he got two strikes, he got cute and on a 3-2 pitch he walked me. Walked in the winning run. Even *that* made me mad. I didn't want any walk, I wanted to hit the damn ball. I threw my bat in the air, and almost didn't go to first base. Del Baker, our first-base coach, had to remind me. I was just disgusted with the whole thing."[515]

1957

Amazing .388 Season Includes Eight Game-Winning Blasts

One could make the argument that—taking everything into account—this was the best season of Ted Williams's career. If not the best, it was right up there. He hit for a .388 batting average. That led both leagues. Second was Mickey Mantle, well behind with .365. If the no-longer-a-kid had managed six more hits—perhaps beating out a few infield hits, which was not as easy to do in his 39th year—he would have hit .402. His .526 on-base percentage also led both leagues, and he hit for power, too, with 38 home runs in only 420 at-bats, which helped him to a slugging percentage of .731, by far tops in the majors. Williams was walked intentionally 33 times.

The Red Sox finished in third place with a respectable 82 wins, but 16 games in back of the perennially-dominant Yankees, who matched Boston at-bat but allowed nearly a run less per game on defense.

A big reason the Red Sox finished over .500 again, of course, was Williams. Eight times a Ted Williams home run produced the run that put the Red Sox ahead for good with a game-winning homer.

Boston Red Sox 4
Chicago White Sox 3

May 7, 1957 — Comiskey Park, Chicago

Ted Williams had a good couple of days in Chicago on May 7 and May 8, 1957. The visiting Boston Red Sox won the May 7 game, 4-3, and Williams figured in three of the four Red Sox runs, including hitting the game-winning homer in the top of the ninth inning.

The following day, he hit three home runs, driving in all four runs in a 4-1 Red Sox victory.

May 7 was a Tuesday night game that drew 25,953 to Comiskey Park. Both starting pitchers went the distance – Dick Donovan pitching for Chicago and Tom Brewer for Boston.[516]

Williams' Two-Run Clout in Ninth Edges White Sox, 4-3
SOX WIN ON TED'S HOMER

Donovan walked leadoff batter Jimmy Piersall, who stole second. Ted Williams singled – to left field – and Piersall scored.[517]

Tom Brewer was right-handed, too. He had three years under his belt and had been 19-9 in 1956 and on the A.L. All-Star team. He didn't let up a hit until the fourth.

Boston threatened, with runners in scoring position in the third and fourth, and loading the bases in the fifth, but the score remained 1-0 until Chicago tied it with a run in their half of the fifth.

The Red Sox took a 2-1 lead in the top of the seventh. Brewer singled to center. Piersall bunted back to Donovan, a sacrifice which moved Brewer to second base. Billy Klaus flied out deep to right field. Brewer tagged and took third base. Williams was walked intentionally a second time. Mickey Vernon had 17 plate appearances (and 13 at-bats) so far in 1957 without a base hit. This time he singled to right field, driving in Brewer.

In the ninth, the Red Sox boosted their lead to 4-1. With his second single of the ballgame, Brewer led off but Piersall hit into a 6-4-3 double play, clearing the bases. Klaus drew a base on balls. Would Williams also be given a fourth walk? Donovan pitched to him. On a 1-0 count, Williams drove a 425-foot home run, "a terrific shot into the lower deck of the extreme edge of the right-field stands."[518] The *Herald* said it "traveled like a bullet into the stands beyond the Red Sox bullpen."[519]

The White Sox got a two-run homer from Larry Doby in the bottom of the ninth, a "high fly to deep center that dropped into the bullpen just beyond a frantic leap by Piersall."[520] Brewer got Sherm Lollar to pop up to Vernon at first base and the game was over.

Brewer threw a three-hitter. Ted Williams figured in three of the four Red Sox runs. In five plate appearances, he'd had a single and three walks (two intentional) and, of course, the ninth-inning home run that made the difference.[521]

Boston Red Sox 4
Chicago White Sox 1

May 8, 1957 — Comiskey Park, Chicago

In a game that lasted less than two hours, Ted Williams hit three home runs. His two solo homers and a two-run homer accounted for all of Boston's four runs. All three were hit off White Sox pitcher Bob Keegan.[522] Clearly, one of the home runs was the game-winner. It was the second one.

Just the day before, his two-run homer in the ninth had won a game in which he had figured in three of Boston's four runs.

This was the 16th game of the season, and the 38-year-old Williams had 16 RBIs and a .474 batting average.

Frank Sullivan was the Red Sox pitcher.

The first Williams homer was in the first inning, after the first two batters made outs. Keegan threw a 3-2 pitch. The *Chicago Tribune* said, "the last seen of the ball it was bouncing around in the lower deck in right center."[523]

In the third inning, the same scenario presented itself – the first two batters made outs and Ted Williams homered on a 0-2 count. The wind helped. White Sox skipper Al Lopez said, "He had a gale blowing for him this afternoon. The one he hit to left center [in the third] ... would have been caught if there hadn't been any wind."[524]

WILLIAMS' 3 HOMERS BEAT WHITE SOX, 4-1
Like Old Man River, Ted Williams Just Keeps Rolling Along

Larry Doby doubled off Sullivan in the fourth, the only hit the White Sox got after the first inning until the eighth when Jim Landis doubled, too.

Ted Williams had his third at-bat leading off the sixth inning. He broke one of his own rules about hitting. "I went for a bad ball with a 3-and-1 count on me and I fouled it off. I could have had a walk, but I wanted to hit it. Then I swung at another bad ball and I popped it up."[525] He lifted a fly ball to medium left-center field. For Williams, whose mantra was "get a good ball to hit," this was a shortcoming that weighed on his mind after the game. It was the only time on either May 7 or 8 that he had been retired.

Other than the two solo homers, Keegan was pitching well. He faced Williams a fourth time in the top of the eighth. Billy Klaus had singled, on first base. The Boston slugger saw what he considered a good ball and swung at the first pitch, hitting his third home run of the game, "20 rows deep into the upper stands in right center."[526] Boston took a 4-0 lead.[527]

Minnie Miñoso, Chicago All-Star, simply said, "He makes 'em all look easy. Like he was bunting the ball."[528]

With two outs and Sullivan on first base, Williams batted again in the ninth, facing reliever Ellis Kinder, who intentionally walked him.[529]

Chicago did get on the scoreboard. With one out, Nellie Fox walked and Miñoso doubled. But Sullivan won a four-hitter. Williams's three hits drove in all Boston's runs.

Al Lopez ordered his team to stay in uniform and hold postgame batting practice.[530]

Boston Red Sox 5
Washington Senators 3

June 2, 1957 — Griffith Stadium, Washington

Ted Williams's come-from-behind home run in the top of the eighth inning propelled his team to victory after nine.

The starting pitchers were a pair of right-handers – Pedro Ramos (4-3, 3.53) for last-place Washington and George Susce (3-1, 2.59) for Boston.

Ramos was touched for one run in the top of the first. He walked leadoff batter Jimmy Piersall. Gene Mauch tripled to right-center field, but he languished on third base.

SOX DOWN NATS ON TED'S HOMER

The Senators loaded the bases in both the second and third innings, but had nothing to show for it.

Williams lined out to short in the first and grounded out to short in the third. In the sixth, he walked with one out, but when Mickey Vernon flied out to right field, he was doubled off first base, having run on a ball he thought was a hit.

In the bottom of the sixth, the first two Senators singled. They tied the score on a productive double play.

Jackie Jensen re-established Boston's one-run edge with a leadoff seventh-inning homer into the center-field stands.

On four consecutive hits, the first off Susce (a double by Eddie Yost which Williams "misjudged" in left) and the next three off reliever Ike Delock, Washington took a 3-2 lead in the bottom half of the seventh inning.[531]

Williams was likely not too happy with himself after two mental lapses. Piersall and Mauch both hit safely leading off the eighth. Williams came to bat. On a 2-0 count, he hit a ball estimated at 400 to 450 feet for a three-run homer, boosting Boston to a 5-3 lead. "The ball went halfway up the center field wall where the 438 numerals are painted."[532] Joe Cashman of the *Record* wrote, "Like the jets he used to fly, the ball tore on a line to deepest center, landing in the Nats' warm-up enclosure, and sending the occupants thereof scattering in all directions."[533]

It was a slow curve, said manager Pinky Higgins. It hit the wall behind the Washington bullpen. The *Herald* put it at 440, a "viciously stroked liner that sizzled some 440 feet on a line into the Washington bull-pen."[534]

Bud Byerly relieved Ramos, and there was no more scoring for either team, though the Senators did get two on in the bottom of the ninth. An "Academy Award" performance helped save at least one run.[535]

As for Ted Williams, he had atoned for his inattention earlier in the game and had hit another game-winning home run.

Boston Red Sox 9
Cleveland Indians 3

June 13, 1957 — Cleveland Stadium, Cleveland

The day had not started well for Ted Williams. He was reportedly "so disgusted with himself in pre-game hitting practice that he threw his bat 50 feet in the air."[536] In an unorthodox move, he actually swapped bats with Cleveland Indians second baseman Bobby Avila. In an effort to beat the "Williams Shift," he had begun 1957 with a heavier bat, hitting the ball more to the left side of the field, since he couldn't whip his bat around quite as quickly. When the opposition noticed him starting to beat the shift, they stopped using it as often, which allowed him to switch back to a lighter bat. He decided to use Avila's lighter-weight bat in this game.[537]

The game itself worked out nicely for the Splendid Splinter.

Cleveland scored first, one run in the bottom of the first inning on Rocky Colavito's bases-loaded walk off Tom Brewer of the Red Sox.

Future Hall of Famer Early Wynn got Williams to ground out in the first inning, but gave up a game-tying solo homer to Frank Malzone in the second.

In the third, with two on base, Williams swung at a 2-2 pitch and "unloaded a line drive over the right-center-field fence."[538] Boston took a 4-1 lead.

After one out in the fifth, Williams hit a solo home run. It came on a 1-0 pitch and left the park, "a high blast over almost the same spot as the first."[539] Malzone doubled in two more runs and scored himself on Gene Mauch's sacrifice fly.

Both Wynn and Indians manager Kerby Farrell complained after the game that umpire Nestor Chylak had failed to call third strikes on Williams. "He'd never have the chance if those good pitches in the strike zone had been called strikes," Wynn griped.[540]

On three hits and an error, the Indians scored twice in the bottom of the eighth. It was 8-3.

The 38-year-old Ted Williams was due to lead off the ninth. He had hoped to be back in the clubhouse at this point. "I wanted to come out after my second homer. It was a cold, crummy night. 'Come on, Mike, take me out.' 'What for? You might hit another one.' Pinky Higgins, my manager, talked me into staying in the game. I got homer number three and a place in the record books."[541]

Bob Lemon had come in to pitch for Cleveland, like Wynn a future Hall of Famer.[542] Williams hit a 2-1 pitch for his third home run of the game, "a long wallop over the right-field fence that narrowly missed going into the pavilion where it is marked 435 feet. The smashes got progressively longer."[543]

Williams was surprised to learn that it was the first time any American League batter had ever hit three homers in a game twice in the same season.[544] And this was three homers off two future Hall of Famers in one game – the two off Early Wynn earlier in the game then the ninth-inning one off Bob Lemon.[545]

POSTSCRIPT

In later comments, the Boston slugger made it clear that hitting home runs was the product of careful study. He told the United Press that "batting isn't a matter of eyesight alone. I know a lot of morons in this racket with better eyes than I have who can't hit a lick. I make a study of hitting and pitchers. I have a checklist when I'm not doing well. I check my stance, the arc of my swing, the pitchers giving me trouble."[546]

He himself wrote, "In my 22 years of professional baseball, I went to bat about 8,000 times, and every trip to the plate was an adventure, one that I could remember and store up as information. I honestly believe I can recall everything there was to know about my first 300 home runs – who the pitcher was, the count, the pitch itself, where the ball landed. I didn't have to keep a written book on pitchers – I *lived* a book on pitchers."[547]

He also said, much later, that one reason he hit to left field more in later years was simply that he had gotten older. "My bat speed slowed down a little. Not all the time, but enough for me to occasionally hit the ball to *left*. So they started laying off that Williams Shift stuff, and when I did hit the ball to right, there were more holes for it to land in."[548]

Williams's study was, we note, done without access to tools which are routine 60 years later – video and computers.

Boston Red Sox 6
New York Yankees 4

August 14, 1957 — Fenway Park

As the 1957 season progressed, there looked to be some serious competition between the nearly 39-year-old Ted Williams and 25-year-old Mickey Mantle of the Yankees, who had won the American League Triple Crown in 1956, and the MVP. Mantle was hitting .384 before this game and Williams was at .388. Mantle had 32 homers and Williams had 30.

The starting pitchers before the capacity crowd at Fenway Park were Tom Brewer for Boston and Whitey Ford for New York. It was Rhode Island Day.

Williams made a mark, defensively, on the first play of the game. Hank Bauer singled off the left-field wall, and Williams fired the ball to second base to erase Bauer.[549] It was one of 140 assists he earned in his major-league career.

In the bottom of the first, with a runner on second and two outs, Ford walked Williams intentionally. Dick Gernert singled and Boston had a 1-0 lead.

In the second inning, Boston third baseman Frank Malzone came up with one out and the bases loaded. Don Larsen (who had thrown a perfect game in the 1956 World Series) had relieved Ford after the first two baserunners reached. Malzone hit a sacrifice fly – and Ted Williams followed that with a three-run homer, "a harshly hit shot high into the left field screen."[550] It was, wrote Lawrence Baldassaro, "not a typical homer by Williams, a notorious pull hitter whose long drives usually landed in the right field bullpens or the stands beyond. Instead, it was a rare opposite-field shot."[551]

The Yankees got their first run with two outs in the fifth when Larsen doubled and Bauer singled him home.

Brewer contributed to the Red Sox offense in the sixth. With one out and catcher Sammy White on first base, Brewer singled and

White went first to third. He scored on a Gene Mauch groundout to second.

Larsen doubled again in the seventh and Bauer homered. And with a runner on third base in the top of the ninth, Larsen singled home New York's fourth run. The three-run Williams home run, however, had given them the edge they needed.

Mantle had singled in the first, but then struck out his next two times and finally grounded out to second base. After the walk and the homer, Williams grounded out to first base unassisted in the fourth and led off the seventh with a single to center field. He was hitting .390 at game's end. Williams, who turned 39 on August 30, ended the season batting. 388. He had hit .454 over the second half of the season. Part of that stretch came September 17-23, when he reached base in 16 consecutive plate appearances, four times via home runs in four consecutive at-bats. He hit 38 homers in 1957.

Boston Red Sox 1
Detroit Tigers 0

August 28, 1957 — Briggs Stadium, Detroit

Detroit's Jim Bunning threw a two-hitter over eight innings, but lost the game 1-0 when Ted Williams finally took it upon himself to swing at a pitch. The Tigers' right-hander was 15-6 on the season with a 2.65 earned run average. He'd already beaten the Red Sox four times in 1957.[552]

Bunning's opponent on the Wednesday afternoon game at Briggs Stadium was right-hander Frank Sullivan. He was 10-9 coming into the game, and also sporting a sub-3.00 ERA at 2.95.[553]

After Bunning retired the first two batters in the top of the first, he walked Ted Williams on five pitches, one of the pitches a called strike. The Red Sox left fielder hadn't taken a cut at even one of Bunning's pitches. He was left stranded on first base when Bunning struck out third baseman Frank Malzone.

The Red Sox got their first base hit when Billy Klaus singled, leading off the fourth. Williams struck out, all three pitches called strikes by home-plate umpire Joe Paparella. No swinging strikes, no foul balls. Again Williams never once swung the bat.

In the fifth inning, both teams got a runner on base and both teams hit into double plays. The score after six was 0-0.

Ted Williams led off the top of the seventh. He didn't swing at any one of the first five pitches he saw. The count built to 3-2. Williams had now seen 14 pitches in the game and was "still without taking the bat off his shoulder. Was he, the fans wondered, ever going to swing at a pitch? What was he waiting for in this, his favorite park?"[554]

On the sixth pitch of the at-bat, the 15th pitch he saw this day, Williams whipped his bat around and slugged one, "the ball landing in the upper deck in deep right-center field, considerably beyond the 400-foot mark in the distance."[555]

Bosox Win On Homer by Williams, 1-0

Joe Falls of the *Detroit Times* wrote, "He didn't take a cut at the ball until the seventh inning. Then, when he did, it was one cut too much for the Tigers...Williams liked the look of No.15."[556]

With the home run, Boston took a 1-0 lead.[557]

Sullivan surrendered two hits in the eighth inning and three hits in the bottom of the ninth. He gave up 10 hits, though no walks. And no runs.

The Williams solo home run, just one of two Red Sox hits, won the game, 1-0. When he finally decided to swing the bat, he made it count.[558]

Boston Red Sox 8
New York Yankees 3

September 21, 1957 — Yankee Stadium, New York

A win on this day would clinch the pennant for the Yankees. The Red Sox were hoping to hold onto third place.

The Red Sox took command early.

The matchup was Bob Turley (12-5) for the Yankees and Willard Nixon (11-12), in his eighth year for the Red Sox.

Boston scored once in the top of the first on a bases-loaded one-out sacrifice fly by Frank Malzone. Ted Williams had been walked intentionally; he was batting .379.

Nixon walked three Yankees in a row, but escaped without a run.

Turley made it through the second inning, but not before giving up seven earned runs. Ken Aspromonte walked. Sammy White singled. Nixon fouled out. Jimmy Piersall walked, loading the bases for the second inning in a row. Klaus hit an infield single, a "topped roller," to third base, Aspromonte scored and the bases remained full for Ted Williams.[559]

On a 2-0 pitch, Williams hit his 15th career grand slam. "The towering smash sailed fairly deep into the lower pavilion in right field," wrote Bob Holbrook.[560] A *New York Times* photograph makes it appear the drive was indeed "towering" but that the ball only landed a few rows into the seats.[561]

Ted's Slam Leads Sox Over Yanks, 8-3

With one swing of the bat, the score was 6-0, Red Sox. Vernon followed with a home run of his own, also into the right-field lower seats, and it was 7-0.

Nixon gave up single runs in the third and in the fifth. In both cases, Hank Bauer scored. In both cases, he scored on a groundout by Yogi Berra.

Leading off the sixth inning was Ted Williams. He walked – his third walk of the game, to go with his grand slam. Being walked prompted "considerable booing."[562] Marty Keough came in to pinch-run, soon scoring on an Aspromonte single.[563]

The only other run in the game was in the bottom of the ninth, off reliever Ike Delock, when Joe Collins hit a solo homer to right field.[564]

Ted Williams faced 15 pitches on the day, and only one was thrown over the plate. That went for a grand slam, the game-winning hit. It was his third home run in three consecutive at-bats. He hit a pinch-hit home run the night before and a pinch-hit homer in Kansas City on the 17th. The *Globe*'s Holbrook declared, "The Yanks walked him three other times. In fact, they are so frightened of Williams at the moment that the only pitch he got to swing at all day was the grand-slam home run."[565]

POSTSCRIPT

All the getting on base was part of a streak in which Williams reached base in 16 consecutive plate appearances – he hit that pinch-hit homer on September 17 and then reached base 15 more times before he was retired. The streak included four homers, two singles, nine walks, and a hit-by-pitch.[566] In fact, the four home runs were hit in consecutive at-bats:

September 17, an eighth-inning pinch-hit home run off Tom Morgan

On September 18, he drew a base on balls.

September 20, a pinch-hit leadoff home run in the top of the ninth inning off Whitey Ford

September 21, the game-winning grand slam in this game, plus three walks

September 22, he walked his first time up and then homered the next, in the top of the fourth off Tom Sturdivant.

He had homered off four different pitchers, in two different parks, twice in night games and twice in day games. He broke up his consecutive homer streak by hitting a single in the sixth inning on the 22nd, then later walked.

Boston Red Sox 2
Washington Senators 1

September 24, 1957 — Griffith Stadium,
Washington

As the 1957 season was in its final week, there was still time for Ted Williams to squeeze in one final home run and for his home run to win one more game for the Boston Red Sox. Of the 38 homers he hit in 1957, eight of them were game-winners.

This one came in the fourth inning of the game at Washington's Griffith Stadium.

Pitching for Cookie Lavagetto's last-place Senators was right-hander Hal Griggs, who breezed through the first inning, striking out leadoff batter Jimmy Piersall and then getting both shortstop Billy Klaus and left fielder Ted Williams to ground out to second base.

The Williams groundout was a routine play, but it ended a record-breaking Ted Williams streak of reaching bases 16 times in a row until the groundout.[567]

Frank Sullivan took the mound for Red Sox manager Pinky Higgins.[568] He gave up a leadoff double to Pete Runnels, but then not another hit until the sixth.

The Red Sox scored a run in the third. With two outs, Sullivan himself singled. He scored from first base when Piersall tripled to right-center field, a ball which "fell off the out-stretched glove of Faye Throneberry."[569]

The score was 1-0 after three innings.

The first batter up in the fourth inning was Ted Williams. On a 2-1 pitch, he "crashed his 38th homer run of the season...a line drive over the right-field fence."[570]

Leading off the sixth inning, Ted Williams struck out. Not only that, he struck out looking, an unusual occurrence.

The Senators put something together in the bottom of the sixth. Runnels singled to center. Clint Courtney reached on an infield single to shortstop. Sievers grounded to third base, but Malzone's only play was to first base and both baserunners moved up. The potential tying run was on second base with just one out. Jim Lemon grounded out, also to third base but the runners had to hold. Killebrew then singled into center field. Runnels scored but "Courtney got too ambitious" – his bid to tie the game was cut short by Piersall's throw home.[571]

Neither team got anyone on base in the seventh. When Malzone threw out Art Schult for the first out of the bottom of the inning, it was the Sox infielder's 10th assist of the game, tying an American League record for assists by a third baseman.[572]

Williams walked in the top of the eighth, the only Boston batter to reach base. Piersall had struck out, leading off – the ninth K of the game for Griggs.

Sullivan closed out the game in the ninth. Lemon led off with a single to left. Killebrew, however, struck out – Sullivan's seventh strikeout of the game. Schult hit a "vicious liner" but into a 4-6-3 game-ending double play.[573]

Autographed 1958 Red Sox Yearbook.

1958

Slow Start Ends With Sixth Batting Title

Ted Williams won his sixth (and final) batting title in 1958, leading the pack among American Leaguers with a .328 average. His .458 on-base percentage led the majors for the 11th time. Appearing in 129 games, Williams homered 26 times and drove in 85 runs—remarkable productivity for a player with 411 at-bats. Seven times he hit a game-winning homer, finishing the year with 103 such home runs for his career. His total production was declining with age, but his ability to get meaningful hits and home runs was as amazing as ever.

As in 1957, the Red Sox finished third in the standings, this year winning 79—again over .500—but again, double figures in games (13) behind New York.

Boston Red Sox 8
Kansas City Athletics 5

May 22, 1958 — Municipal Stadium, Kansas City

The *Kansas City Star* ran a headline on May 22: "What's Wrong with Ted?" Boston's slugger Ted Williams had led the American League with a .388 batting average in 1957 – the year he turned 39. At this point, after 27 games in 1958, he was hitting .225 and had gone 0-for-5 the day before and not one of the balls he had hit had left the infield.

The Red Sox faced sophomore right-hander Jack Urban. Red Sox manager Pinky Higgins had Tom Brewer as his starter. Brewer gave up three runs in the bottom of the second, Urban himself singling to drive in Whitey Herzog for the third run.

Boston got one back, Dick Gernert driving in Don Buddin. Jackie Jensen doubled off the left-field wall to lead off the fourth; it was said the wind prevented the ball from going out.[574] Jimmy Piersall singled and Jensen scored from second. Buddin walked. Pete Runnels reached on a slow roller to third base and the bases were loaded. Williams fouled off Urban's first pitch, and then the second pitch, and then the third pitch. The fourth pitch he hit "onto the right field embankment."[575] It was hit "over the 11-foot right-field fence – 363 feet from the plate. Fifteen farther on, and up an embankment, it hit the base of a light tower."[576] It caromed off the concrete base of the tower and bounded back toward the field. It also catapulted the Red Sox to a 6-3 lead, a grand slam.[577] The ball was hit exceptionally hard, wrote the *Boston Herald*. It "soared through a cross-wind that blew in strongly from centerfield."[578]

The Athletics got one run back in the bottom of the fourth, thanks to a walk and Bob Martyn's triple. They added another, edging to within one run, in the fifth inning. A walk, single, and walk loaded the bases for K.C. with nobody out. Mike Fornieles came in to relieve and Hal Smith's sacrifice fly brought in the one run, but pinch-hitter Vic Power hit into a 6-4-3 inning-ending double play.

The Red Sox added a couple of insurance runs in the top of the ninth, starting with Ted Lepcio's leadoff homer.[579] Fornieles closed it out.

POSTSCRIPT

Whatever might have been wrong with Ted Williams righted itself. He didn't have as spectacular a year as he had enjoyed in 1957, but his .328 batting average did win the American League batting title. His .458 on-base percentage led both leagues. His 26 homers and 85 RBIs helped the Red Sox secure a third-place finish, just a game and a half ahead of the Cleveland Indians and only two games ahead of the fifth-place Tigers.

Boston Red Sox 2
Cleveland Indians 1

June 26, 1958 — Cleveland Stadium

The Thursday afternoon game was light on offense and featured complete games by both Cal McLish of the Indians and Ike Delock of the Red Sox.[580] McLish struck out nine and Delock struck out 12. Delock gave up five hits. McLish gave up six; one of those made all the difference in the game.

The Indians got the first run of the game in the bottom of the fourth. Vic Power reached on an infield single that glanced off Delock's glove. He took second on a passed ball and scored when Rocky Colavito doubled down the left-field line.

There were the scattered base hits and a few walks, but the score remained 1-0, Cleveland, through the first six.

The Red Sox tied the game in the top of the seventh, 1-1, on a one-out solo home run by Dick Gernert to deep left field, a "high drive to left that landed well beyond the fence for his 13th homer of the season."[581]

The game went into the ninth inning, still tied 1-1. Ted Williams took McLish's first pitch for ball one. He hit the next pitch; it "sprung off his bat like a rocket and in its second stage landed in the upper deck of the big Cleveland bowl."[582] As the *Globe* put it, he "bombed a drive 10 rows up in the upper deck in right field, only a few feet inside the foul pole."[583] The *Cleveland Plain Dealer* said it came down "on the first aisleway behind the box seat section. It was his ninth of the season."[584] Given the attendance of only 4,482 at the game, the stands were empty where the ball landed.[585] The Red Sox had taken the lead. The Ted Williams homer won the game.

Delock struck out Colavito. Larry Doby pinch-hit for Nixon. Delock struck him out, too, on a called third strike. Woodie Held hit a fly ball to right field for the final out.[586]

"No. 9 hit No. 9 in the ninth to beat the Indians here today, 2-1," wrote Roger Birtwell for the *Boston Globe*. "That was the ball game."[587]

Boston Red Sox 10
Detroit Tigers 7

June 29, 1958 — Briggs Stadium, Detroit

This was a game which saw the lead bounce back and forth a bit. Both teams were very much in it and the score was tied, 5-5, after the first seven innings. One big blow made a big difference, but the issue remained uncertain right to the end.

Tall righty Frank Sullivan got the win, despite giving up seven runs and faltering just two outs shy of recording a complete game.[588]

Paul Foytack, another right-hander, started for Tigers manager Bill Norman.[589]

The Tigers scored first, once, in the bottom of the second. Gail Harris reached on an infield single to third base, and Charlie Maxwell doubled him home.

Back-to-back doubles to left field by Boston's Marty Keough and Pete Runnels produced one run and, after Ted Williams flied out to right, Frank Malzone singled into center field to give Boston a 2-1 lead.

Foytack singled, leading off the bottom of the third. He scored the game-tying run on another single and a double play.

The Tigers took a 5-2 lead in the fourth, Foytack singling to drive in two of the runs, the third one scoring on an errant throw from Williams.

The Red Sox responded right away, with a Williams single, Malzone's double, and Jackie Jensen's three-run homer – "a high drive into the stands in right-center."[590]

Score tied after seven, Bill Fischer became the fourth Tigers pitcher. A sixth run scored, but when Ted Williams unloaded with a three-run homer, it gave Boston a 9-5 lead. It was "one of the more spectacular home runs of his career – a soaring drive that landed on top of the right-field roof and bounded back on the field....Williams once hit one over the roof in Detroit, but it was considerably nearer the foul line. Today's was farther away, out toward right center."[591] The *Detroit Times'* Joe Falls wrote that Williams's "towering homer...missed by 10 feet of going into Trumbull avenue."[592]

Gene Stephens replaced Williams in left field. In the top of the ninth, Stephens hit a home run, too, one that "struck the facing of the roof-top boxes in right field."[593]

Sullivan ran out of steam and allowed a couple of runs in the bottom of the ninth, but the margin the Williams home run had provided was more than sufficient for a win.

A month later, Ted hit career homer #473 off Fischer, too, in the top of the 11th on July 29. Both were three-run homers and they both won games.

Boston Red Sox 7
Detroit Tigers 6 (12 innings)

July 19, 1958 — Fenway Park

Both starters worked into the ninth, and it seemed like a game Boston didn't want to let get away. Three times they had to take the lead, had to tie it in the ninth to stay alive, and took the lead for good in the 12th on a Ted Williams home run.

The two teams were contending for second place. The starters were Dave Sisler for the Red Sox and Frank Lary for the Tigers.[594]

Boston got on the board first. After back-to-back groundouts, Ted Williams doubled – to left field. Frank Malzone did the same, scoring Williams.

The Tigers tied it in the top of the second with Ozzie Virgil's solo home run into the center-field bleachers.

The Red Sox restored their one-run lead with a second-inning double from Dick Gernert and Sammy White's single.

In the top of the fourth, the Tigers tied it up again, 2-2, on three singles.

The Red Sox wasted little time re-establishing a one-run lead. White tripled and Billy Consolo doubled.

The Tigers tied it again on Harvey Kuenn's seventh-inning solo homer into the left-field screen.

Ted Williams misplayed a ball in the top of the eighth. Al Kaline hit the ball to him and Williams apparently (one wishes there were video replays) achieved "the unusual feat of fielding a one-hop line drive with his posterior."[595] Back-to-back flyballs – the second, Gus Zernial's sacrifice fly – gave Detroit a 4-3 lead.

Detroit bumped up its lead to 5-3 on Jim Hegan's ninth-inning solo homer.

Sammy White homered into the Boston bullpen to bring the Red Sox to within one.[596] Down to their last out, Lou Berberet pinch-hit for reliever Bud Byerly and was hit in the foot by Lary's pitch. Marty Keough came in as a pinch-runner. Gene Stephens singled to right-center field and Keough went first to third. Pete Runnels then grounded a single into center field, and the game was tied.

Hank Aguirre relieved Lary, to pitch to Williams with runners on first and third. Aguirre got the Red Sox slugger to ground out, unassisted, to first base, and the game went into extra innings.

The 12th inning saw the Tigers take a 6-5 lead. With one out, Aguirre singled. Billy Martin doubled to left-center. Kuenn scored all the way from first because of a "wide throw to the plate by Gene Stephens."[597]

Jimmy Piersall pinch-hit and singled. Runnels bunted, a sacrifice, putting Piersall on second. There was a stiff wind heading out to right field. That may well have helped Ted Williams. After initially planning to walk Williams, manager Bill Norman chose not to, because of the cardinal rule "Never put the winning run aboard."[598] Williams jumped on Aguirre's first pitch and "smashed a soaring two-run homer into the right field grandstand."[599]

The *Detroit Times* wrote, "The Tigers thought they had it won not once, but twice, but when the afternoon was over they had nothing more to show for their efforts than their fourth straight defeat."[600]

POSTSCRIPT

After grounding out in the ninth, Williams had told Higgins that Aguirre's ball was sailing in on him and that, in the manager's words, "he'd have to move back in the box to get a good shot at it." Williams said, "I don't know really what I did hit. Ask Aguirre. That guy has been really tough on me. It's about time I hit one."[601]

Of Ted's homer #471, the *Globe* noted, "He's getting closer to Lou Gehrig."[602] Lou had 493 career home runs.

Even with the game going into the bottom of the 12th inning, even with 22 base hits and 13 runs scored, the game was over in less than three hours, with nine minutes to spare.

Boston Red Sox 11
Detroit Tigers 8 (11 innings)

July 29, 1958 — Briggs Stadium, Detroit

It was time for Ted Williams to unload. He came into the game hitless in his last six at-bats, and facing Jim Bunning, against whom he'd been 0-for-7 to this point in 1958. Nine days earlier, Bunning had no-hit the Red Sox at Fenway Park. Williams was 0-for-4 in that game and his flyball to right was the final out.

And just before the game Williams had read a magazine story that angered him. The *Boston Globe*'s Bob Holbrook wrote, "He had been castigated in a vicious magazine story which accused him, bluntly, of being gutless."[603] He'd also been fatigued and some of his teammates thought the manager would give him the night off. He was, however, in the starting lineup.

Williams Hits Slam in Third, Wins Game with 3-Run Homer in 11th

Frank Sullivan started for Boston but gave up four runs and didn't even complete the first inning. Both Billy Martin and Charlie Maxwell hit two-run homers. Ted Bowsfield pitched the next six innings.

With two outs in the third, Bowsfield singled. So did Marty Keough. Pete Runnels walked. Ted Williams lined the second pitch into the right-field seats, but foul by 25 feet. He then swung at the 1-1 pitch and this one stayed fair, hit into the upper deck in right, not far from the foul pole. It was a grand slam, the 17th of Williams's career, placing him second all-time.[604]

The *Boston Herald*'s Arthur Siegel wrote that Bunning "now knows what the older baseball men have always counseled...'Don't get Williams sore...He's tough enough when he's happy.'"[605]

Suddenly, the score was tied. Third baseman Frank Malzone popped up foul, ending the inning. Bowsfield retired the three Tigers he faced.

The Red Sox added a run in the fourth. Billy Hoeft relieved Bunning.

With back-to-back doubles by Gail Harris and pinch-hitter Johnny Groth in the fifth, Detroit tied it, 5-5.

Boston took an 8-5 lead in the seventh on two singles, a wild pitch, a walk, and Jackie Jensen's two-run double.

The Tigers clawed two runs back in the seventh and tied it, 8-8, in the eighth on Red Wilson's leadoff triple and Gus Zernial's pinch hit.

In the ninth, Williams had come up with two runners on and nobody out, but popped up foul. They left the bases loaded.

In the 11th, Bill Fischer took over in relief, the sixth pitcher of the game for the Tigers. (Detroit used 21 players in the game.) Ted Lepcio singled to left. Runnels singled to right. Ted Williams hit a "line-drive wallop into the lower deck that hit a girder and caromed back on the playing field."[606] Brewer put down the Tigers 1-2-3; he'd pitched 4 1/3 innings, blown a save, but got the win.

With a four-run homer at 9:27 P.M. and then a three-run homer at 12:06 A.M., Williams had seven RBIs, and won the game.[607]

Boston Red Sox 3
Cleveland Indians 2

August 3, 1958 — Cleveland Stadium
(first game of a doubleheader)

The Indians came in riding a seven-game winning streak; the Red Sox were saddled with a five-game losing streak which included two losses to the Indians on Friday and another on Saturday.

The Indians started rookie right-hander Gary Bell (5-4, 3.41.) The Red Sox went with Ike Delock, who was 10-2 (2.64); Delock had been undefeated through July 20 but then lost his last two decisions.

Though there had been a couple of shaky moments, neither team scored for the first five innings. Each starting pitcher had allowed but one base hit and both of those had been in the first inning.

The Red Sox scored first, in the top of the sixth, and it was Delock who set it up with a leadoff double.[608] He was sacrificed to third, and then sacrificed home. Delock was disturbed by a play behind him that went for a double and then walked three batters in succession. He was so upset he "flung the resin bag away" and departed the mound before reliever Bud Byerly arrived.[609]

Bell had held the Red Sox to just three base hits over the first eight innings. He'd walked three. The first batter up in the top of the ninth was Pete Runnels, with whom Ted Williams conspired to win the ballgame. Easier said than done, but it worked. Williams reportedly told Runnels, "If you get on, Pete, I'll hit a homer." Runnels said, "I couldn't let a promise like that go by."[610] He swung at the first pitch and singled over second base. Williams ran the count to 3-2, fouling off four pitches in the process, then hit one "high into the upper right field seats."[611]

The pact between Runnels and Williams had produced two runs, and Boston had taken a slim 3-2 lead.

Red Sox reliever Murray Wall was no doubt pleased at the opportunity to add another victory to his record.[612] Larry Doby pinch-hit, leading off the bottom of the ninth. He walked. Billy Harrell then pinch-hit for Bell. He hit a liner right back to Wall, who threw to Runnels at first base and doubled off Mudcat Grant, pinch-running for Doby. Avila flied out.

The Red Sox also won the second game, 4-2. They scored four runs on six base hits, more hits than they had had in any of their five previous games, including the first game of this day's doubleheader.

Boston Red Sox 6
Washington Senators 4

September 28, 1958 — Griffith Stadium, Washington

Forty-year-old Ted Williams closed out his 1958 season hitting home runs three days in a row. His solo home run in the seventh inning of the September 28 Sunday afternoon game at Griffith Stadium dealt defeat to the Washington Senators for their 13th loss in a row – a terrible way for any team to end a season.[613]

Many had been "lured" by the opportunity to see Pete Runnels and Williams battle for the American League batting title.[614] The last time two back-to-back teammates (batting one after the other in the batting order) had battled for the batting crown was in 1921, claimed Huck Finnegan, when Harry Heilmann beat out Ty Cobb.[615] Williams had overtaken Runnels in the race for the batting title just the day before, and they came into the game with Williams at .327 and Runnels at .324.

The starters were Pedro Ramos for the Senators and Tom Brewer for Boston.[616]

Ramos walked the leadoff batter, Don Buddin, who took second on a wild pitch. Ramos walked Runnels. Williams grounded into a double play and Frank Malzone grounded out. Runnels's batting average held at .3244 while Williams's fell to .3259.

The Senators got one run in the bottom of the first. Eddie Yost singled. Brewer struck out Herb Plews. Roy Sievers walked. Clint Courtney hit the ball right back to Brewer, but he threw the ball wildly toward second base and Yost scored from second base.

Neither team scored in the second or third innings. Sievers robbed Runnels of a base hit with a lunging one-handed catch in left-center and then "bounced off the fence with a thud that could be heard in the grandstand."[617]

Red Sox right fielder Jackie Jensen led off the fourth with a solo home run – his 35th of the season – and the game was tied 1-1. The ball went into an exit in the left-field stands.

Boston took a 3-1 lead in the fifth. Buddin singled to center. He was forced out at second by Runnels. But Williams doubled right through first baseman Julio Becquer's legs and Runnels scored all the way from first base. Malzone singled and Williams took third, scoring shortly afterward on a sacrifice fly to left field by Jensen.[618]

The Senators scored three times in the fifth and bumped Brewer out of the game.

Boston's Ted Lepcio led off with a homer to center field in the sixth to tie it. The next three went down in order. The Senators got a walk and a single in the sixth but couldn't score, the inning ending with pinch-runner John Romonosky being picked off second base. Those in attendance who were Senators fans were probably not amused. They had runners on first and second with nobody out in the seventh, but Ramos got picked off second.

The Senators were never truly out of the game. Shirley Povich wrote it was "one of their better performances of the last two weeks."[619]

After Runnels grounded out in the seventh, Williams homered to make it 5-4, Red Sox.[620] Sammy White's homer added an insurance run in the eighth.

Bowsfield walked one in the eighth and one in the ninth, but the score remained 6-4 at the end. The Williams home run was the game-winner.

POSTSCRIPT

The Red Sox won their last four games, and eight of their last nine, climbing from fifth place to third place in the final league standings.

Runnels was 0-for-4 in the game. Williams was 2-for-4 and ended the season batting .328, six points above Runnels' .322. Williams hit .500 over his final 28 at-bats. He'd hit .403 over his last 55 games. It was his sixth batting crown. The year before, Williams had been the oldest player to ever win a batting title. This year, he'd done it again, at the age of 40. Afterwards, he said he thought Runnels deserved the title, noting that Runnels had hit as well as he had with 149 more plate appearances.[621]

Runnels later won A.L. batting titles with the Red Sox both in 1960 and in 1962.

This was the third consecutive game-winner Ramos had allowed Williams. Homers #418 (September 25, 1956) and #430 (June 2, 1957) had also been game-winners.

Williams finished the 1958 season with 26 home runs. There could have been more. Ed Linn writes that during 1958 Williams "ran into a terrible streak of bad luck where by actual count, outfielders reached into the distant right-field bullpen at Fenway Park to take home runs away from him seven separate times in less than two months."[622]

The 26 Ted Williams homers raised $1,850 for the Jimmy Fund, thanks to the preseason pledge from the *Boston Record-American*.

Fortunately for the Jimmy Fund, Jackie Jensen hit more homers than Ted Williams – his 35 homers raised $2,750 for the cause. In all, the Red Sox as a team hit 155 homers and the newspaper donated $9,725 to help finance children's cancer research.

1959

Injuries and Age Result in Only Three Game-Winners

Due to a seriously stiff neck he developed in spring training that forced him to wear a brace, Williams didn't get into a game until May 12th. From there, he played pretty regularly, appearing in 103 games overall, just two-thirds of his team's games. Between age and injury, it was a difficult year for Williams and the results were subpar year for a player of his caliber. He started very slowly, and it was not until June 23 that he edged his batting average over .200. From there he hit pretty well, and his final average of .254 was the highest he reached all season.

Williams's on-base percentage was .372—an excellent figure for nearly everyone except him. His slugging percentage slipped to just .419. He did make the All-Star team, but clearly more out of respect and sentiment than on-the-field production.

In half a season of at-bats, he homered 10 times and drove in 43 runs. Three of the homers were game-winners, but all in all, it was an embarrassing year for Williams and his intense pride. Everyone thought he would retire, and no one would have blamed him if he did, but it wasn't the way he wanted to go out.

Boston Red Sox 8
Baltimore Orioles 3

May 30, 1959 — Fenway Park
(second game of a doubleheader)

The year 1959 was one Ted Williams might have wished he could forget. He suffered a really bad crick in his neck during spring training in Arizona. It turned out to be a pinched nerve and he was in traction for three weeks.[623] He didn't get into a game until May 12, when he went 0-for-5. At the end of May, he was still batting under .200. He entered this day hitting .157.[624]

He was 2-for-4 in the first game.

In the second game, pitcher Ted Wills got first major-league start. The Orioles countered with 20-year-old Jerry Walker (4-0).

A one-out triple by Baltimore right fielder Gene Woodling set up the first run of the game. The Orioles scored single runs in the first, second, and fifth.

Williams had an infield single in the first and grounded out to first base, unassisted, leading off the fourth.

Dick Gernert led off Boston's fifth, homering over everything in deep left field.

Williams walked in the sixth, reaching third on Frank Malzone's double high off the left-field wall. He scored on a balk. The score was 3-2, with the Orioles still in the lead.

With two outs in the bottom of the seventh, Pete Runnels doubled to right-center field. Ted Williams followed with his first home run of the year, a two-run homer that gave the Red Sox the lead, 4-3.

As homers go, it wasn't anything majestic. As described in the *Providence Journal*, it "landed only a dozen feet beyond the foul pole in the near right-field corner and the foul pole is a mere 302 feet from home plate."[625] Bob Holbrook wrote in the *Boston*

Globe, "it was a 310-foot shot that curled around the right-field foul pole"[626] – but it was most welcome nonetheless. "For sheer distance," the *Boston Herald*'s Arthur Sampson wrote, "this probably was one of the shortest homers of Ted's career, but it was hit with his old-time authority as were several other drives stroked by him yesterday."[627] The home run had given the Red Sox the lead. It proved to be a lead that held.

The Red Sox added four insurance runs in the bottom of the eighth, three on Sammy White's bases-clearing double into the left-field corner.

TED'S 1ST HOMER AIDS SOX SWEEP

Still in the game, Ted Williams had been told that the four hits he had on the day had brought his career hit total to 2,499. He was aware of that when he came up to bat and hit a fly ball to deep center field, caught by Willie Tasby on the warning track. It had almost reached the wall, but it was hit into a stiff wind and hadn't been hit quite hard enough.[628] It went for the third out.[629]

With four hits in the doubleheader, he nudged his average up to .203. It wasn't until nearly a month later – on June 26 – that he got it above .200 to stay.

Boston Red Sox 6
Cleveland Indians 4

June 27, 1959 — Cleveland Stadium

It was a Saturday afternoon game at Cleveland Stadium. The Indians (37-29) were in first place. The 30-37 Boston Red Sox were just a half-game above last-place Kansas City in the American League standings. Red Sox manager Pinky Higgins was five days away from being fired from his position. And the Red Sox were a little more than three weeks away from fielding their first Black ballplayer, Pumpsie Green, the last team to have a Black player in a regular-season game.[630]

Mudcat Grant was the starting pitcher for Cleveland. The day was so hot that Red Sox starter Frank Sullivan had to change his uniform twice during the course of the game.[631]

Don Buddin walked, leading off for the Red Sox and scored the first run, going to third on Pete Runnels's double and scoring on a wild pitch.

In the second, Marty Keough doubled and pitcher Sullivan drove him home with a single to center.

With one out in the bottom of the third, Grant singled. Woodie Held walked. Vic Power bounced a single into center, driving in Grant.

After retiring the first two batters in the top of the fifth, Grant gave Buddin a base on balls and then saw Runnels double down the right-field line, to make it 3-1, Red Sox. The Indians infielders kept switching positions. Manager Joe Gordon was said to prefer "the faster-moving Held on the right side of second base."[632]

Ted Williams hit the ball over all the defenders, swinging at the first pitch to send a home run out of the park. He "jammed the first pitch over the improvised fence in right field, catching the stands about 350 feet from home plate."[633]

The score was 5-1, Red Sox. Trekking back to their original positions, the Indians infielders saw another ball leave the park, Jensen's 400-foot home run to the lower deck in left field.

The Indians got two back in the bottom of the fifth. Tito Francona homered into the right-field stands, his fourth home run in the last five games.

Mike Garcia relieved Grant and pitched the sixth and seventh. There were six more infield swaps – three back-and-forths – by Held and Granny Hamner before the game was out. Their defensive positioning for the game reads:

Held: SS-2B-SS-2B-SS-2B-SS-2B-SS-2B-SS-2B-SS-2B-SS-2B-SS

Hamner: 2B-SS-2B-SS-2B-SS-2B-SS-2B-SS-2B-SS-2B-SS-2B-SS-2B[634]

Keough walked in the sixth. After missing a home run to right, foul by only a foot or so, Williams flied out to center in the seventh.

The Indians mounted a minor threat in the bottom of the eighth with a two-out single by Miñoso and a walk to Strickland. Tom Brewer relieved a tiring and depleted Sullivan and struck out Hamner.

In the bottom of the ninth, Held homered into the seats in right field, but Power hit the ball to Brewer, who threw to Dick Gernert for the final out.

Boston Red Sox 7
Detroit Tigers 1

August 22, 1959 — Briggs Stadium, Detroit

Jimmy Dykes took over as Detroit manager in early May. Billy Jurges became Red Sox manager in early July.

Dykes started Don Mossi and Jurges went with Frank Baumann.

Boston managed to score once in the top of the first, but not through any heroics. Jim Busby reached on an error. Pumpsie Green singled and Busby moved to third. Ted Williams was up and he hit into a 4-6-3 double play. Both Green and Williams were out, but Busby scored.

The way the season had been going for Ted Williams (he'd been hitting .236 before the game), there was a real possibility this would be his last season – and his last game playing in Detroit, in what was probably his favorite ballpark in which to hit.[635] He hadn't hit a homer for almost a month; his last one was hit in Kansas City on July 26.

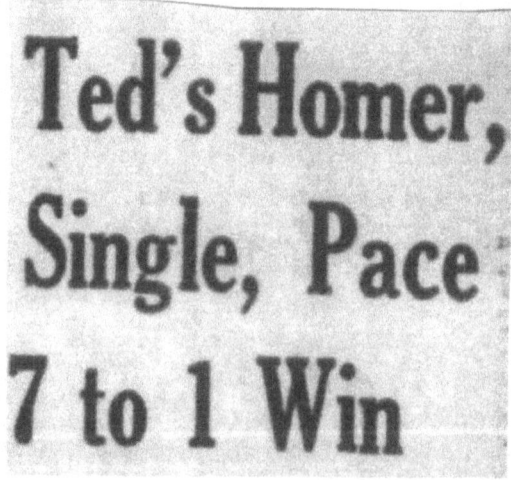

In the Red Sox fourth, Green flied out for the first out. Williams swung at Mossi's first pitch and hit a home run, "high up into the back of the second deck of seats in right field."[636] Joe Falls of the *Detroit Times* detailed the story:

"Mossi's first serve was high and inside – a mistake – and the Williams bat came around in a flash. He connected solidly and the ball sailed majestically toward right field. It was a home run – no doubt of it, just a question how far it would go. It slammed into the 15th row of the upper deck, about 20 feet fair, and nearly knocked a seat from its hinges.

"As Williams circled the bases, the crowd of 8,632 groaned in dismay. Then, as if suddenly sending the significance of the occasion – an artist at work for the last time – the fans arose and began to applaud warmly.

"Ted liked that. He was grinning as he crossed the plate and, wonder of wonders, doffed his cap before disappearing into the darkness of the dugout.

"For the moment, at least, the years of snarling, snapping and spitting at his public were forgotten. Ted Williams, the idol, the enigma, the man of moods, wore the cloak of humility."[637]

In the sixth, the Red Sox broke the game wide open, scoring five runs on five base hits, Williams picking up another RBI on a single and Dick Gernert driving in two.

The Red Sox had a 7-0 lead.

The Tigers manufactured a run in the eighth, escaping a shutout thanks to a parade of pinch-hitters. The third single was Gus Zernial's; Johnny Groth scored from second – only because he ran through third-base coach Billy Hitchcock's stop sign.

Baumann threw a six-hit, 7-1 win for Boston, striking out eight and only walking one. Ted Williams's solo home run in the fourth inning scored the second run of the game – the one needed to win the game.

Autographed 1960 Red Sox yearbook.

1960

A Fabulous Farewell

Ted Williams headed into the season determined to put up strong numbers as he believed he still could, even if others may have doubted him. He demanded a 30% pay cut from owner Tom Yawkey, because he simply felt he hadn't earned his salary in 1959, which if not the highest in baseball, was certainly one of the highest. But whether he could come through was another question.

Come through he did. Williams brought his average up over .300 for the year, finishing at .316. He had come into the season with 492 home runs—tantalizingly close to 500, a figure that at the time only Ruth and Foxx had attained. He reached #500 and went on another 21—29 in all, in only 310 at-bats! Four of Williams's long balls were game-winners. And his 521st home run, though not a game-winner, was one of the most dramatic in baseball history—hit in what everyone knew was to be his last at-bat in major-league baseball.

Boston Red Sox 3
Cleveland Indians 1

June 17, 1960 — Cleveland Stadium

Ted Williams had hit his 499th home run the day before, in Detroit. It had been a discouraging year for the Red Sox slugger.[638] Coming off the 1959 season in which he had hit for a .254 batting average, he hadn't even been doing that well when Boston hosted Cleveland a week earlier. Williams was hitting .235 as recently as June 8, when the Indians had swept a doubleheader.

"Two weeks ago, I was awfully close to quitting," he'd said. "I had a bad cold, was feeling bad and wasn't hitting good. I told Billy Jurges (then the manager), if I can't help the club, I'm going to quit. Then I hit a couple against the wind and decided to stay with it."[639]

He'd started to hit, though, including four homers in seven days, and upped his average to .321.

The Indians were only 1½ games out of first place; they started rookie Wynn Hawkins. The last-place Red Sox (18-34) started Frank Sullivan.[640]

The Indians scored first, in the first, when Harvey Kuenn walked, stole second, and scored on John Romano's bloop single to center. It was the only run they got in the game.

The Red Sox tied it in the second on a single, a stolen base, and two more singles.

In the top of the third, Willie Tasby singled to center. With one out, Williams swung on a 1-2 count and "drove his 500th home run over the left field fence...It was an opposite field smash, not his longest, but it counted just the same. It won a ball game."[641]

Left fielder Tito Francona "stopped in futile pursuit as the ball sailed over the wire fence by a marker with 365 on it."[642]

"Ted didn't say anything much after he hit it," said Higgins, "but you could tell he was overjoyed."[643] It was, after all, home run #500.

"I didn't think I'd be able to get loose tonight," said Williams. "These kinds of nights the cold jars your hands when you hit a ball. But I got that one just right. It felt wonderful."[644]

Ted Clouts 500th Homer
To Give Sox 3-1 Victory

The ball was retrieved, after a "real argument," from a stadium guard by relief pitcher Dave Hillman. The guard wanted to keep the souvenir.[645]

"Well, I've never made a habit of collecting baseballs, but I might like to keep this one," Williams said. "I have a ball autographed by Babe Ruth. I have another autographed by five .400 hitters and the first one I hit off Bob Feller. Yes, I'd maybe like to keep this last one, but if someone came along and offered me some real money for it, I'd be tempted to accept and turn it over to the Jimmy Fund."[646]

Not another run scored in the game. Sullivan struck out 12. Williams hit #501 two days later, and then hit two more on June 21. By season's end, he had 29 and a total of 521.

Boston Red Sox 13
Kansas City Athletics 2

July 3, 1960 — Fenway Park

Willie Tasby hit a grand slam. Vic Wertz hit a three-run homer. But it was the two-run homer in the bottom of the fifth inning that gave the Red Sox their second and third runs – the third run being the one that won them the 13-2 game.

Neither side scored for the first three innings, but Kansas City took a lead when left fielder Norm Siebern hit a leadoff fourth-inning home run off Boston's starting pitcher, Ike Delock.

Ted Williams singled to lead off Boston's fourth. Vic Wertz singled, too, and Williams ran from first to third, sliding into third base on his stomach. Malzone hit into a 6-4-3 double play, but Williams scored the first Red Sox run, tying the score 1-1.

With two outs in the bottom of the fifth, Pete Runnels doubled to right field. Two surprises followed. With first base open, the Athletics pitched to Williams. And then Williams surprised Dick Hall by swinging at the first pitch and struck "a towering 390-footer...which fell five rows up in the right-field pavilion just right of the K.C. bullpen."[647]

Hall figured he'd start off Ted with a high fastball, but missed with the pitch and he said he threw it too high, "up and even with his chin. He was famous for never swinging at bad pitches, but this time, because he was obviously (by hindsight) looking for a high fastball, he swung at it. Problem: He hit it over their part of the bullpen for a home run."[648]

Athletics Pitch To Ted -- WHAM

As to pitching to "the hottest hitter in the American League," the *Boston Globe*'s Harold Kaese just said, "The intentional walk apparently has not reached Kansas City."[649] After a slow start, Williams had hit 11 homers in his last 19 starts.[650] One sportswriter calculated that in 1960 he was hitting one home run in every seven plate appearances.[651]

The Red Sox took a 3-1 lead.

K.C.'s Pete Daley doubled to led off the seventh. He took second on a groundout. With two outs, Hank Bauer doubled down the left-field line, and Daley scored easily. It was 4-2, with runners on second and third. Higgins had Ted Wills take over for Delock to get the third out.

It was a two-run game – until the Red Sox exploded for eight runs in the bottom of the seventh. That's when Wertz hit five foul balls in a row and then greeted Don Larsen with a three-run homer "into the center field end of the Boston bull-pen."[652] The third pitcher of the inning, Ray Blemker, loaded the bases, and walked Ted Wills, forcing in a run. Tasby then hit his grand slam, halfway up and into the screen atop Fenway's left-field wall.

Boston Red Sox 8
Baltimore Orioles 6

August 20, 1960 — Fenway Park
(first game of a doubleheader)

His first time up, Ted Williams drew a walk. It was base on balls #2,000. Only one player had ever walked more – Babe Ruth, who'd earned 2,062 walks.[653] Ted got walk #2,000 in his 2,260[th] game; he wasn't far off from averaging a walk a game.

He is the player with the highest walks percentage in baseball history – 20.64%. More than once in every five times to the plate, he earned a free pass to first base. Ruth's walks percentage was 19.48%.[654]

It was never a personal goal, but instead of by-product of what Williams had been told by Rogers Hornsby and always tried to put into practice – patience. "Get a good ball to hit."[655]

Bob Feller: "You had to throw strikes to him. He would not swing at a ball unless it was over the plate – or he thought it was. He seldom ever took a called third strike that I know of."[656]

It wasn't the walks that got Ted a standing ovation when he came to the plate in the eighth inning. It's because he'd already hit two three-run homers in the game, the first in the fourth and the second one in the sixth. The second one was the game-winning hit.

The pitchers in the game were Bill Monbouquette for Boston and rookie Chuck Estrada for Baltimore.[657]

Monbo got off to a rocky start. Ron Hansen hit a three-run homer in the top of the first.

Williams got his milestone walk in the first and a check-swing single in the third, scoring – after an error – on Russ Nixon's single.

In the fourth, Pete Runnels was hit by a pitch and Willie Tasby singled to left. Ted Williams put the Sox in the lead with "a hightowering hoist"[658] – a three-run homer into the Red Sox bullpen.

Baltimore's Brooks Robinson doubled in the tying run in the fifth, and the Orioles took a 6-4 lead in the sixth on Gene Woodling's pinch-hit triple and a single from Estrada.

In the bottom of the sixth, Runnels and Tasby both singled. Ted Williams swung at Estrada's first pitch and hit a three-run homer, lifting Boston to a 7-6 lead. The home run was pegged at 430 feet. It landed "six or eight rows into the bleacher crowd between the end of the bullpen and the flag pole" in center field.[659]

This was the last multiple home-run game for Ted Williams. He had most recently hit two homers in the August 10 game against Cleveland. This was also the last three-run homer Ted Williams ever hit – though it was his second one of the game. He drove in six of Boston's eight runs, and they needed them. The final score was 8-6.

Hal Brown shut out the Sox, 6-0, in the second game. Williams pinch-hit late in the game and grounded out.

Boston Red Sox 2
Washington Senators 1

September 17, 1960 — Griffith Stadium,
Washington

This was the next-to-last home run Ted Williams ever hit. It was also the fourth game-winner in a row he had hit off Pedro Ramos, who was still only 25 years old but had given up six home runs to Williams, with the four game-winners tying him (with Virgil Trucks) for first place among pitchers who allowed Ted Williams to win a game with a home run.[660]

The game was a 2-1 win for Red Sox pitcher Billy Muffett, who threw a three-hitter just as he had on September 6 in New York.[661]

Manager Cookie Lavagetto had Ramos (11-14) pitching. He had beaten the Red Sox three times before in 1960 and had two non-decisions against them, but both of those were games the Senators also won.[662]

There were only eight hits in this game, Muffett only allowing three.

After five innings, neither team had scored.

That changed in the top of the sixth inning. With one out, Willie Tasby lined a sharp single to center. On the fourth pitch he saw, 42-year-old Ted Williams "swung at the next pitch and it went on a line toward the top of the right-field fence – 31 feet high, 355 feet away, and 30 feet in from the foul line. The ball was on the rise until it was about 15 feet from the top of the fence. Then it leveled off, and cleared the fence by two or three feet."[663] The *Boston Herald* report agreed the ball had barely skimmed the barrier.[664] The home run – #520 of his major-league career, which dated back to 1939 – gave the Red Sox a 2-0 lead. They were the only runs the Red Sox got.

Ted's 520th Homer Wins, 2-1

The Senators only got one. Harmon Killebrew led off the bottom of the seventh, hitting a "towering fly" to Williams in left field.[665] Left fielder Jim Lemon swung at the first pitch and hit the ball into Griffith Stadium's visitors bullpen. It was a home run, Lemon's 38th of the season. It was a one-run game, 2-1. "Unfortunately," wrote the *Washington Post*, "Lemon didn't have the foresight to have a man on base, the way Williams did."[666]

Ramos had allowed just five hits, two of them to "Old Hoss Williams."[667]

All the Senators needed was the one run to tie.

Reno Bertoia got a base on balls to lead off the bottom of the eighth, and manager Cookie Lavagetto pulled out all the stops, putting in three pinch-hitters in a row, one after the other. They all made outs. Muffett retired the Senators in order in the bottom of the ninth.

The game took only one hour and 40 minutes. It had attracted 5,264.

The day ended with the Red Sox still in seventh place.

Ted Williams, by virtue of his sixth-inning home run, had the 110th game-winning home run of his career, a home run that gave the Red Sox the extra run they needed to hold on and win the game.

Using conservative estimates, had Williams not missed five full seasons to military service, he likely would have approached 700 home runs for his career (see pages 268-269).

Notes on Game-Winning Home Runs

Where did Ted Williams hit the game-winning homers?

About half were at home (52) and half were on the road (58). The breakdown is as follows:

Fenway Park, Boston: 52
Briggs Stadium, Detroit: 11
Cleveland Stadium, Cleveland: 10
Comiskey Park, Chicago: 8
Griffith Stadium, Washington: 8
Sportsman's Park, St. Louis: 6
Shibe Park, Philadelphia: 4
League Park, Cleveland: 4
Memorial Stadium, Baltimore: 2
Municipal Stadium, Kansas City: 2
Yankee Stadium, New York: 2
Connie Mack Stadium, Philadelphia: 1

Note: this does not include the All-Star Game home run, hit in Detroit. Against the St. Louis Browns/Baltimore Orioles franchise, he hit a total of 8 road home runs. Against the Philadelphia Athletics/Kansas City Athletics franchise, he hit a total of 7 road home runs.

Among Fenway Park home runs, which teams were most often victimized?

Detroit Tigers: 11
Philadelphia Athletics: 7
St. Louis Browns: 7
Washington Senators: 7
Baltimore Orioles: 5

New York Yankees: 5
Chicago White Sox: 4
Cleveland Indians: 4
Kansas City Athletics: 2

Clearly, home or away, Williams feasted on Tigers pitching. Against visiting teams from the St. Louis Browns/Baltimore Orioles franchise, he hit a total of 12 homers at home. Against the Philadelphia Athletics/Kansas City Athletics franchise, he hit a total of 9 homers at Fenway.

How many RBIs did he collect on the home runs he hit?

Of course, all it takes is one run to win the game, but sometimes the team had to come from two runs down, in which case a three-run homer or grand slam was needed.

Of the 110 game-winning homers, here is the breakdown of the number of runs driven in by the game-winner. In some cases, more runs were driven in than were necessary to win the game in question.

Solo home run: 27
Two-run homer: 49
Three-run homer: 25
Grand slam: 9

We know that Williams hit 17 career grand slams. Nine of them were game-winning ones, but we can see that eight of them were not game-winners.

What is the breakdown by inning of the game-winning home runs?

Sixteen of them were hit in the first inning, but Red Sox pitching in those games was good enough that the number of runs produced by the first-inning homers was enough to win.

First inning: 16
Second inning: 6
Third inning: 17
Fourth inning: 5
Fifth inning: 10
Sixth inning: 9
Seventh inning: 15
Eighth inning: 13
Ninth inning: 8
10th inning: 5
11th inning: 3
12th inning: 3

Walk-off home runs

Of the 19 game-winning homers hit in the ninth or later innings, it's interesting to note that only three were "walk-off" home runs. These were, by definition, hit in the bottom of the inning in question. The Red Sox had to have been the home team to be able to walk off the field with the game thus won. The dates of the three walk-offs were:

May 19, 1957: 9th inning
May 2, 1946: 10th inning
July 19, 1958: 12th inning

None of the games in which Williams provided the game-winning homer were games that lasted fewer than nine innings, such as a seventh-inning second game of a doubleheader called due to darkness, or weather.

One interesting bit of trivia: In 1947, the last four of his 10 game-winning homers that year were all first-inning home runs. In each case, he hit a two- or three-run homer in games the Red Sox won by scores of 12-1, 2-1, 9-1, and 8-1. Three of the four were won by pitcher Joe Dobson.

Who were the pitchers who fell victim to a Ted Williams game-winning homer?

There were many who fell victim once. There were also many who game up multiple home runs to Ted Williams over the years. Virgil Trucks, for instance, gave up 12 of Williams's 521 career home runs. It is perhaps not surprising that Trucks is tied for first among pitchers who gave up homers that count among Williams game-winners. Pedro Ramos gave up half as many – six homers – to Ted Williams, but fully four of them were ones that won games for the Red Sox.

Pedro Ramos: 4
Virgil Trucks: 4
Ned Garver: 3
Jim Bunning: 2
Cliff Fannin: 2
Bill Fischer: 2
Steve Gromek: 2.
Sid Hudson: 2
Bob Keegan: 2
Jack Knott: 2
Walt Masterson: 2
Bob Muncrief; 2
Marino Pieretti: 2
Vic Raschi: 2
Johnny Rigney: 2
Al Widmar: 2

It is interesting to note that Sid Hudson gave up two game-winning homers, as indicated (one in 1942 and one in 1946), but after he was acquired by the Red Sox in 1952, Hudson was also the winning pitcher for the Red Sox in the September 17, 1953 game. Ned Garver gave up the home run to Ted Williams in that game. Traded to the Senators for Hudson were Randy Gumpert and Walt Masterson. Masterson had given up game-winners to Williams in 1940 and 1947, pitched for the Red Sox from June 1949 to June 1952, and then was traded back to Washington.

Which pitchers were credited with the win in games where a Ted Williams home run provided the run that won?

There were the pitchers who were victimized by Williams game-winning homers, but who were the Red Sox pitchers who benefitted most from such home runs that he hit?

Joe Dobson was the big winner. There were the three victories a Williams homer provided Dobson in the two-month stretch from July 26 through September 27, 1947. There were another eight games which Dobson won thanks to a Ted Williams game-winner. In all, Joe Dobson was the winning pitcher in 11 of the 110 games in which Williams hit a game-winning homer. And all that happened in seven seasons (Williams was not on the team in 1943, because he was in military service, and Dobson only pitched a total of 2 2/3 innings in 1954.) Dobson won 106 games for the Red Sox over those seven seasons, and more than 10% of them were won by Ted Williams game-winning homers – 11 of the 106. There were additionally two games which Dobson started, but the win went to others in relief – the June 17, 1941 game was a Dobson start, but Jack Wilson got the win in relief, and the July 14, 1946 game was also a Dobson start, but the win went to Jim Bagby, Jr.

The winning pitchers with more than one win on a Williams game-winning homer are:

Joe Dobson: 11
Ellis Kinder: 10 (5 as a starter, 5 as a reliever)
Frank Sullivan: 10
Tex Hughson: 8 (one of which he started, with Clem Dreisewerd getting the win in relief)
Tom Brewer: 7, one of them in relief
Ike Delock: 5, three of them in relief
Willard Nixon: 5
Mel Parnell: 4
Charlie Wagner: 4
Jim Bagby, Jr.: 3
Boo Ferriss: 3, one in relief
Joe Heving: 3

Leo Kiely: 3, two of them in relief
Denny Galehouse: 2, one in relief
Dave Sisler: 2
Chuck Stobbs: 2

On what days of the week did the game-winning homers get hit?

Given that Mondays and Thursdays have often been travel days, and doubleheaders were more often scheduled on weekend days, the results are perhaps not surprising:

Monday: 9
Tuesday: 15
Wednesday: 19
Thursday: 10
Friday: 15
Saturday: 22
Sunday: 20

In what months were the game-winning homers hit?

It's worth keeping in mind that in Williams's day, the season typically did not start until mid-April. There were very few regular-season games played in early October. Then, as now, the All-Star Break ate up several days in mid-July. These were the months in which Williams hit his game-winning homers. There were, of course, a couple of years he had late starts, a couple which were curtailed by his Korean War service, and 1950, when he suffered the broken elbow in the All-Star Game.

April: 3
May: 25
June: 20
July: 17
August: 23

September: 21
October: 1

Hitting a home run on the first pitch

One thing that Ted Williams preached was to take the first pitch. As he put it in *The Science of Hitting*, "For me as a batter hitting third in the lineup, there was one thing that was 95 per cent certain: I was going to *take the first pitch*. Even a strike right down the middle....

"But what advantage is there in taking the first pitch in a game (the rule doesn't apply in succeeding times up) if the pitch is a strike and you've automatically reduced by 33 per cent the number of strikes you'll get? These advantages: You've refreshed your memory of the pitcher's speed and his delivery. You see if he's got it on this particular day. You've given yourself a little time to get settled, to get the tempo....It's simple arithmetic: You figure to face a pitcher at least three or four times in a game. The more information you log the first time up, the better your chances the next three. The more you make him pitch, the more information you get."[668] He did add, "The reason I swung on the other 5 per cent was that occasionally I got one that was so tempting, such a big balloon coming in, that I took a cut to keep the pitcher honest."

Apparently he got a few of those big balloons. Thirteen of the game-winning homers he hit were on first pitches. Most of those did come in later innings. This list shows the dates and (in parentheses) the inning in which he hit the game-winner. Eight of the 13 were hit in the park where he was most accustomed to hitting: Fenway Park. The at-home homers are marked with an asterisk.

June 15, 1939 (8)
July 14, 1946 (8)*
June 4, 1947 (6)
May 28, 1949 (5)*
May 30, 1949 (8)*
May 5, 1950 (7)*

July 17, 1956 (6)*
May 8, 1957 (3)
July 19, 1958 (12)*
June 27, 1959 (5)
August 22, 1959 (4)
July 3, 1960 (5)*
August 20, 1960 (8)*

There is, as noted in the text, some question regarding on which pitch he hit the May 30, 1949 home run but we list it here, because almost all sources indicated it was a first-pitch homer.

The home run that he hit on May 8, 1957 came early in the game, but it was in his second at-bat, and he had already hit one home run (on a 3-2 count) off pitcher Bob Keegan his first time up.

Had it not been for his nearly five years in military service, how many game-winning homers might Ted Williams have hit?

Ted Williams hit 521 home runs over the course of his career, but he lost approximately 4.7 years due to military service – most of five seasons. He lost time due to injury, of course – the broken elbow in the 1950 All-Star Game, the broken collarbone in 1954, the pinched nerve in 1959. Injuries occur. But spending most of five seasons in military service is outside what one might normally expect. Inevitably one wonders how many more homers he might have hit had World War II not broken out, and had he not been summoned back to service during the Korean War.

There are different ways one could try to guess how many homers he might have hit had it not been for the wars. We will look at just one – how many he hit in the two years before his service and the two years after.

1941 – 37
1942 – 36
1943 – 0
1944 – 0

1945 – 0
1946 – 38
1947 – 32

The average of the two years immediately preceding World War II was 36.5 home runs and the average for the two years after the war was 35 home runs. Averaging all four shows 35.75 home runs per year. Fill in the three years 1943 through 1945 with 35.75 homers per year, and one gets an additional 107.25 home runs. Were we to add 107 homers to the 521 he did hit, one gets a total of 628.

If we do the same thing for the two years preceding 1952 and 1953, we find:

1950 – 28 (that he missed a large part of the season due to the injury is, as suggested, something we will not treat differently)

1951 – 30
1954 – 29
1955 - 28

The average comes to 28.75 home runs per year. Double that for the two years, and round down the fraction, and one adds another 57 home runs (from which we could subtract the 14 he did hit during the truncated years of 1952 and 1953), and we could argue that he should be hypothetically "credited" an additional 43 home runs. Add that 43 to the 628 projected total from the WWII years, and one gets a grand total of 671 career home runs.

How many game-winning homers would this mean he would (arguably) have hit? In the two years before WWII, he hit 14 and in the two years after he hit 13. At an average of 7.5 game-winning homers over the WWII years, one could project an additional 22.5 game-winning homers. Do the same for the Korean War years, the average of the two years before Korea and two years after was 5.75, or 11.5 for the two years. Subtract the four he did hit, one can add 7.5 more homers. Add 22.5 and 7.5, and the projected total could be an additional 30 game-winning homers. Thus, instead of 110 career game-winning homers, he might have hit 140.

Sources and Endnotes

In addition to the sources cited in the Notes, the author consulted Baseball-Reference.com and Retrosheet.org. Thanks to Malcolm Allen, Ian Browne, John Fredland, Evan Katz, Herm Krabbenhoft, Kevin Larkin, Pete Palmer, Carl Riechers, and Tom Ruane.

Notes

1   Ted Williams and Jim Prime, *Ted Williams' Hit List* (Indianapolis: Masters Press, 1996), 19. The wording was nearly the same as the way he had begun *The Science of Hitting*: "Hitting a baseball – I've said it a thousand times –is the single most difficult thing to do in sport." Ted Williams and John Underwood, *The Science of Hitting* (New York: Fireside Books, 1970), 7.

2   Ted Williams and Jim Prime, *Ted Williams' Hit List,* 22.

3   Ted Williams and Jim Prime, *Ted Williams' Hit List,* 10.

4   Ted Williams and John Underwood, *The Science of Hitting*, 25.

5   Bruce Weber, "Another Season, and Baseball Still Seeks Truth in Numbers," *New York Times*, April 9, 1989: section 4, 1.

6   Larry Granillo, "Wezen-Ball: The Drawbacks and Demise of a Stat," BaseballProspectus.com, February 16, 2012, at https://www.baseballprospectus.com/news/article/16054/wezen-ball-the-drawbacks-and-demise-of-a-stat/

7   Gerry Moore, "Ted Williams Scores Five Runs with Two Homers," *Boston Globe*, May 5, 1939: 1. The May 4 game account is adapted from one which first appeared in *Tigers By The Tale: Great Games at Michigan and Trumbull* (Phoenix: SABR, 2016), edited by Scott Ferkovich.

8   All ballpark measurements are from Philip J. Lowry, *Green Cathedrals* (New York: Walker & Company, 2006), 83, 84. A second deck in right had been added after the 1935 season. It overhung the lower deck by 10 feet, and there was a "315" marker attached to the second deck.

9   Moore, "Ted Williams Scores Five Runs with Two Homers."

10   Burt Whitman, "Williams' Two Homers Send Across Five Runs As Sox Trip Tigers, 7-6," *Boston Herald*, May 5, 1939: 35.

11   Whitman, "Williams' Two Homers Send Across Five Runs As Sox Trip Tigers, 7-6."

12   Moore, "Ted Williams Scores Five Runs with Two Homers."

13   The story is also told in Ted Williams' autobiography, Ted Williams with John Underwood, *My Turn At Bat* (New York: Simon & Schuster, 1969), 64.

14 Moore, "Ted Williams Scores Five Runs with Two Homers." The reporter may have not realized that Ruth's last year in the American League was 1934, before the upper deck was built following the 1935 season.

15 Detroit sportswriter Joe Falls remembered a late-career batting practice in the Motor City. There was already a large crowd in the park. Williams stepped into the cage to take his seven swings. "The first one he lines down the right-field line just inside the foul pole. Crash! Home run into the upper deck. The second one went a little further into the upper deck. The third one a little further. And now the crowd starts to pick up on this. The fourth one — BOOM, a little further. He did it seven straight times — seven times in the upper deck, each one a little longer than the last one and by the time the seventh ball went out, the place was up in uproar. I'd say 25,000 were roaring because they saw what he was doing. He turned around, went back to the dugout, went down the steps, didn't say hello, good-bye, kiss my ass, tip his hat, nothing. That's a true story." Jim Prime and Bill Nowlin, *Ted Williams: The Pursuit of Perfection* (New York: Sports Publishing, 2002), 195.

16 Martin J. Haley, "Red Sox Trip Browns in Tenth, 10-8, on Williams' Homer," *St. Louis Globe-Democrat*, May 10, 1939: 13.

17 Gerry Moore, "Red Sox Win in 10th to Hold Lead in League," *Boston Globe*, May 10, 1939: 25. Haley's article said Foxx's homer left the field of play "above the 425-foot mark ... one of the longest drives ever hit into that sector."

18 Associated Press, "Red Sox Beat Browns, 10-8, in 10th, Keep Lead," *Washington Post*, May 10, 1939: 21.

19 Vosmik had played just one season for the Browns – 1937 – but hit .325 with 93 runs batted in.

20 Burt Whitman, "Williams' Homer in 10th with Two On Gives Sox 10-8 Win over Browns," *Boston Herald*, May 10, 1939: 15.

21 Moore, "Red Sox Win in 10th to Hold Lead in League."

22 On May 30, the 20-year-old rookie right fielder had hit a first-inning homer off Red Ruffing – his first off a Yankees pitcher and first off a future Hall of Famer – but it had been Jimmie Foxx's second-inning homer that won that game.

23 The game was the first of a Sunday afternoon doubleheader at Fenway Park. Lou Gehrig had played the final game of his career on April 30, but he continued to travel with the team. When he came out to present the Yankees' batting order, Red Sox owner Tom Yawkey came out to greet him.

24 Gerry Moore, "Sox Split with Yankees as Injuries Fell Three," *Boston Globe*, July 3, 1939: 1, 5.

25   Desautels was able to return to play just two days later, on July
      4. There were three injuries in the first game, and four lesser
      ones in the second.

26   The right-field bullpens, which shortened the home-run
      distance by 23 feet, were not added until the 1940 season.
      When added, they were dubbed "Williamsburg," seen as
      constructed in large part to help Boston's new left-handed
      slugger hit more homers.

27   James P. Dawson, "Grove Prevails, 7-3, at Boston, Then
      Yankees Rout Red Sox, 9-3," *New York Times*, July 3, 1939: 10.
      Henrich suffered a severe concussion and a lacerated scalp and
      spent the night in a local hospital.

28   Ruffing was a good hitter, used with some frequency as a pinch-
      hitter. At the end of his 22 years in the majors (which had
      begun with the Red Sox in 1924), he had a .269 lifetime batting
      average. Ruffing was 55-for-212 lifetime as a pinch-hitter
      (.259), with 2 homers and 44 RBIs.

29   Meredith Perri, "Do Boston Red Sox' Games Against New York
      Yankees Take Longer Than Average Game?" masslive.com,
      May 19, 2019. masslive.com/redsox/2017/07/do_boston_red_
      sox_games_agains.html, accessed November 29, 2020.

30   It wasn't his first. This was the fifth of his career, building
      toward of total of 258 intentional walks.

31   Burt Whitman, "Red Sox 9-5 Victors; Bees Win, 7-3," *Boston
      Herald*, July 15, 1939: 23.

32   Hy Hurwitz, "Williams Puts Red Sox Over for 10 in Row,"
      Boston Globe, July 16, 1939: B1.

33   Whitman, "Red Sox 9-5 Victors; Bees Win, 7-3."

34   Shirley Povich, "Nats and Red Sox Split Two," *Washington
      Post*, August 20, 1939: X1.

35   The stage was set. Arthur Sampson of the *Boston Herald* wrote,
      "Young Ted was born for the sensational and here he found the
      situation tailor made for his vanity. To win a game on a home
      run with two out in the ninth is a feat to thrill any drama-loving
      soul, and such a climax has been glamorous Ted's ambition
      ever since joining the Red Sox.
      "He strode to the plate with the swagger of Mickey Rooney
      playing a serious part in an Andy Hardy movie. It was easy to
      see he had his heart on the thing, a home run over the right-
      field wall." Arthur Sampson, "Williams Homer Gives Sox Split,"
      Boston Herald, August 20, 1939: 31. This was Ted Williams's
      18th career home run, and he'd already homered off two
      pitchers who had changed their names –Appleton (born Peter
      Jablonowski) and Ed Cole (born Edward William Kisleauskas).

36   Povich, "Nats and Red Sox Split Two."

37   Gerry Moore, "Titanic Ted Williams Hits a Four-Run Homer,"
      Boston Globe, August 20, 1939: B23.

38   Moore, "Titanic Ted Williams Hits a Four-Run Homer."

39   Arthur Sampson, "Sox Beat Indians, 6-5, on Williams Home
      Run," *Boston Herald*, August 29, 1939: 18.

40   Gerry Moore, "'Timely Ted,' Williams' New Nickname with
      Six," *Boston Globe*, August 30, 1939: 20.

41   Gerry Moore, "Ted Williams Poles Homer to Win for Red Sox,
      7 to 4," *Boston Globe*, August 30, 1939: 21.

42   Eugene J. Whitney, "Williams Lashes Homer with Bases
      Full to Beat Tribe Again," *Cleveland Plain Dealer*, August 30,
      1939: 16.

43   As a point of interest, on June 10, 1938, Lefebvre had hit a
      Fenway Park home run in his first at-bat in the major leagues.
      This was before he ever played a game in the minor leagues.

44   Kaese offered, "He thought of everything, even when he was a
      kid." See Harold Kaese, "Ted Pulls Punches as Memoirs Start,"
      Boston Globe, April 17, 1954: 13.

45   Indeed, he may actually have been born on August 20. The
      story is explored in detail in Bill Nowlin, *Ted Williams:
      First Latino in the Baseball Hall of Fame* (Cambridge,
      Massachusetts: Rounder Books, 2018), 19, 79-82.

46   Melville Webb, "Williams Hits 2 Homers as Sox Take A's
      Twice," *Boston Globe*, September 11, 1939: 6.

47   Webb, "Williams Hits 2 Homers as Sox Take A's Twice."

48   Ted Williams and John Underwood, *The Science of Hitting*, 32.

49   Burt Whitman, "Red Sox Club Six Home Runs, Beat Chisox
      Twice, 4-3,14-5," *Boston Herald*, June 17, 1940: 12.

50   Shirley Povich, "Nats Beaten, 9-4, by Bosox Hard Hitting,"
      Washington Post, July 6, 1940: 11.

51   John Drohan, "Sox Set Off Fireworks Late, Blow Nats out of
      Park, 9-4," *Boston Herald*, July 6, 1940: 6.

52   Hy Hurwitz, "Sox Trample Senators, 9-4," *Boston Globe*, July
      6, 1940: 7. The bat flew over first baseman Bonura's head.

53   Drohan, "Sox Set Off Fireworks Late, Blow Nats out of Park,
      9-4."

54   "Reporter Surprised to Hear Baseball Gab, Not Gossip, In
      Stands on Ladies' Day," *Evening Star*, July 6, 1940:

55   Ted Williams and John Underwood, *The Science of Hitting*, 23.

56   Burt Whitman, "Williams 'Homer Nips Chisox in 11th," *Boston
      Herald*, May 8, 1941: 34.

57   Charlie Wagner to Bill Nowlin. Jim Prime and Bill Nowlin,
      Ted Williams – The Pursuit of Perfection, 37. See also Leigh
      Montville, *Ted Williams* (New York: Doubleday, 2004), 81.

58   Melville Webb, "Wagner Pitches Red Sox to Win," *Boston Globe*, May 8, 1941: 20.

59   Webb, "Wagner Pitches Red Sox to Win."

60   Bill Nowlin, "Charlie Wagner," SABR BioProject. https://sabr. org/bioproj/person/charlie-wagner/

61   Burt Whitman, "Red Sox Win, 5-2; A's Retaliate, 11-1," *Boston Herald*, May 28, 1941: 16. The *Globe* simply dubbed it "a slam into the center-field bleachers." See James C. O'Leary, "Red Sox Win, 5-2, then Lose, 11 to 1," *Boston Globe*, May 27, 1941: 21. The Associated Press story said it was "a bristling home run into the distant right field stands." See Associated Press, "Athletics Bow, 5-2, Then Halt Red Sox," *New York Times*, May 27, 1941: 34. Ed Rumill of the *Christian Science Monitor* wrote that it "carried over the visiting bull pen and into the distant right-center field bleachers." See Ed Rumill, "Little Professor Knows Trick of Getting On Base," *Christian Science Monitor*, May 27, 1941: 16. At the time, the visitors' bullpen was the one more toward center field and the Red Sox bullpen was the one closest to the right-field line, the opposite of the way it has been for more than half a century since.

62   Burt Whitman, "Williams' Homer Chills Macks, 6-4," *Boston Herald*, May 30, 1941: 24.

63   Hy Hurwitz, "Three Homers Spell 6-3 Win," *Boston Globe*, June 7, 1941: 8.

64   Williams was unsparing in a later comment on Rigney: "The trouble with the average pitcher is his hardheadedness. He has too inflated an opinion of what he's got. Say it's his fast ball. He thinks he can throw it anytime, anyplace, anywhere. If you hit his fast ball, he still gives it to you again. John Rigney was like that. He would put it in there, and you would put it out." Ted Williams and John Underwood, *The Science of Hitting,* 71.

65   Hurwitz, "Three Homers Spell 6-3 Win."

66   Irving Vaughan, "Three Red Sox Homers Defeat White Sox, 6-3," *Chicago Tribune*, June 7, 1941: 15.

67   John Drohan, "Ryba, Williams Give Sox 3-2 Nightcap Win," *Boston Herald*, June 13, 1941: 33. The *St. Louis Globe-Democrat* agreed the ball had left the park and gone to Grand. See Glen L. Wallar, "Relief Hurlers Shine As Browns Split Bill," *St. Louis Globe-Democrat*, June 13, 1941: 3B.

68   Hy Hurwitz, "Ryba's Relief Work Saves Sox," *Boston Globe*, June 13, 1941: 28.

69   In an interview with the author on July 13, 1997, Thomas said, "He hit his first home run off me. The first one he ever hit. In Fenway Park. 1939. Spring of '39. He hit a sort of a change of pace, like it was a slow ball. He pulled it hard. It was just

a fair ball way down the right-Stadium line." Bill Nowlin, *521 - The Story of Ted Williams' Home Runs* (Cambridge, Massachusetts: Rounder Books, 2013), 7.

70   Burt Whitman, "Sox Explode, 14-6, Then Tumble, 8-5," *Boston Herald*, June 18, 1941: 26.

71   James C. O'Leary, "Red Sox Win, 14-6; Lose, 8-5," *Boston Globe*, June 18, 1941: 21.

72   Whitman, "Sox Explode, 14-6, Then Tumble, 8-5."

73   "Bob Dunbar's Comment," *Boston Herald*, September 1, 1941: 32.

74   Burt Whitman, "Ted's Homer Gives Sox Split," *Boston Herald*, September 1, 1941: 33.

75   Whitman, "Ted's Homer Gives Sox Split."

76   Whitman, "Ted's Homer Gives Sox Split."

77   We say "game days" because there was one game in the stretch when he did not homer – the second game of the August 31 doubleheader. One might argue that part of the reason he did not homer is that he was walked three times. His batting average dipped from .408 to .407, but his on-base percentage increased from .549 to .550.

78   Hy Hurwitz, "Ted Lifts Hit Mark to .401 Before 22,577 Sox Fans," *Boston Globe*, September 2, 1941: 1, 4. The *Boston Herald* dubbed it a "wind-aided sock." See Burt Whitman, "Williams Wallops 3 Homers as Sox Win Two," *Boston Herald*, September 2, 1941: 1, 14.

79   Bill Nowlin, *521 – The Story of Ted Williams' Home Runs*, 61.

80   Whitman, "Williams Wallops 3 Homers as Sox Win Two."

81   Hurwitz, "Ted Lifts Hit Mark to .401 Before 22,577 Sox Fans,"

82   Hurwitz, "Ted Lifts Hit Mark to .402 Before 22,577 Sox Fans." The ball landed "in the sixth row of the center-field stands." See "8 Pitchers Fail to Halt Boston Bats," *Washington Post*, September 2, 1941: 20.

83   Ben Bradlee, Jr. *The Kid: The Immortal Life of Ted Williams* (New York: Little, Brown, 2013), 196.

84   Ted Williams with John Underwood, *My Turn at Bat*, 87.

85   Ed Rumill, "Ted Williams Writes Fictional Finish to Memorable Farewell at Fens: Red Sox Star Hits Game Winning Homer," *Christian Science Monitor*, May 1, 1952: 14.

86   Ted Williams and John Underwood, *The Science of Hitting*, 33.

87   J.G. Taylor Spink, "That Toe-Tingling Thump by Ted the Terror," *The Sporting News*, July 17, 1941: 4.

88   See also Leigh Montville, *Ted Williams*, 84-86.

89   Marc Lancaster, "Listen, You Lug...," in Scott Ferkovich, ed., *Tigers by the Tale: Great Games at Michigan and Trumbull* (Phoenix: SABR, 2016), 70.

90   Ted Williams with David Pietrusza, *My Life in Pictures*, 42.
91   Ted Williams with John Underwood, *My Turn at Bat,* 89.
92   J.G. Taylor Spink, "That Toe-Tingling Thump by Ted the
        Terror."
93   J.G. Taylor Spink, "That Toe-Tingling Thump by Ted the
        Terror."
94   "All-Star Game Does Baseball Proud," *The Sporting News*, July
        17, 1941: 4.
95   Williams later also hit homers # 177, 187, and 195 off Muncrief.
96   Burt Whitman, "Tex Hughson Gives 2 Hits in 4-2 Victory,"
        Boston Herald, May 17, 1942: 39, 40.
97   Whitman, "Tex Hughson Gives 2 Hits in 4-2 Victory."
98   Harold Kaese, "Hughson Allows Only Two Hits," *Boston Globe*,
        May 17, 1942: B24.
99   Arthur Sampson, "Sox Make Merry in Philadelphia, 14-2,"
        Boston Herald, May 30, 1942: 9.
100   Melville Webb, "Hughson Pitches A Swell Ball Game," *Boston
        Globe*, May 30, 1942: 8.
101   Pesky was on his way to 205 base hits in his rookie season,
        leading both leagues. He then lost the next three seasons to
        World War II, return to record two more 200-hit seasons in
        1946 (208) and 1947 (207). For more on his extraordinary
        start, see Bill Nowlin, *Mr. Red Sox: The Johnny Pesky Story*
        (Cambridge, Massachusetts: Rounder Books, 2004).
102   Webb, "Hughson Pitches A Swell Ball Game."
103   Leo Macdonell, "3 Red Sox Combine to Beat Tigers, 1 to 0,"
        Detroit Times, June 25, 1942: 25. The *Boston Globe*'s Melville
        Webb, wrote, "Just as the ball came down, he placed one hand
        on top of the little barrier...Dom's timing was perfect. He pulled
        down the ball with his gloved hand at full reach above his head.
        It was one corking bit of work." See "Ted Williams'17th Homer
        wins 1-0," *Boston Globe*, June 25, 1942: 21. The account in the
        Boston Herald said DiMaggio grabbed onto the netting and
        pulled himself up as much as four or five feet to catch the ball.
104   Burt Whitman, "Sox Win on Williams Homer," *Boston Herald*,
        June 25, 1942: 12.
105   Macdonell, "3 Red Sox Combine to Beat Tigers, 1 to 0."
106   Whitman, "Sox Win on Williams Homer."
107   The 12 homers Williams hit off Trucks spanned career home
        run #108 (this one) to home run #444 on July 16, 1957, more
        than 15 years later and also a one-run homer. The 12: 108, 115,
        146, 174, 189, 226, 236, 243, 320, 342, 437, and 444. Five of
        the 12 were one-run homers, five were two-run homers, and
        two were three-run homers. Four of them were game-winners,

#174 (May 19, 1947), #189 (August 2, 1947), and #243 (July 16, 1949) being the others.

108   Ralph Wheeler, "Hughson Cops 15th as Nats Bow, 2-1, 7-6," *Boston Herald*, August 16, 1942: 29.

109   Shirley Povich, "Nats' Streak Halted as Bosox Win Two," *Washington Post,* August 16, 1942: SP1.

110   Gerry Moore, "Williams, Finney Spark Sox Double Win," *Boston Globe*, August 16, 1942: A22.

111   Spence was 5-for-8 in the doubleheader.

112   Moore, "Williams, Finney Spark Sox Double Win."

113   Moore, "Williams, Finney Spark Sox Double Win."

114   He had been 5-3 in 1941. Hughson's ERA in 1942 was 2.59.

115   Burt Whitman, "Williams' 30th Homer Erases Athletics, 8-7," *Boston Herald*, September 7, 1942: 26.

116   He came into the game with a 2.36 earned run average. He had relieved earlier in the year but joined the starting rotation on August 6 and won every one of his six starts, two of them shutouts. Ross was 5-5 with a 4.68 ERA.

117   Burt Whitman, "Hose Win Pairs' Ted Hits No. 32," *Boston Herald*, September 14, 1942: 13.

118   His name was "Iron Lung" Burke and he was from Toledo. Williams laughed at some of the antics and after his home run, Williams "made an elaborate bow and doffed his cap to the balcony hecklers as he crossed the plate." Edgar Munzel, "Sox Drop Pair to Boston, 6-1, 5-0," *Chicago Sun*, September 14, 1942: 15, 17.

119   Fred Knight, "Freak Accidents Enliven Red Sox Week-end Games," *Boston Traveler*, September 14, 1942: 25. Newman's cheek was cut and he had to go to Mercy Hospital for examination. The *Boston Traveler* said he lost two teeth.

120   The author often vents that the 1942 A.L. MVP award went to New York's Joe Gordon, who had half as many homers (18), drove in 34 fewer runs, and hit for an average that was 34 points lower with an on-base percentage that was 90 points lower. Gordon led the league in only two categories in 1942: strikeouts (95) and grounding into double plays (22). And he committed 28 errors. This season was one of several in which Williams had more homers (37) than strikeouts (27).

121   Leigh Montville, *Ted Williams*, 124.

122   Melville Webb, "Williams' Homer in 10th Inning Wins for Sox, 5-4," *Boston Globe*, May 3, 1946: 1, 16.

123   Burt Whitman, "Williams Homer in 10th Wins 5-4," *Boston Herald*, May 3, 1946: 1, 31.

124   Arthur Sampson, "Routed Tigers Sing Praises of Red Sox," *Boston Herald*, May 3, 1946: 31. Ted could return home and

nurse his cold. Whitman wrote, "That clutch homer was the best self-administered cold medicine that Williams could have." Ben Bradlee Jr. says that John F. Kennedy was at the game, age 28 and running for Congress. Kennedy had reportedly lost a bet, saying that Williams would not homer at the time he did. See Ben Bradlee Jr., *The Kid: The Immortal Life of Ted Williams*, 253.

125   Burt Whitman, "Ted Homers in 12th, Sox Top Indians, 7-4," *Boston Herald*, May 23, 1946: 15.

126   Alex Zirin, "Williams' 2-Run Homer in 12th Beats Tribe, 7-4; Harder is Injured," *Cleveland Plain Dealer*, May 23, 1946: 18.

127   Hy Hurwitz, "Williams Belts Homer in 12th, Sox Win, 7-4," *Boston Globe*, May 23, 1946: 1, 10.

128   Whitman, "Ted Homers in 12th, Sox Top Indians, 7-4."

129   Burt Whitman, "Sox Twin Wins, 11-1, 9-4, Over Nats Boost Lead," *Boston Herald*, July 8, 1946: 1, 12. The Red Sox won the second game, 9-4. DiMaggio had three hits and two RBIs in the first game and five hits on the day. Rudy York also had a five-hit day and drove in three in the opener. Doerr had two RBIs.

130   Vernon had been named to the American League starting lineup for the All-Star Game – as had Pesky, Williams, DiMaggio, and Doerr – later immortalized as "The Teammates" by a David Halberstam book of that name and also a statue outside Fenway Park.

131   Shirley Povich, "28,961 See Nats Routed By Red Sox, 11-1 and 9-4," *Washington Post*, July 8, 1946: 1, 18. Roger Birtwell of the *Boston Globe* counted three of the walks as intentional. It might be difficult to know what aggravated Williams more – the two errors he'd made or being walked and walked. "The Senators got Williams out only once in each game," wrote Roger Birtwell, on both occasions by a grounder to Vernon. Roger Birtwell, "Williams Belts No 23, Sox Win Two to Increase Lead," *Boston Globe*, July 8, 1946: 1, 4.

132   Burt Whitman, "Williams Pounds Out Three Home Runs, Sox Win, 11-10, 6-4, Lead By 11 Games," *Boston Herald*, July 15, 1946: 1,11. Gromek gave up six home runs to Ted Williams over the course of their overlapping careers. He also surrendered homers #155, 205, 263, 437, and 354. Gromek finished the 1946 season with a 5 -15 record.

133   At the time, the visitors' bullpen was the one that extended to center field and the Red Sox bullpen was the one closest to the right-field grandstand.

134   Gerry Moore, "Sox Beat Indians Twice to Take 11-Game Lead," *Boston Globe*, July 15, 1946: 1, 6.

135   This is the foul pole known in later years as the Pesky Pole. The sports page cartoon on page 11 in the July 15 *Boston Herald* shows the locations of the three home runs, as does the front-page cartoon by Gene Mack in the *Boston Globe.*

136   Hitting three homers in a game at Fenway had been done once before, but by a visiting player – Ken Keltner, on May 25, 1939.

137   Jim Prime and Bill Nowlin, *Ted Williams: The Pursuit of Perfection*, 119.

138   On both counts, see Ben Bradlee Jr., *The Kid: The Immortal Life of Ted Williams*, 258, 265.

139   The Red Sox starter had quite a first couple of years in the big leagues. In 1945, he was 21-5 with five shutouts. He won every one of his first seven starts, embracing three shutouts during that stretch. He was 8-0 before he lost a game, and he lost that one in part because his team only produced two runs. In 1946, he got off to an even better start, going to 10-0 before losing his first game. Among those 10 wins were four shutouts. He was 16-4 with a 2.86 ERA coming into this game.

140   For the years 1932 through 1946, the Indians played some of their home games at League Park, but the ones that looked likely to draw larger crowds were played at Cleveland Stadium, which had a much larger capacity.

141   In this first postwar year, cities that tried to maintain darkness for fear of enemy air raids removed any such restrictions. Some parks, such as Fenway Park in Boston, installed lighting for the first time and began to hold their first night games. The Red Sox played their first home night game the following year on July 13, 1947. This game was the 12th the Red Sox played under the lights. Some of the games had attracted very large crowds – the July 2 night game at Yankee Stadium had drawn 68,617 and the July 23 game at Comiskey Park was played before 49,376.

142   Alex Zirin, "Ferriss Shuts Out Indians with Three Hits to Snare 17th Victory, 4 to 0," *Cleveland Plain Dealer*, July 31, 1946: 14.

143   Burt Whitman, "Sox Blank Indians, 4-0, As Ted Hits 28th Homer," *Boston Herald*, July 31, 1946: 1, 11.

144   Gerry Moore, "Williams, Russell Homer As Ferriss Wins 17th, 4-0," *Boston Globe*, July 31, 1946: 1, 16.

145   Moore, "Williams, Russell Homer As Ferriss Wins 17th, 4-0."

146   Whitman, "Sox Blank Indians, 4-0, As Ted Hits 28th Homer."

147   So began the account of Ted Williams's 165th career home run in Bill Nowlin, *521 - The Story of Ted Williams' Home Runs*, 108.

148   Hy Hurwitz, "Weird Indian Defense Finally Boomerangs to Give Sox Pennant," *Boston Globe,* September 14, 1946: 2.

149   This paragraph comes in its entirety from Bill Nowlin, *521:
       The Story of Ted Williams' Home Runs,* with permission.
       Heilmann's advice had come two days earlier. Heilmann, a
       local broadcaster in Detroit at the time, sat on the bench with
       Williams before the game and told him he ought to be able to
       hit .400 again (as Heilmann had done himself in 1923) if he'd
       consistently bunt toward third base whenever they pulled the
       shift on him. "You can bunt yourself into leading the league
       in hitting…What Ty Cobb would do with that sort of defense
       would be to get 4-for-4 every game." See Burt Whitman,
       "Tigers Clout Ferriss, Check Sox 7-3," *Boston Herald,*
       September 12, 1946: 15.
150   Alex Zirin, "Red Sox Nail First Flag in 28 Years, *Plain Dealer,*
       September 14, 1946: 11.
151   Embree was sacrificed to second, then took third base when
       Seerey singled to right field. Embree might have scored the
       tying run, but wisely was held as Red Sox right fielder Tom
       McBride "made a perfect relay to the plate." See Zirin.
152   Ed Linn, *Hitter: The Life and Turmoils of Ted Williams* (New
       York: Harcourt & Brace, 2003), 212.
153   Ted Williams with John Underwood, *My Turn At Bat*, 111.
154   The pennant was the first one the Red Sox had won in 28 years.
       It was manager Joe Cronin's second, though. He had won one
       with the Washington Senators in 1933.
155   See, for instance, Leigh Montville, *Ted Williams*, 126.
156   Red Smith, "Kid's Bunt Bigger Thrill for Spectators Than York's
       Wallop," *Boston Globe*, October 10, 1946: 22.
157   The dropoff was most dramatic for Boo Ferriss, who had won
       more than 20 games in 1945 and 1946 but only 12 in 1947,
       due to a shoulder injury. Hughson, another two-time 20-game
       winner, required orthopedic surgery before the season was
       done.
158   Hy Hurwitz, "Sox Win Third," *Boston Globe*, April 19, 1947: 1,
       8.
159   Arthur Sampson, "Ferriss Rules A's, 9-3," *Boston Herald*, April
       19, 1947: 11.
160   Hurwitz, "Sox Win Third."
161   Sampson, "Ferriss Rules A's, 9-3." Hy Hurwitz wrote it was "off
       the fence in left center."
162   Hurwitz, "Sox Win Third."
163   Hy Hurwitz, "Williams' Homers Tie Game in Ninth, Win It in
       11th, 6-5," *Boston Globe*, May 7, 1947: 1, 18.
164   It was early in the season. The hosting St. Louis Browns were
       6-9; the visiting Boston Red Sox were 8-8. Kramer had won
       half of the Browns' victories to date; he was already 3-0.

165   J. Roy Stockton, "Browns Turn On Lights Tonight, But There'll
        Be No Williams with A's," *St. Louis Post-Dispatch*, May 7,
        1947: 20.
166   Hurwitz, "Sox Win Third."
167   Hurwitz, "Sox Win Third." The *Herald* writer said, "We could
        see it bound up to the third story of a house on the other side of
        the boulevard, and conservative estimates of its penetration, on
        level ground, would be 475 feet." See Burt Whitman, "Williams
        2 Homers Win, 6-5," *Boston Herald*, May 7, 1947: 1, 29.
168   Stockton, "Browns Turn On Lights Tonight, But There'll Be No
        Williams with A's."
169   Melville Webb, "Williams' Grand Slam Clout Third of Career
        at Fenway; Dorish Coasts to 12-7 Win," *Boston Globe*, May 17,
        1947: 6.
170   Dent McSkiming, "Browns Bow to Red Sox, 12-7; Williams
        Wallops Grand Slam Homer," *St. Louis Post-Dispatch*, May 16,
        1947: 30.
171   Doerr drove in three runs without a base hit, on three sacrifice
        flies. He also made two putouts and had 10 assists.
172   Melville Webb, "Williams' Grand Slam Clout Third of Career
        at Fenway; Dorish Coasts to 12-7 Win," *Boston Globe*, May 17,
        1947: 6.
173   Webb, "Williams' Grand Slam Clout Third of Career at Fenway;
        Dorish Coasts to 12-7 Win." Burt Whitman agreed on the
        distance and location: "more than 400 feet before falling in the
        10th row, or thereabouts, of the very last section of the right-
        field grandstand." See Burt Whitman, "Ted Grand Slams As Sox
        Win," *Boston Herald*, May 17, 1947: 11. Vic Johnson's sports
        page cartoon in the *Herald* depicted it landing in what is today
        Section 1, and it was 11-0, Red Sox. See Vic Johnson, cartoon
        "Salaam for a Grand Slam," *Boston Herald*, May 17, 1947: 11.
174   "Cronin wanted the boy to have the satisfaction of going all the
        way." Webb, "Williams' Grand Slam Clout Third of Career at
        Fenway; Dorish Coasts to 12-7 Win."
175   Mele had played right and Moses played center in the first
        game, but they switched positions for the second game. Burt
        Whitman, "Red Sox Split on Ted's Merriwell Homer," *Boston
        Herald*, May 20, 1947: 16.
176   Bill Nowlin, *521 - The Story of Ted Williams' Home Runs*,
        116. Burt Whitman wrote, "With the count 3-0, Williams had
        looked to manager Joe Cronin, coaching at third base. There
        was no take sign. Cronin had signaled him to swing if he saw
        a pitch he liked. In came the pitch, "a very fast ball right up off
        Ted's letters. With those eyes of his, he saw it was good, took
        his lethal swing and down into the east wind the ball rifled its

way into the fifth or sixth row of seats in the deep right field
wing of the grandstand." *Herald* sportswriter Whitman added,
"That sock might have landed on top of the grandstand out
there with a favoring west wind. A preposterous statement or
claim? Not so when you recall that in batting practice one day
at Fenway Park, with a favoring wind, Ted hit one onto the
top of the Post Office garage beyond the right field end of the
grandstand." Williams hit 12 home runs off Trucks, the most he
hit off any pitcher. His 12 homers off Trucks were career home
runs 108, 115, 146, 174, 189, 226, 236, 243, 320, 342, 437, and
444. Tagged with the loss in this game, the *Detroit Times* noted
that Trucks had pitched a total of two-thirds of an inning in his
last two appearances and lost both games. He'd started against
Philadelphia on May 16 and was pulled after allowing six runs
while only recording one out. See Leo Macdonell, "Trucks Sets
Mark for Losing 'em Fast," *Detroit Times*, May 20, 1947: 20.

177   Williams had hit homers off Bob Muncrief before – two of them
on August 19, 1941 and a game-winner on May 16, 1942. Two
more followed later in 1947, a two-run homer at Fenway Park
on July 26 and a three-run homer on September 17, also at
Fenway.

178   Harold Kaese, "Browns Pitchers Couldn't Believe Anyone Could
Hit like Williams, Says Heath," *Boston Globe*, March 3, 1948:
21.

179   Ben Bradlee, Jr. *The Kid: The Immortal Life of Ted Williams*,
23.

180   Glen L. Wallar, "Two Red Sox Homers Hand Muncrief Loss,"
St. Louis Globe-Democrat, June 4, 1947: 19.

181   Hy Hurwitz, "Williams, Mele Connect; Dobson Scores 5th Win,"
Boston Globe, June 5, 1947: 18.

182   Burt Whitman, "Braves Trip Cards, 3-1; Red Sox Whip Browns,
5-2," *Boston Herald*, June 5, 1947: 13.

183   Hurwitz, "Williams, Mele Connect; Dobson Scores 5th Win."

184   The year 1947 was the final one of his 22 seasons in the game,
which had started with the Red Sox back in 1924. Despite
being 37 years old, he was drafted into non-combatant military
service for two years during World War II. This was just his
second start of the season; due to an injured knee, he'd only
worked one inning in his previous start, back on May 4.

185   Roger Birtwell, "Galehouse 8-Hitter, Williams' Home Pace
Hose Victory Over Chisox, 7-2," *Boston Globe*, July 17, 1947: 8.

186   Burt Whitman, "Red Sox Ramp, 7-2," *Boston Herald*, July 17,
1947: 19. Aside from the 1939 home run and this one, Williams
had also hit two others off Ruffing, both at Yankee Stadium,
career homer #47 on August 14, 1940 and his next-to-last home

run before leaving the game for three years of Navy service, homer #146 on September 20, 1942.

187   #45 and 45 – July 26, 1940 at Sportsman's Park against the St. Louis Browns

#111 and 112 – July 26, 1942 at Sportsman's Park against the St. Louis Browns

#186 and 187 – July 26, 1947 against the St. Louis Browns, but at Boston's Fenway Park (the first of the two was a game-winning home run)

#313 – July 26, 1951 – against the Chicago White Sox at Fenway Park

#382 – July 26, 1955 – against the Cleveland Indians at Fenway Park

#403 – July 26, 1956 – against the Kansas City Athletics at Municipal Stadium (the only other July 26 home run that was a game-winner)

#490 – July 26, 1959 - against the Kansas City Athletics at Municipal Stadium.

One notes that Williams couldn't have hit any more home runs against the Browns after 1953 because the franchise had relocated and become the Baltimore Orioles. He couldn't have hit any against the Kansas City Athletics before 1955 because the Athletics were based in Philadelphia through that season. He couldn't have hit any in 1943, 1944, 1945, 1952, or 1953 because he was in military service or (in 1953) just returning from same. He couldn't have hit any in 1948 because the Red Sox didn't play a game on July 26. He couldn't hit any in 1950 because he had broken his elbow in the All-Star Game and didn't play any regular-season games at all from July 10 through September 6. He couldn't have hit any in 1954 because the Red Sox didn't play a game on July 26.

188   Burt Whitman, "Red Sox Bombard Browns, 12-1," *Boston Herald*, July 27, 1947: 42.

189   Whitman, "Red Sox Bombard Browns, 12-1."

190   This was also his third home run off Fannin in an eight-day stretch. He'd driven in five of the runs the Red Sox had scored in the July 18 game, with two runs off Fannin in that game.

191   Jack Barry, "Williams Belts Two More as Sox Picnic, 12-1," *Boston Globe*, July 27, 1947: C26.

192   It was the second of the six homers the Browns pitcher teed up for him. Williams had his first game-winner off him on May 16, 1942.

193   Glen L. Waller, "Bosox Beast Browns, 12-1; Williams Hits 2 Homers," *St. Louis Globe-Democrat*, July 27, 1947: 1E.

194   He received both a one-ton Chevrolet truck and a tractor to be delivered to his ranch in Oregon, a Cadillac, a radio, clock, barometer, a red leather chair with ottoman, an outboard motor, a juke box, an electric blanket, a $2,500 mink stole for his wife Monica Doerr and a few live mink for their ranch. A dozen other gifts are listed, and 5-year-old son Donnie got a bicycle, a wagon, an electric train set, and more. Red Sox owner Tom Yawkey presented him the promise of a power lighting plant for the ranch, which lacked any public utilities. See "Santa Visits Doerr at Fenway," *Boston Herald*, August 3, 1947: 63.

195   Harold Kaese, "Boston Infielder Given $25,000 in Presents, Including Live Mink," *Boston Globe*, August 3, 1947: 1, 28.

196   Jack Barry, "Williams' Two-Run Homer Sets Back Tiger, 2 to 1," *Boston Globe*, August 3, 1947: 28.

197   Burt Whitman, "Sox Win on Ted's Homer to Climax Doerr Night," *Boston Herald*, August 3, 1947: 1, 33.

198   Ultimately, Ted Williams hit 12 home runs off Virgil Trucks, more than off any other pitcher. Of his 521 home runs, he hit these home runs off Trucks: 108, 115, 146, 174, 189, 226, 236, 243, 320, 342, 437, and 444.This one was #189. Four of them were game winners. Williams also hit four game-winners off Pedro Ramos.

199   Doerr said Trucks had given him something for Doerr Night, too: "He gave me some good pitches, but I couldn't do anything with them." See Kaese, "Boston Infielder Given $25,000 in Presents, Including Live Mink," 28.

200   Leo Macdonell, "Red Sox Beat Tigers in Night Game, 2-1," *Detroit Times*, August 3, 1947: C2-1.

201   The Red Sox were 12 ½ games behind the New York Yankees and the Tigers were 13 games behind. The Athletics were one game behind the Tigers and the Indians half a game behind the Athletics. The Red Sox were due to play back-to-back twin bills on the 26th and 27th at Briggs Stadium. Detroit won the first game, 12-1, a first-inning Ted Williams sacrifice fly scoring the only Red Sox run. After the first inning, no Red Sox runner got past second base. The second game on the 27th was a makeup for a rained-out game.

202   Burt Whitman, "Hose Break Even, Keep Second Place," *Boston Herald*, August 27, 1947: 15.

203   Leo Macdonell, "Tigers Get into 2d, But Stay is Brief," *Detroit Times*, August 27,1947: 22-C.

204   Roger Birtwell, "Red Sox Battered in Opener, 12-1; Tex Victor in 2d, 9-1; Ted Homers," *Boston Globe*, August 27, 1947: 20.

205 Birtwell, "Red Sox Battered in Opener, 12-1; Tex Victor in 2d, 9-1; Ted Homers."

206 No one had a shot at first place; the Tigers were 13 games behind the New York Yankees.

207 Walter Haight, "Bosox Pounds Bats, 8 to 1," *Washington Post*, September 28, 1947: C1.

208 Haight, "Bosox Pounds Bats, 8 to 1."

209 "Tribe Tops Brooks, 2-1; Red Sox Win, 8-1," *Boston Herald*, September 28, 1947: 63.

210 During the game, the Red Sox were watching the scoreboard and saw the Tigers beat the Indians. The Tigers won their final two games (in fact, they ended the season winning their final five games) and held on to second place.

211 Williams hit five home runs off Walt Masterson, dating back to 1939 – career homers #6, 42, 197, 218, and 402.

212 He was 5-6 before this game, a future Hall of Fame pitcher who was the only pitcher on the Indians staff with a losing record.

213 Harry Jones, "Red Sox Hand Feller Fifth Setback in Row, Defeat Indians, 7-4," *Cleveland Plain Dealer*, June 17, 1948: 20.

214 Burt Whitman, "Williams' Four Hits Pace Sox, 7 to 4," *Boston Herald*, June 17, 1948: 33.

215 Campbell. The *Herald*'s Burt Whitman pointed out that Dobson actually had two strikes on each of the three batters before walking him.

216 Jones, "Red Sox Hand Feller Fifth Setback in Row, Defeat Indians, 7-4."

217 "Williams Clouts Homer to Help Red Sox Win, 10-5," *San Diego Union*, August 28, 1948: 10. Henry McKenna's article clarified it was the right-center bleachers. Henry McKenna, "Hose Erupt, 10-5, Add to Lead; Braves Bow to Cubs in 9th, 1-0," *Boston Herald*, August 28, 1948: 1. Hurwitz's story in the *Globe* said it landed behind the Chicago bullpen. Ted had come close to hitting a grand slam in the second inning but White Sox center fielder Dave Philley backed up to the Boston bullpen and caught the ball. His sixth-inning homer reached the third row of the bleachers, comfortably coming down on the other side of the Chicago bullpen. Frank Bell of Needham was one of many who scrambled for the souvenir; he came out with some scrapes that had to be treated by team doctor Ralph McCarthy, and he didn't even get the ball to show for his effort. See Hy Hurwitz, "Yanks, Indians Split, Sox Lead by 1 Game," *Boston Globe*, August 28, 1948: 4.

218 Irving Vaughan, "Sox Power Only Half As Good As Boston," *Chicago Tribune*, August 28, 1948: A2.

219   Burt Whitman, "Browns Pummeled, 10-2, Then Come Back, 12-4," *Boston Herald*, August 30, 1948: 1, 13.

220   Hy Hurwitz, "Doerr Out Indefinitely as Sox Split, Retain 1 1/2-Game Lead: Dobson Coasts to 14th, 10-2, Then Browns Retaliate, 12-4," *Boston Globe*, August 30, 1948: 4. Doerr pulled a muscle late in the second game. In fact, he was back two days later and didn't miss a game. Gene Mack's sports page cartoon in the *Boston Globe* showed Williams's home run going over the bullpen and landing several rows into the seats, with Tebbetts's home run maybe five feet fair inside the left-field foul pole. See Gene Mack, cartoon, "Oh Well, No Ground Lost," *Boston Globe*, August 30, 1948: 4.

221   The Boston Braves had already clinched. Should the Red Sox win the American League pennant, the two teams located about a mile apart from each other would go head-to-head in the World Series.

222   On September 25, Kramer had beaten New York at Yankee Stadium, 7-2 and he was 9-1 in games at Fenway Park.

223   Burt Whitman, "Hose Must Win, Indians Lose to Bring A L Flag Tie," *Boston Herald*, October 3, 1948: 27.

224   John Drebinger, "Bombers Bow, 5-1," *New York Times*, October 3, 1948: S1. Williams' home run was only his second in six weeks. He'd hit one on August 29, but the only one before this one was on September 19. He'd been battling a heavy cold.

225   Hy Hurwitz, "Sox Can Still Win Flag," *Boston Globe*, October 3, 1948: C1.

226   Jack Hand, "Kramer Makes It 5 Over New York," *Cleveland Plain Dealer*, October 3, 1948: C1, 3.

227   Dave Heller, ed., *Facing Ted Williams* (New York: Sports Publishing, 2013), 67.

228   Bill Nowlin, *521 – The Story of Ted Williams' Home Runs*, 141.

229   Kinder was a 34-year-old right-hander in his fourth season. Righty Pieretti, a native of Lucca, Italy who had grown up in San Francisco, was in his fifth season. Kinder finished the 1949 season with a record of 23-6, the best winning percentage in the major leagues. His six shutouts also led both leagues.

230   Irving Vaughan, "White Sox Lose, 7-4," *Chicago Tribune*, May 19, 1949: A1. The spelling of Scala's first name was Vaughan's. His first name was Gerard. Clif Keane's *Boston Globe* account said that Jerry Scala had "misplayed" the ball. Clif Keane, "Williams, Doerr Hit Home Runs; Kinder Wins 3rd," *Boston Globe*, May 19, 1949: 1.

231   Will Cloney, "Red Sox Triumph, 7-4," *Boston Herald*, May 19, 1949: 37.

232   Vaughan. The "right-field grandstand," wrote Keane. See "Williams, Doerr Hit Home Runs; Kinder Wins 3rd."

233   Cloney, "Red Sox Triumph, 7-4."

234   Tebbetts talked about pitching to Zernial: "Kinder had him struck out in the fifth, and I dropped the foul tip. Then he got an inside pitch and hit a three-run homer. Kinder got the ball a little more over the middle of the plate in the ninth and he hit that long double to center for another run." Keane, "Williams, Doerr Hit Home Runs; Kinder Wins 3rd."

235   The other two games in which Williams provided the winning run with a homer were against the White Sox on May 18 and against the Athletics on May 30. This Saturday afternoon game began with both Boston and Washington 5½ games behind the Yankees in league standings. The Red Sox were percentage points ahead of the Senators.

236   Shirley Povich, "Bosox Halts Griffs with Bases Full," *Washington Post*, May 29, 1949: C1.

237   A hospital visit showed that no bones had been broken. He had a concussion and was kept overnight. See Jack Barry, "Sox Climb to 2d Place; Braves Regain N.L. Top," *Boston Globe*, May 29, 1949: 1, 14.

238   Barry, "Sox Climb to 2d Place; Braves Regain N.L. Top."

239   After the 1947 season, Hughson had orthopedic surgery to address ongoing numbness in his right shoulder. He was never again the dominant pitcher he had been. He hadn't worked that much in 1948 – only 19 1/3 innings – and only in relief. He'd had a couple of starts in April and May 1949, but was otherwise a reliever for the rest of the year, his last year in baseball, ending the season with a 5.33 ERA. For a contemporaneous look at Hughson's situation, see Will Cloney, "Tex Again Craving for Starting Role," *Boston Herald*, May 29, 1949: 13, 14.

240   Arthur Sampson, "Sox, Braves Win on Homers," *Boston Herald*, May 29, 1949: 13.

241   With one out, Sherry Robertson doubled down the right-field line, his third hit. Clyde Vollmer hit a ball that dropped in amongst three fielders, and he made a double out of it, but Robertson was uncertain whether or not Al Zarilla would catch it, and had to hold at third base. Eddie Robinson then walked, loading the bases with just one out. A deep fly ball would have tied the game. Hughson then struck out Eddie Yost on four pitches and got Sam Dente to ground out to Goodman, Hughson covering first base and taking the throw for the final out.

242   Right fielder Al Zarilla drove in six of the 10 Red Sox runs, a grand slam accounting for four of the six runs. One unusual feature of the first game was that no one from either team struck out.

243   For Parnell, this was his second full year in the majors. He had enjoyed a 15-8 season in 1948, with a 3.14 earned run average. He was off to an excellent start in 1949, and was already 6-1 with an ERA of 1.75. He'd started the season with back-to-back shutouts. Every one of his previous eight starts had been a complete game. The one game he lost was a 4-3 defeat at the hands of the reigning world champion Cleveland Indians, in Cleveland, on May 7 – a game he took into the 12th inning before losing by the one run. This was the same Indians team which had beaten the 1948 Red Sox in a single-game playoff that determined that year's American League pennant winner.

244   Jack Barry, "Ted's Homer Gives Sox Sweep," *Boston Globe*, May 31, 1949: 16.

245   Arthur Sampson, "Williams and Zarilla Jolt A's; Phillies Keep Tribe in N.L. Tie," *Boston Herald*, May 31, 1949: 1, 8.

246   Bill Cunningham, "Red Sox Must Fight for Top," *Boston Herald*, May 31, 1949: 6. Cunningham said Williams swung on a 3-2 count, but all other accounts, such as Sampson's game story and the Associated Press story, say that Williams swung at the first pitch. Sampson's game story said, "The towering drive stayed up long enough to give the fans a thrill. When it came down it was well over the screen in front of the Sox bullpen." Sampson, "Williams and Zarilla Jolt A's; Phillies Keep Tribe in N.L. Tie."

247   Scheib later talked about the at-bat. "I pitched him curveballs low and inside and got him out three times at bat. A story later was that he told the guys on the bench, if I started him again on curveballs, he would hit a home run...and he did. It beat me in the ball game." See Heller, *Facing Ted Williams*, 177, 178.

248   Will Cloney, "Teddy Calls Winning Clout," *Boston Herald*, May 31, 1949: 8.

249   Ed Rumill, "Ted Calls the Turn on Killing Curve," *Christian Science Monitor*, May 31, 1949: 16. (Emphasis added.) Parnell threw 27 complete games in 1949, leading both the American and National Leagues. His 25 wins also led both leagues. He was 25-7, and his 2.77 ERA led the American League.

250   Kinder, who had broken into the majors at age 31 with the Browns and attracted the nickname "Old Folks," had started as a reliever and became one again (in both 1951 and 1953 he led the league in appearances). In 1949, he finished with a 23-7 record, leading both leagues in winning percentage. He did a

fine job in this game, holding his former team to just five hits while only walking one.

251 A left-hander, he'd also broken into the majors with the Browns at age 31. His nickname was "Specs" or "Professor," though, due to the eyeglasses he wore. He was 2-2 with a 4.08 ERA before the game. Dom DiMaggio singled to center field. Pesky got his first hit, a double to right field.

252 Jack Barry, "Ted Belts Two Homers, Goodman Gets Five Hits in Mayhem at Fenway," *Boston Globe*, June 25, 1949: 4.

253 *St. Louis Globe-Democrat* sportswriter Harry Mittauer began his article writing, "Manager Zach Taylor wasn't kidding the other day when he said that he was hard-pressed for pitchers." Harry Mittauer, "Bosox Sticks Browns with 21-2 Loss," *St. Louis Globe-Democrat*, June 25, 1949: 13.

254 *Boston Post*, as quoted in Bill Nowlin, *521 – The Story of Ted Williams' Home Runs,* 150.

255 After the game, Red Sox manager Joe McCarthy was asked why he hadn't taken out some of the regulars to give them a breather. His response, in part, was: "Heck, they don't want to come out when they're hitting. Did you ever see any ball player that did?" See Barry, "Ted Belts Two Homers, Goodman Gets Five Hits in Mayhem at Fenway."

256 Ted Williams and John Underwood, *The Science of Hitting,* 27.

257 The Red Sox were 9 ½ games behind the first-place New York Yankees. The Tigers were only two games behind the Red Sox, in fifth place. At this juncture, the Red Sox probably wouldn't have believed they would eliminate that nearly 10-game gap and end the season tied with the Yankees for first place.

258 Jack Barry, "Four Red Sox Homers Rip Tigers as Parnell Wins 12th, 11-1," *Boston Globe*, July 17, 1949: B-31.

259 Leo Macdonell, "Bosox Belt 4 Homers, Blast Tigers, 11-1," *Detroit Times*, July 17, 1949: C-1.

260 Parnell led the American and National leagues with 27 complete games in 1949.

261 *Boston Post*, quoted in Bill Nowlin, *521 – The Story of Ted Williams' Home Runs,* 151.

262 Will Cloney, "Hose Homers Ruin Tigers," *Boston Herald*, July 17, 1949: 29, 31.

263 It was his third win of the season against Detroit; his career record against the Tigers improved to 8-0. As the season played out, he won 15 of his next 17 decisions and finished with a record of 25-7 (2.77), the best winning percentage in both the American and National Leagues.

264 Jim Prime and Bill Nowlin, *Ted Williams: The Pursuit of Perfection,* 120.

265   Jack Barry, "Sox Beat Yankees, 6-3; Dom Hitless," *Boston Globe*, August 10, 1949: 1, 20.

266   Barry, "Sox Beat Yankees, 6-3; Dom Hitless." He had "parked his 28th homer of the year into the Red Sox bullpen in right-center." Arthur Sampson, "Sox Defeat Yankees, 6-3; Tebbetts, Williams Homer," *Boston Herald*, August 10, 1949: 24.

267   This was the first home run Williams had hit off Raschi. The first homer he hit in 1950 was off Raschi, too, another game-winning homer, on April 19 at Fenway Park. Later that year, he hit two other homers (#292 and 293), both on September 24 at Yankee Stadium. And Williams home run #321 won a third game at Raschi's expense, on September 5, 1951, also at the Stadium.

268   Ed Rumill, "Ellis Kinder Among Top Right-Handers," *Christian Science Monitor*, August 10, 1949: 12.

269   John Drebinger, "Homers by Williams and Tebbetts Sink Bombers for Red Sox, 6 to 3," *New York Times*, August 10, 1949: 28.

270   The next day's column by George C. Carens looked at the end of the streak in detail. See "Dom Went Down with Head Up," *Boston Traveler*, August 10, 1949: 23. Through the 2021 season, this remains the Red Sox record for a player hitting in consecutive games.

271   The Red Sox and Yankees engaged in a single-game playoff at Yankee Stadium on October 2. Red Sox fans would rather not remember the outcome.

272   Kinder was on his way to a 23-6 record that proved the best won/loss percentage in either the American or National League. He started 30 games in the 1949 season and, at age 34, threw 19 complete games. He threw six shutouts, also leading both leagues.

273   Attendance was 13,196. They saw a nicely-pitched game, with only 10 base hits total and no errors. Bases on balls were almost as much of a problem as base hits. Detroit Tigers starter Hal Newhouser walked five Boston batters. Kinder walked three. None of the walks resulted in any runs, though. Each team left five men on base.

274   Detroit hit into four; Boston into three.

275   Hy Hurwitz, "Sox Win, But Yanks Take Two," *Boston Globe*, September 15, 1949: 1, 16.

276   Louis Effrat, "Kinder of Red Sox Takes 20th, 1-0, on Williams's Blow Against Tigers," *New York Times*, September 15, 1949: 36.

277   Williams ended the season with 43 homers and 159 RBIs, leading both leagues in both categories, though tied with teammate Vern Stephens in the runs batted in department.

278   For what it was worth, all in the press box thought it had gone into the screen, too. See Hy Hurwitz, "Sox Win, But Yanks Take Two."

279   Newhouser credited him after the game: "We got the lead-off batter on base in four of the first seven innings and couldn't' score. Boy, when a pitcher throws so a batter grinds the ball into the dirt and grounds into a double play, that's pitching." Will Cloney, "Ted Great Hitter, Says Hal," *Boston Herald*, September 15, 1949: 17. Newhouser was also quoted at length about Williams as a hitter, saying he thought Williams could "hit about .390 or .400 every year if he wanted to" – and explained how.

280   Just the year before, he'd been 18-5 with the best winning percentage in the American League, but he had declined and by 1950 was used more in relief.

281   Hy Hurwitz of the *Boston Globe* wrote, "The scrap and confidence which has been oozing from the Sox since they returned home 10 days ago was never more apparent than yesterday. Twice they came from behind to go ahead." Hy Hurwitz, "Red Sox Defeat Indians 9 to 6 on Ted's Homer; Yanks Lose," *Boston Globe*, September 22, 1949: 1, 22.

282   Arthur Sampson, "Kinder Saves Day," *Boston Herald*, September 22, 1949: 1, 29.

283   The home run was one of six Williams hit off Gromek.

284   Every one of the six Cleveland pitchers gave up at least one base hit. *Cleveland Plain Dealer* writer Harry Jones called it a "tee-off party." Harry Jones, "Williams Clouts 41st to Break Tie," *Cleveland Plain Dealer*, September 22, 1949: 26.

285   Ted Williams with David Pietrusza, *My Life in Pictures*, 73.

286   Ted Williams with John Underwood, *My Turn at Bat,* 159.

287   Dobson had been with the Red Sox since 1941, and in the four postwar years had averaged more than 15 wins a season. Raschi was a native of Western Massachusetts. He had been 21-10 in 1949, his first full season with the Yankees. He had beaten the Red Sox four times, including the single-game playoff for the 1949 pennant.

288   Arthur Sampson, "Sox Win, 6-3; Yanks, 16-7," *Boston Herald*, April 20, 1950: 26. The *Boston Globe* characterized it as "a towering, well-belted blast." See Hy Hurwitz, "Sox Slugged by Yanks, 16-7, After Dobson Hurls 6-3 Win," *Boston Globe*, April 20, 1950: 1, 12.

289   Pesky walked three times and hit two singles, reaching base five times in five plate appearances.

290   John Drebinger," Yanks Chase Kinder and Gain Even Break With Red Sox," *New York Times*, April 20, 1950: 40.

291   Left-hander Billy Pierce, 23, was in his third season and 1-0
        in 1950. He had yet to give up a run in three appearances.
        Dobson, 33, had been with Boston since 1941. He was He was
        2-1, with a 3.38 ERA over his first three appearances in 1950.
292   Hy Hurwitz, "Williams Homer Give Red Sox Victory Over
        White Sox, 5-2," *Boston Globe*, May 6, 1950: 4.
293   Stephens and Ted Williams tied with 159 RBIs apiece, tops in
        both the American and National Leagues. Walt Dropo made
        this third out of the inning. Dropo was 0-for-4 in this game, but
        at year's end he led the two leagues in runs batted in, with 144.
294   John C. Hoffman, "White Sox Do Boston Swoon, Tumble 5-2,"
        Chicago Sun-Times, May 6, 1950: 27.
295   Will Cloney, "Onslow and Cast Outdo Vaudeville," *Boston
        Herald*, May 6, 1950: 6.
296   Edward Burns, "Boston Homers Beat Sox, 5-2," *Chicago
        Tribune*, May 6, 1950: A1.
297   F. C. Matzek, "Stephens', Williams' Drives Give Boston 5-2
        Victory," *Providence Journal*, May 5, 1950: 6.
298   Hoffman wrote that they had "walked everyone but the peanut
        vendors."
299   Matzek, "Stephens', Williams' Drives Give Boston 5-2 Victory."
300   He hit 12 homers in the month of June. This was the year
        he broke his elbow in the All-Star Game. By mid-season, he
        already had 25 home runs and 83 runs batted in. He wasn't
        able to start in another game until September 15. He still
        finished the year with 97 RBIs – just three short of 100 –
        despite only appearing in 89 games. This game was one of an
        astonishing 34 games in which the 1950 Red Sox scored 10 or
        more runs. And that was with Ted Williams missing 65 games.
301   After the game, Luke Appling of the White Sox declared that
        Fenway's left-field wall should be outlawed. "That fence is
        disgraceful. It's all right with the fans if the home team is
        doing it. But it's a bad park and it's why those Red Sox lose the
        pennant when everybody thinks they're a cinch to win. They
        get 61 wins out of 77 games last year and still lose." Clif Keane,
        "Fenway Left Field Fence Should be Outlawed – Appling,"
        Boston Globe, May 7, 1950: C-47.
302   John C. Hoffman, "Bosox' 6 Homers Drub Sox 11-1," *Chicago
        Sun-Times*, May 7, 1950: 82. The wind was cited by more
        than one newspaper as having aided the ball to carry. See, for
        instance, Hy Hurwitz, "2 Tebbetts Clouts Pace 11-1 Victory,"
        Boston Globe, May 7, 1950: C-46.
303   Arthur Sampson, "Hose Slug White Sox, 11-1," *Boston Herald*,
        May 7, 1950: 55.

304   The *Herald*'s Arthur Sampson wrote that the White Sox had at this point lost 41 of their last 48 games at Fenway Park. The *Chicago Sun-Times* correspondent painted a picture: "Boston – This is a place where people eat scrod and baked potato for breakfast, where smut is not permitted to rear its ugly head in literature and the drama and you can see a parade almost any day in the week. It is also a place where the White Sox should never try to play baseball." Hoffman, "Bosox' 6 Homers Drub Sox 11-1."

305   The *Boston Herald* said the ball really took "a freak hop and bounced away toward right field." Arthur Sampson, "Four Sox Homers Blast Tigers, 6-1," *Boston Herald*, May 17, 1950: 16.

306   Kell became the 1949 batting champion, by a ten-thousandth of a point. His final batting average was .3429118 to Ted Williams' .32427561.

307   Sampson, "Four Sox Homers Blast Tigers, 6-1."

308   Leo Macdonell, "Belting of Williams, Stephens Tumbles Tigers from Top Rung," *Detroit Times*, May 17, 1950: 29. The last Boston batter to come to the plate was Stephens. He "made quite a bid for a third homer. Hoot Evers caught his drive a foot from the barrier in left center – 365 feet from the plate." See Hy Hurwitz, "Williams and Stephens Homer Twice as Sox, Dobson Defeat Tigers, 6-1," *Boston Globe*, May 17, 1950: 20.

309   Edgar Hayes, Williams In Assault on Bambino's record," *Detroit Times*, May 17, 1950: 29. This was the year in which Williams broke his elbow in the All-Star Game, squelching what was truly shaping up to be an historic season.

310   Boston's Mel Parnell had won 25 games in 1949. His 2.77 earned run average had been second-best in the American League (to Cleveland's Mike Garcia) and his 27 complete games had also led both the A.L. and N.L.

311   Arthur Sampson, "Indians Bow As Williams Poles No. 13," *Boston Herald*, June 4, 1950: 54.

312   Bearden had had a superb 1948 season, his 2.43 ERA helping lead the Indians through the single-game playoff against the Red Sox for the American League pennant (his 20th win) and through the World Series against the Boston Braves, throwing a shutout in Game Five. He was, frankly, mediocre from 1949 on.

313   Hy Hurwitz, "Red Sox Sweep Indians Series, 11 to 9," *Boston Globe*, June 4, 1950: C46. (Fenway Park used to have a flagpole that was in the field of play in straightway center field, and a little bit to the left.)

314   Birdie Tebbetts lined out to left field. Doerr scored – or thought he had. Umpire Bill McKinley ruled that Doerr had left third

base too early; the ball thrown in to Boudreau was relayed to Al Rosen at third base and Doerr was called out. Parnell flied out to Joe Gordon at second base.

315   Sampson, "Indians Bow As Williams Poles No. 13."

316   Hurwitz, "Red Sox Sweep Indians Series, 11 to 9."

317   George B. Kelleher, "Sox and Braves Score Triumphs, 11-9, 10-6," *Springfield Union* (Springfield, Massachusetts), June 4, 1950: 1B.

318   Harry Jones, "Red Sox Again Tally 6 in 1st; Edge Indians, 11-9," *Cleveland Plain Dealer*, June 4, 1950: 1-B

319   Given the 154-game schedule that major-league teams played at the time, that was a pace that would have seen them score 1,777.99 runs for the season. As it was, they scored 1,027 – the largest total in Red Sox franchise history, even including the 162-game schedule that has been in place since 1961. Of the 29 games the Red Sox played during June 1950, there were 14 games in which one team or another scored 10 or more runs.

320   Clyde Vollmer hit two homers in that game and so did Vern Stephens. Walt Dropo hit one. Vollmer and Stephens each drove in five runs; Dropo and Ted Williams each drove in three.

321   The *Boston Herald* said 10; the *Boston Globe* said a dozen.

322   With the score 20-3 after four, the Red Sox public-address announcer invited the bleacherites to move out of the sun and enter the grandstand. There was plenty of room; attendance for the game was 5,105. F.C. Matzek, "Bosox Rewrite Record Book by Blasting Browns, 29-4," *Providence Journal*, June 9, 1950: 12.

323   Arthur Sampson, "Red Sox Crack Records Galore, Crush Browns, 29-4," *Boston Herald*, June 9, 1950: 34.

324   Hy Hurwitz, "Sox Break 5 Major Records in 29-4 Rout of Browns," *Boston Globe*, June 9, 1950: 36. As compiled by Hurwitz, the five records were:
Runs scored in a game (29), eclipsing the 28 scored in a game by the 1929 St. Louis Cardinals;
Runs batted in, in a game (29); the previous record was 28 by the 1929 St. Louis Cardinals;
Total bases in a game (60), five more than the 1893 Cincinnati Reds had;
Most runs scored in two consecutive games (49); the 1925 Pittsburgh Pirates had 45;
Most hits in two consecutive games (51); the 1922 Pirates had once hit 49.
There were other records broken at the time, enough that the *Boston Traveler* wrote, "Like the atomic bomb, the full results of the Red Sox demolition may not be known for several days.

New records may be popping up the more the statisticians dig into the ruins and come up with new discoveries." John Drohan, "Thunder of Red Sox Bats Echoes in Hurlers' Ears," *Boston Traveler*, June 9, 1950: 34.

325 It was Mack's last season managing the Philadelphia Athletics. He had managed them in every year of the team's existence, 1901 through 1950. Brissie was a 16-game winner the year before, but came into this game with a very disappointing record of 2-11. His ERA was 4.60.

326 Will Cloney, "Three Sox Homers Beat A's, 6-2," *Boston Herald*, June 29, 1950: 36.

327 Hy Hurwitz, "Williams Homer Beats Athletics, 6-2; Red Sox Win Sixth Straight on Road," *Boston Globe*, June 29, 1950: 27.

328 Cloney, "Three Sox Homers Beat A's, 6-2."

329 Arthur Sampson, "Sox Edge Browns, 5-4, Bow, 8-2," *Boston Herald*, May 7, 1951: 7.

330 Sampson, "Sox Edge Browns, 5-4, Bow, 8-2."

331 The phrase was Clif Keane's. See "Widmar Baffles Hose as Mates K.O. Parnell; Boston Strands 16 in Opener," *Boston Globe*, May 7, 1951: 9. The Red Sox stranded 17, including the final one in the 10th. The Browns left 11 men on base. Had it not been for Upton's two errors, resulting in two unearned runs, Sleater might have won the game.

332 For Sleater, 1951 was a rough first full year. He finished with a 1-9 record and with a 5.11 ERA. But he was a big-league pitcher and he fashioned a seven-year career that saw him work in 131 games. Wight pitched for eight different teams in 12 seasons, but it was Kinder who got the win on this May 6, improving to 2-0. The Red Sox improved to 9-8 on the young season. The Browns fell to 4-14. They did win the day's second game, though, and finished the day ahead of the last-place 3-16 Philadelphia Athletics. The second game was 8-2, Browns, Al Widmar out-pitching Mel Parnell.

333 Harold Kaese, "Williams' Big Day Makes Rolfe Prophet," *Boston Globe*, May 11, 1951: 11.

334 Associated Press, "Williams not a Great Hitter in the Opinion of Ty Cobb," *Christian Science Monitor*, May 18, 1951: 9.

335 The game was played before a sparse Ladies Day crowd of 5,934. Even with the ladies present, the total came to 6,977 – the park was about 75% empty.

336 Kaese, "Williams' Big Day Makes Rolfe Prophet."

337 After the game, longtime Boston sportswriter Melville Webb (the "dean of Boston ball writers") recalled how manager Ed Barrow had tried to talk another left-handed Boston slugger into hitting the left field: "'Oh, I can hit to left if I want to,'

growled [Babe] Ruth, 'but I don't want to. But I'll show you
today I can.' By Webbie's memory, Ruth hit slashing doubles
to left his first three times at bat. Convinced that he had shown
Barrow, Ruth then hit a home run – to right." Kaese.

338   Taylor had started his career with the Brooklyn Dodgers
and then spent a couple of years pitching for St. Paul. Late
in September 1950, the Red Sox purchased his contract. He
started two games for them and won them both. In 1951, he lost
his first three decisions and then won a pair.

339   He was a Cuban righty, in his second year, with a record of 1-1
and a very good 2.83 ERA in 27 2/3 innings before this game.
He'd been 1-1 in four games in 1950.

340   The ball had actually bounced off shortstop Sam Dente's chest,
and fans reportedly laughed when it was announced that it was
ruled a base hit. See Herb Heft, "Grand Slam by Williams, 2 Big
Innings Sink Griffs," *Washington Post*, May 28, 1951: 11.

341   Ed Costello, "Williams' Slam Highlights Double Win by Sox,9-
3, 7-1," *Boston Herald*, May 28, 1951: 13. Burton Hawkins of
Washington's *Evening Star* agreed, as did the *Boston Globe*
accounts. See Burton Hawkins, "Nats Meet A's Here Tonight
after 'Escape' from Boston," *Evening Star* (Washington, DC),
May 28, 1951: A-17. The *Washington Post* was out of step with
the other papers, saying he hit it "deep into the right-field
bleachers." See Heft. One way or another, it was a grand slam.

342   Vic Johnson, "Holiday for Strings," (sports page cartoon),
Boston Herald, May 28, 1951: 13.

343   Jack Barry, "Williams' Grand Slam Highlights Sox Double
Victory," *Boston Globe*, May 28, 1951: 6.

344   See Williams' comments in Jack McCarthy, "Ted's Mark
Zooms; Hits to Left Pile Up – Unintentionally," *Boston Herald*,
May 28, 1951: 13.

345   By season's end, the Red Sox had swept 10 times and been
swept five times. They split seven.

346   The Browns' Jim Suchecki was the losing pitcher. Dom
DiMaggio (on a bases-loaded walk) and Bobby Doerr (a solo
home run) each had one RBI. There was one unearned run.
Ted Williams got the other two runs batted in, one on another
bases-loaded walk. He drove in the fifth and ultimately
deciding run on a single in the bottom of the eighth.

347   Joe McHenry, "Williams Paces 5-4, 3-0 Bosox Victories,"
Providence Journal, June 18, 1951: 8. Ted Williams hit three
career home runs off Widmar, all in 1951. This was the first. He
also homered off Widmar on July 16 and September 14.

348   Jack Barry, "Sox Beat Browns, 5-4, 3-0," *Boston Globe*, June
18, 1951: 6. Arthur Sampson wrote that the throw had Williams

beat by several feet. "Sox in Fifth Sweep, Beating Browns, 5-4, 3-0," *Boston Herald*, June 18, 1951: 15.

349   Harry Mitauer, "Browns Choke on Boots, 5-4, then Go Hungry, 3-0," *St. Louis Globe-Democrat*, June 18, 1951: 1B.

350   Hy Hurwitz, "Red Sox Knock Yankees Off Top, 4-2," *Boston Globe*, September 6, 1951: 1, 26.

351   Ed Costello, "Kiely, Red Sox Knock Yankees Off Peak," *Boston Herald*, September 6, 1951: 1, 22.

352   John Drebinger, "Bombers Lose, 4-2, as 58,462 Look On," *New York Times*, September 6, 1951: 40,

353   Hurwitz, "Red Sox Knock Yankees Off Top, 4-2."

354   Costello, "Kiely, Red Sox Knock Yankees Off Peak."

355   The loss cost the Yankees a bit in the standings, but they hosted the Washington Senators for the next four games and won them all, getting themselves back in a tie for first place. They dropped back again but re-tied once more on September 19 and then went 8-2 over their last 10 games, beating Boston in seven of the eight games the two teams played. The Yankees finished strong, five games ahead of the Indians with the Red Sox in third place, but a full 11 games behind due to losing 12 of their last 13 games.

356   Bill Nowlin, *521 – The Story of Ted Williams' Home Runs*, 187. For information on Nieman's background and some of his comments on the game, see Will Cloney, "Home Run Hitting Nieman Studying to Write Sports," *Boston Herald*, September 15, 1951: 5. Nieman had spent most of the year at Triple-A Oklahoma City, where he hit a Texas-League-leading .328 with 10 homers in 409 at-bats. He got his call to the majors and this was his debut, playing left field and batting fifth for Zack Taylor's Browns. He had reported to the Browns that very morning. See also United Press, "Red Sox' 14 Hits Trip Browns, 9-6," *New York Times*, September 15, 1951: 9.

357   Sanford had lasted just one-third of an inning. Sadly for him, the six batters he faced were the last batters he faced in the big leagues.

358   Clif Keane, "Sox Beat Browns, 9-6, 3 Games from Top," *Boston Globe*, September 15, 1951: 1, 4.

359   It was the third home run he'd hit off Widmar that year (the only three he ever hit off him); he had homered at Fenway on June 17 and at Sportsman's Park on July 16. Both had also been two-run homers, and both in the first inning. The June 17 one was a game-winner.

360   It has been done once since, by catcher Keith McDonald over two games in July 2000. In McDonald's case, it was as a pinch-hitter for another St. Louis team, the Cardinals.

His second at-bat was a couple of days later, on July 6, also against the visiting Cincinnati Reds, this time a home run at Busch leading off the bottom of the second inning. Four other players have homered twice in their first game: Bert Campaneris (July 23, 1964), Mark Quinn (September 14, 1999), J.P. Arencibia (August 7, 2010), and Trevor Story (April 4, 2016) are the only others to do so. None of the others hit them in their first two at-bats.

361 Clif Keane, "Browns Rookie Makes Home Run History; Ted Has Tantrum As Ol' Satch Fools Him," *Boston Globe*, September 15, 1951: 4. The *Globe* ran a photo of Nieman with comedian/coach Max Patkin, who had worked in the coaching box for one inning.

362 Keane, "Browns Rookie Makes Home Run History; Ted Has Tantrum As Ol' Satch Fools Him."

363 Will Cloney, "Home Run Hitting Nieman Studying to Write Sports," *Boston Herald*, September 15, 1951: 5.

364 Tom Monahan, "Williams Not Mad at Satchmo, Just at Himself," *Boston Traveler*, September 15, 1951: 5.

365 Keane, "Sox Beat Browns, 9-6, 3 Games from Top"

366 Williams' handwritten notes for the speech may be seen here: https://collection.baseballhall.org/PASTIME/ted-williams-baseball-hall-fame-induction-speech-1966-july-25#page/1/mode/1up

367 Earlier home runs that Williams hit off Trout were homers number #107, 144, 164, 221, and 283.

368 Williams was given a "day" where fans in Boston could say goodbye as he left baseball to re-join the United States Marine Corps. Even though he was turning 34 years old and had a wife and child, he'd been recalled to service because of the shortage of Marine aviators at the time of the Korean War. The full story of Ted Williams' two stints in U.S. military service during both World War II and the Korean War is told in Bill Nowlin, *Ted Williams At War* (Burlington, Massachusetts: Rounder Books, 2007).

369 Ted Williams with David Pietrusza, *My Life in Pictures* (Kingston, New York: Total Sports Illustrated, 2001), 90.

370 Jack Barry, "Ted Says Au Revoir with Game-Winning Homer," *Boston Globe,* May 1, 1952: 8.

371 Joe Cashman, "Ted's Farewell Homer Wins for Red Sox, 5-3," *Boston Record,* May 1, 1952: 25.

372 See photograph accompanying Jack McCarthy, "Auld Lang Syne Affects Happy, Trembling Teddy," *Boston Herald*, May 1, 1952: 22.

373   Ed Rumill, "Ted Williams Writes Fictional Finish to Memorable Farewell at Fens: Red Sox Star Hits Game Winning Homer," *Christian Science Monitor*, May 1, 1952: 14.

374   Rumill, "Ted Williams Writes Fictional Finish to Memorable Farewell at Fens: Red Sox Star Hits Game Winning Homer."

375   Murray Kramer, "Hollywood End Provided by Ted," *Boston Record,* May 1, 1952: 25.

376   Barry, "Ted Says Au Revoir with Game-Winning Homer."

377   Dave Egan, "Ted Undeserving of Fans' Tribute," *Boston Daily Record*, April 30, 1952: 24. Egan often got on Williams' case, a story we need not explore here.

378   Kramer, "Hollywood End Provided by Ted."

379   Ted Williams with John Underwood, *My Turn at Bat,* 175, 176.

380   The mark wasn't equaled until the Los Angeles Dodgers' Mike Marshall obliterated it with a major-league record 13 consecutive games from June 18 through July 3, 1974, a mark matched by Dale Mohorcic of the Texas Rangers from August 6 through 20, 1986.

381   He shut out the St. Louis Browns, 5-0. He lost his next two starts, the Red Sox scoring a total of only two runs in the two games combined. This was his fourth start for manager Lou Boudreau.

382   Piersall had to leave the game after spiking himself on a headfirst slide into second base. Piersall "was cut badly on the right leg yesterday by his own spikes as he tried to stretch a fourth-inning single into a double...His left shoe caught him inside the right thing above the knee, cutting him severely, He was taken to Sancta Maria Hospital for six or seven stitches. Piersall apologized to Ted Williams for making the third out and depriving Williams of an at-bat. Bob Holbrook, "Injured Piersall 'Apologizes' to Ted," *Boston Globe*, August 20, 1953: 1, 6. The number of stitches was reported by the *Boston American*.

383   Policeman Roger Thayer worked in that area and he said it had gone 430 feet; it was described as landing in Row 28. Harold Kaese, "Only 3 Weeks in Uniform and Ted's Ahead of Pitchers," *Boston Globe*, August 20, 1953: 1.

384   Clif Keane, "Piersall Makes Surgeon Wait Until Game is Over," *Boston Globe*, August 20, 1953: 15.

385   On August 31, the Red Sox played a night game at Cleveland Stadium. The Indians were riding a six-game winning streak that included sweeping two from the Red Sox the day before. Cleveland was only 1 ½ games out of first place.

386   Harry Jones, "Williams' Homer Sinks Indians, 6-4," *Cleveland Plain Dealer*, September 1, 1953: 21.

387   Hy Hurwitz, "Boudreau, Piersall Hail Williams as 'the
        Greatest'," *Boston Globe*, September 1, 1953: 28.

388   Associated Press, "Williams' Homer Tops Tribe, 6-4," *San
        Diego Union*, September 1, 1953: 18.

389   Jones, "Williams' Homer Sinks Indians, 6-4." The home run
        was the 331st of his career and tied him with Hank Greenberg.

390   What kind of pitch was it? "I thought it was a slider," Williams
        said after the game, "but I suppose Garcia will say it was a fast
        ball. I thought I hit a slider off Feller yesterday but he said
        it was a fast ball. I don't know, maybe those guys are using
        psychology on me." Hurwitz, "Boudreau, Piersall Hail Williams
        as 'the Greatest'."

391   Henry McKenna, "Ted's Three-Run Homer Wins for Sox,"
        Boston Herald, September 1, 1953: 15. Tris Speaker was at the
        game. He said of Williams, "He's marvelous. I don't know, but
        I think Mike was fooling him with a certain pitch, probably his
        fast ball, until that time...But you can't keep getting away with
        one pitch against Ted. Sooner or later, he'll catch up with you."
        He added that Williams, not long out of the Marines, "doesn't
        look to be in too good shape, and that's to be expected" but "his
        swing is as good as ever."

392   "Ted Out of Lineup - Is 'Stiff and Aching'," *Boston Globe*,
        September 1, 1953: 1.

393   F. C. Matzek, "Kinder Sets American League Pitching Mark;
        Ted Connects Again," *Providence Journal*, September 18,
        1953: 11.

394   Bob Nieman caught it; his throw to second was fast enough to
        double off Tommy Umphlett, and Sammy White's crossing the
        plate didn't count. Joe Cashman, "Ted's 13th HR Trips Tigers,
        2-1," *Boston Daily Record*, September 18, 1953: 29.

395   Leo Macdonell, "Tigers Back in Town for Last Home Stand,"
        Detroit Times, September 18, 1953: 25. The *Globe* put it at 15
        rows up, in Section 2.

396   Hy Hurwitz, "Williams' 2-Run Homer in 8th Beats Tigers for
        Sox," *Boston Globe*, September 18, 1953:

397   Mike Gillooly, "Ted Hides Behind Kinder," *Boston American*,
        September 18, 1953: 24.

398   Heller, *Facing Ted Williams,* 63, 64.

399   "Watch that wind and get on your horse," the 39-year-old
        Kinder purportedly told Piersall as he ran in from the bullpen.
        All three Detroit batters hit fly balls to the outfield, one to
        center and then two to right field, both of which were hauled in
        by Piersall but only after running both down. See Ed Costello,
        "Sox Shade Tigers, 2-1, on Ted's Homer," *Boston Herald*,
        September 18, 1953: 21.

400   Williams hit 10 home runs off Garver over the years. This was his 337th home run. The ones he'd hit off Garver were #213, 245, 272, 282, 337, 375, 385, 422, 436, and 459. Two others were game-winning homers, both in 1955, on June 21 and July 31.

401   Hy Hurwitz, "Williams' Homer in 10th Gives Red Sox 3-1 Victory," *Boston Globe*, August 7, 1954: 4.

402   There had been a spectacular play that saved a run in the bottom of the seventh. With two outs in the bottom of the inning, and a runner on second base, Dick Kryhoski pinch-hit for Coleman. He "whacked one down the first base line an inch about the ground. Agganis made a diving stab for the ball and came up with it." Umpire Red Flaherty didn't think he had caught it, though, When Agganis realized that, he "took one look and then sprinted for the bag. He just nipped Kryhoski with a running slide to first as Fridley was crossing home plate." Hurwitz, "Williams' Homer in 10th Gives Red Sox 3-1 Victory."

403   Ted Williams batted second in the lineup, a very rare event. He walked; that was not so rare. His 136 walks led both leagues in 1954, the eighth year he led the American League in walks. He was placed second in the lineup to give him more plate appearances in a year when he had missed a lot of time at the start of the season, and thus give him a shot at the batting title.

404   Hurwitz, "Williams' Homer in 10th Gives Red Sox 3-1 Victory."

405   Henry McKenna, "Red Sox Win, 3-1, on Ted's Homer," *Boston Herald*, August 7, 1954: 6.

406   Hurwitz, "Williams' Homer in 10th Gives Red Sox 3-1 Victory." The lesson, Hurwitz wrote in his lead sentences, was: "You can't heckle an old pro. At least, not one like Ted Williams."

407   Bob Holbrook, "Ted Needled, Sox Afire," *Boston Globe*, August 7, 1954: 6. That Williams would be playing in the game was given a big buildup in the Baltimore papers beforehand and Holbrook added that among the "partisan Baltimore crowd...a good many of them rose to their feet and gave the loping Williams a tremendous hand. After all, they came to the ballpark for two reasons – one, to see Baltimore win and the second to see Ted Williams hit a home run."

408   Joe Cashman, "Sox Slam Nats, 10-1; Two Homers for Ted," *Boston Daily Record*, August 12, 1954: 40.

409   Ed Costello, "Sox Beat Nats, 10-1, Then Lose 5-4," *Boston Herald*, August 12, 1954: 21.

410   Cashman, "Sox Slam Nats, 10-1; Two Homers for Ted."

411   Clif Keane, "Nats Score Three in 9th to Score Split with Red Sox," *Boston Globe*, August 12, 1954: 18. It was Consolo's first home run of the year.

412   Burton Hawkins, "Senators' Hopes Fall As Sievers Slumps Again," *Evening Star* (Washington, DC), August 12, 1954: C1, C2.

413   Before September 3, seven games and 30 plate appearances passed without him hitting that next one. He had walked 12 times (twice intentionally, and others perhaps due to extra caution), hit five singles, two doubles, six groundouts (one into a double play), four fly outs, and one popup.

414   Clif Keane, "Ted Hits 362d Homer to Pass DiMag as Sox Win, 11-1," *Boston Globe*, September 4, 1954: 4.

415   After the game, sportswriter Ed Rumill of the *Christian Science Monitor* helped retrieve the home run ball for Ted Williams. Rumill said it was only the second baseball he ever asked for. The first homer was the first homer he had hit off Bob Feller, back on May 4, 1946. Williams ultimately hit 10 home runs off the future Hall of Famer. Rumill elaborated: "This writer arranged for a 20th Street resident to return the ball, in exchange for which he received a new ball autographed as follows: 'To Bill: this is in exchange for my record-breaking home run number 362. Thanks, Ted Williams.'" Ed Rumill, "Ted Williams Collects Record-Breaking Ball," *Christian Science Monitor*, September 4, 1954: 11.

416   Keane, "Ted Hits 362d Homer to Pass DiMag as Sox Win, 11-1."

417   Ed Costello, "Williams Homers, Sox Win, 11-1," *Boston Herald*, September 4, 1954: 8. Next on the career home run list was Lou Gehrig, who had 493 home runs. That seemed impossibly far away, particularly since Williams claimed at the time that he was retiring at the end of the 1954 campaign. Beyond Gehrig were Mel Ott (511), Jimmie Foxx (534), and Babe Ruth (714).

418   John Drohan, "Williams Gets Epic Home Run Ball," *Boston Traveler*, September 4, 1954: 6.

419   John Gillooly, "Sox Tip A's, 5-2; Ted Belts #28," *Boston Daily Record*, September 21, 1954: 23.

420   Hy Hurwitz, "Sox Beat A's, 5-2; Brewer Wins 10th; Williams Clouts 28th Home Run," *Boston Globe*, September 21, 1954: 8.

421   Ed Costello, "Red Sox Win Over A's, 5-2, Behind Brewer," *Boston Herald*, September 21, 1954: 13.

422   The Red Sox held onto fourth place, where they finished the season. The Athletics finished last. It didn't help that the Red Sox swept them in a doubleheader the next day, September 21 by scores of 4-3 (in 10 innings) and 4-3.

423   Ed Rumill, "One of 1954's Pleasant Surprises on Red Sox," *Christian Science Monitor*, September 21, 1954: 10, Brewer had expected to be spending another season in Triple A. He credited coach Del Baker for giving him confidence in spring

training, and Sammy White for calling good games when it was
his turn to pitch.

424 Associated Press, "Frisky Williams Bombs Tigers," *Grand
Rapids Press*, June 11, 1955: 27.

425 Associated Press, "Frisky Williams Bombs Tigers." Ted
Williams missed a couple of games in Cleveland as he was
fighting off a heavy cold, but he always loved to hit in Briggs
Stadium so when the Red Sox arrived for a Friday afternoon
game, he was in the lineup.

426 Henry McKenna, "Ailing Williams Hits Two Homers As Red
Sox Subdue Tigers, 5-2," *Boston Herald*, June 11, 1955: 6.

427 "Mike [Higgins] told us to watch the situation," he said after
the game. "I think I could have made second, all right. But if I
do, Ted Williams comes up and they automatically walk him
with first base open." Mike Gillooly, "Klaus Does Right Thing at
Right Time," *Boston American*, June 11, 1955: 18.

428 Both home runs took advantage of the closer left-field stands in
Detroit; both of Williams's hits might have been outs at Fenway
Park. The slugger himself said as much: "Both would have been
outs in Boston. Easy outs." Associated Press, "Ted Williams
Says His Home Runs Just Outs at Fenway Park," *Springfield
Union* (Springfield, Massachusetts), June 11, 1955: 42.

429 McKenna, "Ailing Williams Hits Two Homers As Red Sox
Subdue Tigers, 5-2."

430 Center fielder Bill Tuttle singled. Al Kaline followed with
a single of his own. Ferris Fain walked and the bases were
loaded. Left fielder Jim Delsing singled to left field and two
runs scored.

431 Hy Hurwitz, "Williams Clouts 3-Run Homer for 5-4 Red Sox
Win," *Boston Globe*, June 22, 1955: 1, 8.

432 Some of the Boston sportswriters called on the weather to
create more of a sense of melodrama. Henry McKenna of the
Herald began his story: "Lightning flashed across the skies,
thunder roared and Ted Williams, like the mighty Zeus,
tossed one of his famous thunderbolts into the firmament in
another bristling, battling thriller last night at Fenway Park."
Henry McKenna, "Red Sox Win, 5-4, on Ted's Homer," *Boston
Herald*, June 22, 1955: 1.

433 Bob Holbrook, "Garver Takes Chance on Ted, Finds it Costly,"
Boston Globe, June 22, 1955: 8.

434 Holbrook, "Garver Takes Chance on Ted, Finds it Costly."
Williams had other opportunities against Garver. He later hit
four more homers off Garver, including a fourth-inning grand
slam that won the game on July 31. Garver himself later said,
"I loved to pitch against guys like Mantle and DiMaggio and

people that were recognized as the great ones. If they got a hit off you, well what the heck, he's supposed get a hit; he's a great one. But if you got him out, well that was an accomplishment." He added, "Walk Williams? People came from Arizona and Wyoming and places like that to see him hit when we were in Kansas City. They didn't come to see him walk to first. So I figured, what the heck, I ought to pitch to him." Heller, *Facing Ted Williams*, 62.

435   Henry McKenna, "Nixon, Williams Spark Sox 5-0 Win," *Boston Herald*, July 30, 1955: 1, 5.

436   One of the outfield putouts was by Ted Williams in the fifth inning, described by Matzek as "a spectacular back-handed and overhead stop of Boone's drive to the left-field scoreboard." F. C. Matzek, "Red Sox Blanks Tigers, 5-0," *Providence Journal*, July 30, 1955: 1, 9. The *Boston Globe* called it "a spectacular stab...going toward the wall full tilt." Bob Holbrook, "Nixon, Sox Halt Tigers, 5-0," *Boston Globe*, July 30, 1955: 1, 4.

437   Jim Prime and Bill Nowlin, *Ted Williams: The Pursuit of Perfection*, 97.

438   It was his first grand slam since he returned from the Korean War in the latter half of 1953. The last time he had hit a grand slam was on May 27, 1951.

439   Bob Holbrook, "Sox Win on Williams Slam, 8-3; On Piersall Homer in 9th, 3-2," *Boston Globe*, August 1, 1955: 1, 4.

440   Associated Press, "Terrible Ted Again Paces Bosox in Double Tiger Licking," *Grand Rapids Press*, August 1, 1955: 33.

441   Baumann had thrown 5 2/3 innings of scoreless relief. It was the first walkoff home run of Piersall's career.

442   Ted Williams and John Underwood, *The Science of Hitting*, 20.

443   Pedro Ramos, in Danny Peary, ed., *We Played the Game* (New York: Hyperion, 1994), 377.

444   Williams hit six career home runs off Ramos, but only this one off Abernathy.

445   Bob Holbrook, "Williams' Slam Leads Sox 8-4 Win," *Boston Globe*, August 16, 1955: 1, 8.

446   Norm Zauchin walked, loading the bases. Catcher Sammy White hit the ball deep but right-fielder Carlos Paula ran it down and caught it for the third out.

447   Bob Addie, "Bosox Lead Nats, 8-4; Williams Has Grand Slam," *Washington Post*, August 16, 1955: 14.

448   Henry McKenna, "Sox Win, 8-4; Ted Clouts Slam," *Boston Herald*, August 16, 1955: 1, 15. It was the 13th grand slam of Williams' career. McKenna noted that Williams had collected his 2,000[th] hit just a few days before, on August 11. The ball was pulled out of play and both ball and bat were donated to the

Jimmy Fund for a contest, the winner to be the person judged to have best completed, in 15 words or less: "I would like to help the Red Sox fight cancer in children because...."

449   Manager Chuck Dressen left Abernathy in. Jensen walked – and then stole second. Abernathy got out of the inning, though not before he walked Hatton once more. He'd walked six men in the second inning alone; the record at the time was eight, according to the *Boston Globe*. See Holbrook, "Williams' Slam Leads Sox 8-4 Win." The record of eight walks in an inning was set by another Washington pitcher, William "Dolly" Gray, on August 28, 1909, seven of the eight walks in succession.

450   Williams struck out again in the eight, a two-K game, but the game-winning grand slam may have made up for it.

451   He had been hammered for four runs by the Yankees in New York and only recorded three outs, leaving after back-to-back triples in the bottom of the second. He had won a game in relief in one prior outing.

452   It was to catcher Frank House, according to databases consulted in 2021. The *Boston Herald* account said he fouled out to Bubba Phillips in left field.

453   Williams had hit a home run off Aber before, on July 14, into the right-field upper deck at Briggs Stadium.

454   Hy Hurwitz, "Ted's Grand Slam in 9th Puts Red Sox Nearer Top," *Boston Globe*, August 28, 1955: C1. Williams never really complained about balls and strikes, and never showed an umpire up. Right-hander Charlie Beamon once explained, "If they happened to call something he didn't think was a strike, he never said anything. All he needed was one pitch anyway, you know!" See Heller, *Facing Ted Williams*, 17.

455   Aber's first pitch went for a ball. Ted fouled off the second pitch, hitting a ground ball past first base. Another ball followed. Aber's fourth pitch was over the plate. Sampson wrote: "Mighty Casey DID NOT strike out." See Arthur Sampson, "Williams Silences Critics," *Boston Herald*, August 28, 1955: 47. He said the ball went halfway up into the upper-deck stands. Hy Hurwitz wrote it landed about 10 rows up into the seats.

456   The two previous ones had come on July 31 against the Tigers in Boston and August 15, against the Washington Senators, likewise at Fenway Park. Taking Ted Williams's slot in the batting order, Ellis Kinder pitched the ninth inning for the Red Sox. Hurd got the win. Kinder picked up his 17th save. The 40-year-old reliever led both leagues, closing 38 games in 1955.

457   Ted Williams and Jim Prime, *Ted Williams' Hit List*, 44.

458   Harold Kaese, "Hose Nearer Yanks, Fielding Picks Up, Outlook
       Improves," *Boston Globe*, July 9, 1956: 5. Ben Bradlee Jr.
       wrote, "He slipped on one of the clogs he wore in the shower
       and hurt the arch in his foot, an inglorious injury that sidelined
       him for five weeks." Ben Bradlee Jr., *The Kid: The Immortal
       Life of Ted Williams*, 415.

459   Harold Kaese, "Hose Nearer Yanks, Fielding Picks Up, Outlook
       Improves."

460   "Ted at Peak, Bats .368, Drives in 1,500[th] Run," *Boston Globe*,
       July 9, 1956: 1. It was his second home run off Moore; in
       September 1955, he had hit #392 off Moore. The score was 2-0,
       Red Sox. Two fly balls followed, one by Mickey Vernon to right
       field and the other by Jackie Jensen to center.

461   Joe Cashman, "Red Sox Beat Orioles, 9-0, 8-4," *Boston Daily
       Record*, July 9, 1956: 8.

462   Ted Williams was involved with another Sullivan this day
       – CBS television's Ed Sullivan. Ted Williams was national
       campaign chairman of Boston's Jimmy Fund and he appeared
       in a three-minute cut-in on *The Ed Sullivan Show*. At the end
       of his remarks on fighting cancer in children, he took a moment
       to ask the kidnapper of 5-week-old Peter Weinberger of Long
       Island to return the child to his parents. Joe Looney, "Ted's
       Biggest Hit on Sullivan TV," *Boston Herald*, July 9, 1956: 11.
       See also "Kidnapper Stays in Hiding," *Boston Globe*, July 9,
       1956: 1, 3. Tragically, Angelo LaMarca killed the young boy. He
       was himself executed at Sing Sing in August 1958. Bill Nowlin,
       521 – The Story of Ted Williams' Home Runs, 234.

463   Tom Brewer of the Boston Red Sox shut out the visiting Kansas
       City Athletics, allowing just four base hits. In so doing, he had
       run his scoreless innings streak against the Athletics to 38
       innings and his record against them to 6-0. The Red Sox won,
       10-0 on 16 hits, with the three RBIs by Don Buddin leading the
       offense. All 10 runs were scored off starter Art Ditmar. Billy
       Goodman drove in two.

464   Porterfield had been acquired by the Red Sox over the previous
       winter and came into the game with a season record of 2-8 and
       an ERA of 6.19. He hadn't won a game since May 31.

465   Hy Hurwitz, "Williams Hits 400th Homer; Joins Baseball
       Immortals," *Boston Globe*, July 18, 1956: 1, 12.

466   Henry McKenna, "Williams Slugs 400th Homer," *Boston
       Herald*, July 18, 1956: 1, 25.

467   Hurwitz, "Williams Hits 400th Homer; Joins Baseball
       Immortals." The ball wound up in the hands of 24-year-old
       Peter Hickey of Winthrop Street, Waltham. Bullpen coach
       Mickey Owen and a couple of ushers approached Hickey and he

got to meet Ted, get a couple of autographed balls and a pair of tickets to a future game in exchange for the memento. He said he would save one of the autographed balls for his son, Jimmy Hickey.

468   Hy Hurwitz, "Brewer, Porterfield Shut Out A's 10-0, 1-0," *Boston Globe*, July 18, 1956: 11.

469   Had the Red Sox ever shut out the opposition in both games of a doubleheader at home? Writers at the time said no one could remember it. It had been nearly 30 years; on September 17, 1926 the Red Sox beat the St. Louis Browns 2-0 and 4-0.

470   Ed Rumill spoke with Williams after the game about some of the home runs that stood out in Williams's memory. Ed Rumill, "Red Sox Star Recalls Some High-Light Homers," *Christian Science Monitor*, July 18, 1956: 11. Asked about how he might have made it to 500 by now, had it not been for two hitches of military service, and some injuries, Williams said, "Maybe. But I'll never make it now and, of course, we'll never know what it might have been."

471   Hurwitz, "Williams Hits 400th Homer; Joins Baseball Immortals." It's perhaps of interest that another milestone was reached the same evening. Stan Musial collected his 2,700th major-league base hit.

472   "Ted Aiming At Only Few Sports Scribes," *Boston Traveler*, July 18, 1956: 29. Bud Collins told more of the story in the *Boston Herald*. See "Disdain Shown for Newsmen," *Boston Herald*, July 18, 1956: 25.

473   Joe McGuff, "Ted 's Homer Jolts A's," *Kansas City Times*, July 27, 1956: 28.

474   Mickey Vernon letter to Michael Seidel; see Seidel, *Ted Williams: A Baseball Life* (Chicago: Contemporary Books, 1991), 281.

475   McGuff, "Ted 's Homer Jolts A's."

476   Bob Holbrook, "Sox Overcome A's in 10th, 5-3," *Boston Globe*, July 27, 1956: 31.

477   Arthur Sampson, "Sox Bound Back, 5-3," *Boston Herald,* July 27, 1956: 35. After the Red Sox slugger had crossed the plate, a fan in a white t-shirt jumped out of the stands, ran to shake Williams's hand, and then kept running and hopped back into the stands on the other side.

478   Dave Sisler was the son of Hall of Famer George Sisler. This was his first year in the majors. He came into the August 5 game with a 4-5 record and a 4.73 earned run average. He was the younger brother (by 11 years) of first baseman and left fielder Dick Sisler, who had wrapped up a solid eight-year career in 1954.

479   Harry Jones, "Red Sox Homers Beat Indians, 2-1," *Cleveland Plain Dealer*, August 6, 1956: 31.

480   Joe Cashman, "Red Sox Win On Homers, 2-1," *Boston Daily Record*, August 6, 1956: 7.

481   Bob Holbrook, "Jensen, Williams Homers Beat Tribe, 2-1," *Boston Globe*, August 6, 1956: 4. Ted Williams hit four homers off the future Hall of Famer. This was the second of the four. They were #307, at Fenway Park back in 1951, and (later) two in 1957, one in June and one in July, both also hit at Cleveland Stadium. Unfortunately, we can't pin down which of the homers hit off Lemon was the one he described when talking about how he felt it was good policy for a batter to (almost) always take the first pitch. "Despite taking that first pitch, I was still pitched to carefully - an indication of respect, I guess, or maybe that the pitchers didn't trust me. (I hit a home run off Bob Lemon on a first pitch one time, and he yelled, 'What the hell are you doing?' He was one guy I didn't want to get ahead of me.)" See Ted Williams and John Underwood, *The Science of Hitting*, 49.

482   Michael Seidel, *Ted Williams: A Baseball Life*, xiv. Williams told Jimmy Piersall, "Kid, there's only one way for you to become a hitter. Go up to the plate and get mad. Get mad at yourself and mad at the pitcher." See Bob Holbrook, "Sox Rookie Piersall Super Fielder; Ted, Pesky Strive to Aid Boy's Batting," *Boston Globe*, March 21, 1951: 31. He even told Ted Ashby of the *Boston Globe,* straight out: "I hit better when I'm mad. I'm sharper. My reactions are quicker. My sensibilities keener." Seidel, *Ted Williams: A Baseball Life*, xiv, citing the *Boston Globe*, June 25, 1949. See also Gordon Edes, "Gone," *Boston Globe*, July 6, 2002: G5.

483   Ben Bradlee, Jr., *The Kid: The Immortal Life of Ted Williams,* 17.

484   For more on how some fans felt, see "Fan's Reaction to Ted Fine," *Boston Globe*, August 9, 1956: 20. There were two other columns in the *Globe* as well, both reporting the reaction amongst the populace. See also David Wilson, "Sox Fans Rally to Ted's Defense" *Boston Herald*, August 9, 1956: 1. The *Globe*'s Clif Keane went out to watch the game from the left-field grandstand seats, and all but a very few hecklers were solidly in Ted's corner. Williams was cheered when he first came out on the field. Clif Keane, "Bleacher Fans Show Loyalty to Ted at Game," *Boston Globe*, August 9, 1956: 1.

485   John Gillooly, "Yawkey at Fenway Park to Settle Williams Row," *Boston Daily Record*, August 9, 1956: 53.

486   Associated Press, "'Do It Again if I get Mad Enough' – Ted," *Providence Journal*, August 9, 1956: 8.

487   Arthur Sampson, "Red Sox Victors, 7-2," *Boston Herald*, August 9, 1956: 25. There was a front-page eight-column banner headline on the next day's *Boston Globe* that read "Williams Hits Homer, Covers Mouth Before 30,338."

488   Bob Holbrook, "Parnell Wins 4th Straight, Tops Orioles," *Boston Globe*, August 9, 1956: 21.

489   Ted Williams with John Underwood, *My Turn at Bat*, 136.

490   John Gillooly, "Hasty Retreat for Williams," *Boston American*, September 2, 1956: 10.

491   Hy Hurwitz, "Sox Win, 4-2, on Ted's 2-Run Homer," *Boston Globe*, September 2, 1956: 10.

492   Joe Cashman, "Sox Win on Ted's HR, 4-2; Sully Fans 8 Orioles; Jensen Smacks HR," *Boston American*, September 2, 1956: 10.

493   There had been a defensive play by Ted Williams that might have saved the game. Kell's ball was hit hard into the left-field corner. "[Ted] Williams went back into the corner, braced his back against the wall and leaped. He reached the ball and held it. The snare robbed Kell of a double." See Cashman.

494   Henry McKenna, "Sully Sleeps On Something New," *Boston Herald*, September 2, 1956: 22.

495   Hurwitz, "Sox Win, 4-2, on Ted's 2-Run Homer."

496   Cashman, "Sox Win on Ted's HR, 4-2; Sully Fans 8 Orioles; Jensen Smacks HR."

497   F.C. Matzek, "Williams' Homer Wins for Sox; Yanks Beaten by Nats," *Providence Journal*. September 2, 1956: 57. McKenna wrote that the ball went about four rows deep and was about 20 feet from the foul pole. McKenna, "Sully Sleeps On Something New."

498   Winning the game with the eighth-inning home run might have been "heart-warming, temper-softening...a game-winner to make a guy glow." Instead, he "beat Baltimore and then he beat it to the parking lot." Gillooly somewhat facetiously suggested that he might have wanted to keep his stern public demeanor: "might have been that he was so delighted that he dashed for his automobile lest anyone see him grinning in glee, from lobe to lobe." Gillooly, "Hasty Retreat for Williams."

499   Joe Cashman, "Loes Jibes Williams," *Boston Daily Record*, July 2, 1956: 2. Loes was a right-hander who'd begun his career with the Brooklyn Dodgers and been purchased by the Orioles in May. During that June 30 game, he'd been heckling Ted Williams and Jimmy Piersall. When Williams singled through the open shortstop hole in the sixth, Loes called over to him at first base, "Why don't a strong guy like you pull the ball and

hit it out of the park instead of settling for those lousy taps to left?" Loes and Piersall later exchanged jibes during a Piersall at-bat on July 7. No stories of the day indicated that the banter was anything other than light-hearted, but of course it might nonetheless have seemed irritating.

At one point, while Loes was jawing with Jimmy Piersall, who he'd hit with a pitch that he said got away from him, umpire Ed Runge "suggested that Loes cut out the clowning," to which Loes replied, "Who invited you into the act?" Later in the game, Williams was back on first base again and saw Loes gabbing with batter Mickey Vernon. He would have had second base stolen, except that Vernon fouled off the pitch.

500 Gregory H. Wolf, "Billy Loes," SABR BioProject, at https://sabr.org/bioproj/person/billy-loes/

501 Loes did come back with a strong 12-7 season in 1957 and made the All-Star team.

502 Henry McKenna, "Ted Homers as Sox Beat Orioles, 6-1," *Boston Herald,* September 9, 1956: 63.

503 Hy Hurwitz, "Brewer Holds Orioles to 4 Hits for 19th Win," *Boston Globe*, September 9, 1956: 42.

504 McKenna, "Ted Homers as Sox Beat Orioles, 6-1."

505 He'd hit one off Connie Johnson on August 8 and one off Morrie Martin on September 1. This one was his seventh game-winning four-base hit of the year. Two more followed, on September 11 and September 25.

506 The right-hander had enjoyed a very strong 1954 season, but been beset with arm problems in the latter part of that year. He never got back to the form he had shown. He came into this game 5-6 with a 3.30 ERA.

507 Robert Cromie, "Sox Lose to Boston, 503; Slip to Third," *Chicago Tribune*, September 12, 1956: C1.

508 Henry McKenna, "Red Sox Win, 5-3," *Boston Herald*, September 12, 1956: 33.

509 See for instance, Joe Cashman, "Ted Homers As Sox Win," *Boston Daily Record*, September 12, 1956: 46.

510 The home run was the fourth Williams had hit off Keegan. In 1957, he hit three, all in the same May 8 game. See Gregory H. Wolf, "Ted Williams smashes three home runs in the Windy City," at https://sabr.org/gamesproj/game/may-8-1957-the-splendid-splinter-smashes-three-in-the-windy-city/ .

511 Ramos had won games on April 25, May 25, May 27, August 11, August 17, and August 19. He had been laid low for three weeks with some illness – a "bug" – and when he returned had been hammered for 12 runs in his final 3 2/3 innings of the season. See Burton Hawkins, "Ramos' Failure Proves Jolt to Worried

Griffs," *Evening Star* (Washington, DC). September 26, 1956: C1, 4.

512   Mantle finished the season with a .353 batting average and Williams was second at .345.

513   Ted Williams with David Pietrusza, *My Life in Pictures*, 111.

514   Ted Williams with John Underwood, *My Turn at Bat*, 135.

515   Ted Williams with John Underwood, *My Turn at Bat*, 135, 136. The spitting incident famously cost Williams a $5,000 fine levied by team owner Tom Yawkey. A good treatment of this whole incident is found in Leigh Montville, *Ted Williams*, 196-199.

516   Donovan was a right-hander, a native of Boston, who had worked his first big-league game for the Boston Braves back in 1950. He'd had only scattered appearances in the majors until 1955 when he had a 15-9 year for the White Sox. He was just beginning a 1957 season which proved to be his best. Before this game, he'd won his only decision having beaten the Washington Senators, 6-1, on May 2.

517   Williams' first run batted in came with his "well-placed single through the vacant spot in an over-shifted infield." Arthur Sampson, "Sox Win On Ted's Homer," *Boston Herald*, May 8, 1957: 39.

518   Hy Hurwitz, "Sox Beat Chisox, 4-3," *Boston Globe*, May 8, 1957: 32.

519   Sampson. "Sox Win On Ted's Homer." It was the only home run Williams ever hit off Donovan, but it had been another game-winner. At season's end, Donovan's 16-6 record had tied him with Tom Sturdivant for the best winning percentage in the major leagues, but this homer cost him one of his six losses. He threw an American League-leading 16 complete games. His ERA was 2.77 and he placed second in the Cy Young Award balloting.

520   Sampson, "Sox Win On Ted's Homer."

521   In his book on hitting, Williams later wrote, "Most pitchers are hardheaded enough not to realize you have figured them out. Dick Donovan of the White Sox was a good pitcher and should have been one of the best. He had an exceptionally good slider. He got everybody out on it, but he threw it too often, and for six or seven years I laid for that one pitch and hit a tune on it. Then one day he threw me a big, slow-breaking curve and I looked so bad on it it must have woke him up, because after that he threw me more curves and became a tougher pitcher for me." See Ted Williams and John Underwood, *The Science of Hitting*, 31-32.

522   Later in the year, on August 20, Keegan no-hit the Washington Senators, 6-0.

523   Irving Vaughan, "Williams' 3 Homers Beat White Sox, 4-1,"
       Chicago Tribune, May 9, 1957: D1.

524   Hy Hurwitz, "'I Broke My Own Rule,' Why Ted Williams
       'Failed' to Have Perfect Day," *Boston Globe*, May 8, 1957: 16.

525   Hurwitz, "'I Broke My Own Rule,' Why Ted Williams 'Failed' to
       Have Perfect Day."

526   Arthur Sampson, "Williams Raps in All Runs, Sox Win, 4-1.
       Ted Crushes Three Homers," *Boston Herald*, May 9, 1937: 35.

527   He wasn't the first Red Sox batter to hit three in a game. Jim
       Tabor had in 1939, and so had Bobby Doerr (1950), Clyde
       Vollmer (1951), and Norm Zauchin (1955). But he was the first
       to have done so twice. He had also done so against Cleveland
       on July 14, 1946. Through 2020, there have been 33 times
       that a Red Sox batter hit three home runs in one game. Ted
       Williams did it a third time; see June 13, 1957, when his first of
       three was a game-winner.

528   Hurwitz, "'I Broke My Own Rule,' Why Ted Williams 'Failed' to
       Have Perfect Day."

529   Even some of the White Sox partisans disapproved; they
       wanted to see history. Chicago manager Al Lopez, though,
       wanted to win. "I don't care if it's Williams or Mantle or
       anybody else," said Lopez. "We're still in the ballgame. We're
       out to win. To hell with four home runs in a ballgame." Mike
       Gillooly, "Ted's Dizzy Pace Stuns Baseball," *Boston American*,
       May 9, 1957: 50.

530   Vaughan of the *Chicago Tribune* wrote, "The senor should have
       requested Williams to help out as an instructor." See Vaughan,
       "Williams' 3 Homers Beat White Sox, 4-1."

531   Bob Addie, "Ted's 3-Run Blast Beats Pete Ramos for Bosox,"
       Washington Post, June 3, 1957: A12. The ball went over
       Williams's head.

532   Bob Holbrook, "Sox Down Nats on Ted's Homer," *Boston
       Globe*, June 3, 1957: 4.

533   Joe Cashman, "Red Sox Beat Solons, 5-3, On 3-Run Homer by
       Ted," *Boston Daily Record*, June 3, 1957: 21.

534   Henry McKenna, "Ted's Bat Wins, 5-3," *Boston Herald*, June 3,
       1957: 23.

535   They had the tying run on first and the winning run coming
       to bat in the person of Jim Lemon. Lemon lofted the ball
       toward Jensen in right field. He had no chance to catch the
       ball, but neither baserunner could know that. Jensen deked the
       opposition, with, explained Bob Addie of the *Washington Post*,
       "a great bit of faking...he extended his hands as if he were going
       to catch the ball. The ball fell in front of him. Sievers hung up
       long enough to be forced at second as Jensen whipped the ball

to Billy Klaus." The *Post*'s Addie dubbed it an "academy award" performance. Mike Gillooly of the *Boston American* devoted an entire article to it. See Mike Gillooly, "Jensen's 'Decoy' Saved Sox Bacon," *Boston American*, June 3, 1957: 31.

536 Chuck Such, "Williams Squares Off Against Indians With Some Mighty Wallops," *Repository* (Canton, Ohio), June 14, 1957: 35, 37.

537 Chuck Heaton, "Ted Uses Avila's Bat to Set Record," *Cleveland Plain Dealer*, June 14, 1957: 32. Even before he made the majors, Williams knew there could be a benefit to a lighter-weight bat. "I switched to a light bat as early as 1938, when I was with Minneapolis, the year before I went up with the Red Sox. It was in late August, and the weather was awful – hotter than I had ever seen it on the West Coast. I was having my first real good year in professional baseball, leading the American Association in batting, home runs, runs batted in, everything. But I was on base so much, swinging and running and sweating, that I felt wrung out.

"One night we were in Columbus, another hot muggy night, and I happened to pick up one of Stan Spence's bats. What a light bat. A toothpick, the lightest in the rack. It was real pumpkin wood, too...It felt good in my hands. I'd been swinging a 35-ouncer, so I asked Stan if I could use it.

"First time up, bases loaded, a little left-hander pitching, and the count went to 3 and 2. As I usually did in those cases, I choked up and said to myself, 'I'm not going to strike out now, I'm going to get some good wood on that ball,' and he threw me a good pitch, low and away but just over the plate. I gave this bat a little flip, and I could hardly believe it – a home run to center field. Not the longest poke in the world, only 410 feet, but long enough...I always used light bats from then on. I kept six or seven bats ready all the time, some as light as 32 ounces, but never over 34 ounces." Ted Williams and John Underwood, *The Science of Hitting*, 16, 18.

538 Bob Holbrook, "Ted's 3 Homers Pace Sox over Indians, 9-3," *Boston Globe*, June 14, 1957: 38.

539 Holbrook, "Ted's 3 Homers Pace Sox over Indians, 9-3."

540 Heaton, "Ted Uses Avila's Bat to Set Record."

541 Ted Williams with John Underwood, *My Turn at Bat*, 199.

542 Lemon was pitching just to get a little work in, coming back as he was after being out for three weeks due to a pulled leg muscle.

543 Holbrook, "Ted's 3 Homers Pace Sox over Indians, 9-3."

544   It had been done before in the National League. Johnny Mize
        had done it with the Cardinals in 1938 and again in 1940.
        Ralph Kiner had done it with Pittsburgh in 1947.

545   Bill Liston, "Ted Chooses Fast Balls at 20 Paces," *Boston
        Traveler*, June 14, 1957: 24.

546   Liston, "Ted Chooses Fast Balls at 20 Paces."

547   Ted Williams and John Underwood, *The Science of Hitting*, 18.

548   Ted Williams with David Pietrusza, *My Life in Pictures*, 120.

549   The *Times* noted that Williams fielded it "calmly" on one
        bounce and opined, "That kid of hit at the Fens is a single and
        the harder it's hit the more certain this is." John Drebinger,
        "Boston Slugger's Homer, Single Send Bombers to 6-4
        Setback," *New York Times*, August 15, 1957: 24.

550   F. C. Matzek, "Ted Wallops 3-Run Homer," *Providence
        Journal*, August 15, 1957: 1. The traffic was so bad that Gov.
        Dennis J. Roberts of Rhode Island got to Fenway Park too late
        to throw the ceremonial first pitch.

551   Lawrence Baldassaro, "August 14, 1957: Ted Williams' rare
        opposite-field homer," SABR Games Project, https://sabr.org/
        gamesproj/game/august-14-1957-ted-williams-rare-opposite-
        field-homer/

552   Manager Jack Tighe could hardly ask for a better performance,
        but at the end of the day it was another loss in the books and
        the Tigers had lost a bit of ground in their hope to reach third
        place in the standings. The Boston Red Sox were the team just
        above them in the American League. The Red Sox were 14 ½
        games behind the New York Yankees. The Tigers were 17 games
        behind.

553   It was something of a rainy day and the game only attracted
        8.308 paying customers. Those who came saw a pitchers' duel.

554   Ed Rumill, "Struck At One Pitch for Winning Home Run,"
        Christian Science Monitor, August 29, 1957: 14.

555   Ed Rumill, "Struck At One Pitch for Winning Home Run."

556   Joe Falls, "How 'Bout Getting Ted to Give Tigers That Lift?,"
        Detroit Times, August 29, 1957: 10.

557   The game-inning homer was one of eight which Ted Williams
        hit off the future United States Senator from Kentucky: #383,
        439, 440, 451, 472, 498, 504, and 519. This one was #451.
        Earlier in the season, on July 12, he'd hit #439 and 440 in the
        same game. Those two homers kicked off a spurt in which from
        July 12 through July 14, he hit five home runs.

558   Why had he prompted such drama, not swinging at all those
        pitches, five of which were called strikes? "There was a reason,"
        he said after the game. "But I'd rather not tell you what it was,
        because it might be something the other clubs could use in the

future." As to the pitch he did swing at, he said, "Yeah, I saw that." Rumill, "Struck At One Pitch for Winning Home Run."

559   Bill Cunningham, "N.Y. Scribes Concede Nothing Like Ted in Game," *Boston Herald*, September 22, 1957: 55.

560   Bob Holbrook, "Ted's Slam Leads Sox Over Yanks, 8-3," *Boston Globe*, September 22, 1957: 57.

561   John Drebinger, "Williams Excels," *New York Times*, September 22, 1957: 27. The *Boston Herald* said it fell eight to 10 rows deep. See Henry McKenna, "Ted Grand Slam Beast Yanks, 8-3," *Boston Herald*, September 22, 1957: 55. It was, wrote the *Herald*'s Bill Cunningham, "a sky-wiper whereas last night's was a line drive, and out near the end of its flight, it seemed to hang and suddenly drop straight down." Cunningham, "N.Y. Scribes Concede Nothing Like Ted in Game."

562   Drebinger, "Williams Excels." Drebinger wrote that Yankee Stadium fans would have loved to see Williams strike out, "but they don't care to have him by-passed with a walk in his bid for the batting crown." He did win his fifth American League batting title with a .388 average.

563   This game was Ted Williams's first start since August 31. He had been laid up for more than two weeks with a severe cold.

564   This was a game full of bases on balls – 18 of them, in all. Yankees pitchers walked 11 Boston batters. Boston pitchers walked seven. The Yankees left 14 men on base. The Red Sox left 12.

565   Holbrook, "Ted's Slam Leads Sox Over Yanks, 8-3." The *New York Times* said that Williams had been thrown 14 balls, and the only one that was over the plate was swiftly deposited into the seats in right. See Drebinger, "Williams Excels."

566   More than 60 years later, the record still stands.

567   After missing more than two weeks due to a severe cold, Williams hit a pinch-hit homer on September 17. He walked in his one plate appearance on the 18th. He hit another pinch-hit home run on September 20. On the 21st, he started the game and hit a game-winning home run and drew three bases on balls. On the 22nd, he singled, homered, and walked two times. On the 23rd, he was hit by a pitch, singled, and walked three more times. It's a record that still stands more than 60 years later. Griggs retired him on his 17th plate appearance.

568   Sullivan came into the game with a 13-11 record. It was his fourth full season in the majors and he had an excellent 2.80 earned run average. He'd pitched 12 complete games in 1957. In eight of his 11 losses, the Red Sox had scored two or fewer runs.

569   Henry McKenna, "Ted Hits No. 38," *Boston Herald*, September 25, 1957: 33.

570   McKenna, "Ted Hits No. 38."

571   Bob Addie, "Sullivan Outduels Griggs, 2-1," *Washington Post*, September 25, 1957: C1.

572   The National League record was 11, first set in 1884, matched in 1890, and most recently tied by the Boston Braves' Dee Phillips in 1944. Malzone shared the A.L. record with Luke Appling, Vern Stephens, and Heinie Majeski. See McKenna, "Ted Hits No. 38."

573   Addie, "Sullivan Outduels Griggs, 2-1." It was "sparkling… banged far to Aspromonte's right. Ken backhanded it and made a quick, one-handed toss to Billy Klaus who completed the twin killing." Bob Holbrook, "Sox Win on Ted's 38ᵗʰ Home Run," *Boston Globe*, September 25, 1957: 25. The *Herald*'s McKenna enthused, "You never saw a better one." McKenna, "Ted Hits No. 38."

574   Henry McKenna, "Sox Defeat Athletics, 8-5," *Boston Herald*, May 23, 1958: 41.

575   Joe McGuff, "Ted's Slam Shakes A'," *Kansas City Star*, May 23, 1958: 32.

576   Bob Holbrook, "Ted's Homer Wins," *Boston Globe*, May 23, 1958: 37. Ed Rumill of the *Monitor* agreed: the ball was hit "well up on the right field banking, behind the fence." See Ed Rumill, "Better than All Except League-Leading Yankees," *Christian Science Monitor*, May 23, 1958: 19.

577   The four-run homer by Ted Williams in the top of the fourth was the game-winning hit. It was the 16ᵗʰ grand slam of his career. Two months later, he hit one more, off the Tigers' Jim Bunning, for what proved to be a final career total of 17. Williams' 17ᵗʰ grand slam was hit at Tiger Stadium on July 29, 1958. He also hit a three-run homer later in the same game.

578   McKenna, "Sox Defeat Athletics, 8-5."

579   It was a "jet-blast over the 375-foot marker in left-center field with a strong, gusty wind trying to beat the ball back all the way." Mike Gillooly, "Mike Blasts Lane After Lepcio HR," *Boston American*, May 23, 1958: 41. Lepcio told Gillooly, "Before I went up to bat, I was talking with Ted (Williams). He told me that because I hadn't batted much this season, I should go up there and relax, take it easy and get a ball I could really see. Then, just meet it. I guess I followed his instructions to the letter." See Gillooly, "Lane Pain in Neck, Explodes Higgins," *Boston American*, May 23, 1958: 58.

580   Delock hadn't lost yet; he was 4-0, but this was his first start of the season.

581 Arthur Sampson, "Homers Nip Indians, 2-1," *Boston Herald*, June 27, 1958: 41.

582 Mike Gillooly, "Ted Called Shot, Umpire Claims," *Boston American*, June 27, 1958: 45. Third-base umpire Johnny Stevens said that Williams had called his shot as he came in from his position in left field, saying, "The next time I come up McLish is going to throw me a curve ball and I'll hit it into the upper deck." See Bob Holbrook, "Ted Called His Shot on Upper Deck Homer," *Boston Globe*, June 27, 1958: 32.

583 Roger Birtwell, "Gernert, Ted Flatten Indians," *Boston Globe*, June 27, 1958: 33.

584 Harry Jones, "Ted Belts Homer to Trip Tribe," *Cleveland Plain Dealer*, June 27, 1958: 29.

585 Joe Cashman, "Sox Win on Ted's HR," *Boston Record*, June 27, 1958: 31.

586 Delock improved his record to 5-0. He continued to start games and continued to win without losing until he reached 10-0 on the season, making it 13 victories in a row (he'd won his last three decisions in 1957.) Going for #11, he got hammered for seven runs in four innings. He finished the season 14-8 with a 3.38 ERA. Cal McLish had an even better season, going 16-8 with a 2.99 ERA. Ted Williams, who turned 40 years old at the end of August, hit .328 and won the American League batting title. His .458 on-base percentage led both leagues.

587 Birtwell, "Gernert, Ted Flatten Indians."

588 He did throw 10 complete games in 1958, tying him with Tom Brewer for the team lead. Sullivan was coming off four seasons for Boston in which he had won more than a dozen games in each. His record was just 4-2 (with an ERA of 3.17) coming into this game right at the end of June. By season's end, Sullivan won 13 games. His record was 13-9 (3.57).

589 Norman had taken over managing from Jack Tighe a little less than three weeks earlier. Foytack was 6-7 (3.49) and coming off a shutout of the Orioles five days earlier.

590 Arthur Sampson, "Sox Slam Tigers," *Boston Herald*, June 30, 1958: 23. It was Jensen's seventh home run on the road trip, his 14th home run in the month of June.

591 Roger Birtwell, "Homers Spark Sox Victory," *Boston Globe*. June 30, 1958: 25.
The earlier rooftop home run was way back in 1939 – his second home run in the major leagues, on May 4. In fact, he hit two onto the right-field roof that day, off two different Tigers pitchers. See Bill Nowlin, "May 4, 1939: Who is that Kid? Ted Williams homers in dramatic Detroit debut," at https://

sabr.org/gamesproj/game/may-4-1939-who-is-that-kid-ted-williams-homers-in-dramatic-detroit-debut/.

592   Joe Falls, "Tigers Better in '57," *Detroit Times*, June 30, 1958: 11. Gene Stephens replaced Williams in left field. In the top of the ninth, Stephens hit a home run, too, one that "struck the facing of the roof-top boxes in right field."

593   "Williams Sparks and Spikes Sox to Win," *Boston Traveler*, June 30, 1958: 24.

594   Both right-handers, Sisler was 6-4 coming into the game, with a 4.38 ERA. Lary had been a 21-game winner two years before, leading the American League in wins. He came into this game 9-8 with a 3.15 ERA.

595   Roger Birtwell, "Ted Wins it in 12th," *Boston Globe*, July 20, 1958: 53. No error was assessed, and Kaline was credited with a double. "[Williams] played a single into a double," wrote the *Detroit Times'* Joe Falls. See Joe Falls, "Mighty Ted Clips Detroit," *Detroit Times*, July 20, 1958: D1.

596   "First time I ever hit one in the bullpen," White said. Henry McKenna, "Norman Shifts on Passing Ted," *Boston Herald*, July 20, 1958: 39.

597   Arthur Sampson, "Ted's Homer Nips Tigers, 7-6," *Boston Herald*, July 20, 1958: 39. On a ball Kuenn hit, Aguirre had been forced out at second and so Kuenn was the baserunner on first.

598   McKenna, "Norman Shifts on Passing Ted."

599   Sampson, "Ted's Homer Nips Tigers, 7-6." The jeers changed to cheers. It was another game-winning home run, giving the Red Sox a 6-5 victory. It was "miles high but not far fair." Joe Cashman, "Sox 7-6 on Ted's Homer," *Boston American*, July 20, 1958: 35. "It was fair by this much," said first base umpire Frank Umont, "holding his hands four feet apart." See Birtwell, "Ted Wins it in 12th."

600   Falls, "Tigers Better in '57." It was so stunning a reversal that the Tigers seemed unable to believe it. "I never saw anything like it," said Higgins. "I had to look at the scoreboard to make sure we weren't tied. That Detroit team didn't move from the field. It was the doggonedest thing." See Bob Holbrook, "Tigers Can't Believe It! Refuse to Leave the Field," *Boston Globe*, July 20, 1958: 54.

601   Holbrook. Williams later hit home run #499 off Aguirre on June 16, 1960 in Detroit.

602   Birtwell, "Ted Wins it in 12th."

603   Bob Holbrook, "Ired Ted Has Best Day of Year," *Boston Globe*, July 30, 1958: 35. The article "alleged that Williams was approached by gamblers in 1941 and failed to report it to

headquarters." John Gillooly, "Ted's At It Again: Sox Gate to Soar," *Boston Daily Record*, July 30, 1958: 19. None of the newspaper accounts named the magazine.

604   Lou Gehrig ranked first, with 23 grand slams. This was, as it happened, the last slam of Ted's career.) To see a listing of all Williams' grand slams, see Bill Nowlin, *521 - The Story of Ted Williams' Home Runs*, 331, 332.

605   Arthur Siegel, "Doesn't Pay to Get Ted Riled Up," *Boston Herald*, July 30, 1958: 38.

606   Henry McKenna, "Red Sox Down Tigers, 11-8," *Boston Herald*, July 30, 1958: 25.

607   The times of the homers come from the July 30, 1958 *Detroit Times* on page 29. Williams wasn't quite 40 yet. He turned 40 on August 30. Tigers manager Bill Norman was stunned to be told that Williams had been saying he wasn't at his best. "I don't ever want to see him in more of a groove than he is right now. He's 40 and the only reason I know that is by the record books...The only thing I can say to sum up my feeling is that he does the expected. When he has you in a tight spot, you expect him to hit a home run. He does that very thing." See "Ted Claims He Still Isn't in the Groove," *Boston Herald*, July 30, 1958: 38. After it was all over, the fatigue Williams had felt seemed to be gone: "He felt like a kid again. He'd been challenged and he answered the challenge with his best day of the year."

608   The ball went between third baseman Power and the bag and into left field. It was only his second hit of the year. Delock finished the season with three hits, and an .063 batting average. His career batting average was .086 in 425 plate appearances. He did hit one home run, in 1959.

609   "Stephens misjudged Minoso's line drive directly at him and it went for a double." Henry McKenna, "Sox Sweep, 3-2,4-2," *Boston Herald,* August 4, 1958: 13, 14. See also Harry Jones, "Indians Halted at 7 in Row, 3-2, 4-2," *Cleveland Plain Dealer,* August 4, 1958: 23. On Delock being disturbed, see Hy Hurwitz, "Hose Sweep Indians," *Boston Globe*, August 4, 1958: 9.

610   "Monbouquette Faces Washington Tomorrow," *Boston Traveler*, August 4, 1958: 10.

611   Jones, "Indians Halted at 7 in Row, 3-2, 4-2."

612   In 1958, Wall finished appeared in 52 games with a 3.62 ERA, comparatively better than the team's collective ERA of 3.92. His record was 8-9. As an aside, Wall committed suicide at age 45, one of 58 known major-league baseball player suicides

613   through the year 2020. See a listing at: http://www.baseball-almanac.com/legendary/suicides_baseball.shtml

613   Seven of those 13 losses came at the hands of the Red Sox. The Senators had long been out of the race. They finished 13 games behind the New York Yankees. As the saying went, "First in war, first in peace, and last in the American League."

614   Bob Addie, "Williams Captures Batting Title," *Washington Post*, September 29, 1958: A14.

615   Huck Finnegan, "Final Day Heroics," *Boston American*, September 29, 1958: 37.

616   Ramos was wrapping up his third season with a 14-17 record and a 4.15 ERA, with four more wins than any other Senator and an ERA below the 4.53 team average. Brewer was in his fifth season, and was 12-12 (3.68).

617   "Ted Gains 6th Title," *Boston Globe,* September 29, 1958: 1, 13.

618   Jensen's 122 RBIs led the league. He was voted A.L. MVP.

619   Shirley Povich, "This Morning...with Shirley Povich," *Washington Post*, September 29, 1958: A14.

620   There was so much attention paid to the batting race that newspapers almost forgot to tell readers where Williams's home run went, but the words the *Globe* allotted Lepcio's homer provide the answer: "Lepcio hit a 400-foot homer to the left of center – almost to the same spot Williams later hit his, but a bit farther up." See John Gillooly, "Sox Injured Get Full Series Share," *Boston American*, September 29, 1958: 37. The *Herald* said Ted fouled off the first pitch but then hit the homer about halfway up in the center-field stands. See Henry McKenna, "Ted's .328 Wins Sixth Batting Title," *Boston Herald*, September 29, 1958: 1, 26.

621   John Gillooly, "Sox Injured Get Full Series Share," *Boston American*, September 29, 1958: 37.

622   Ed Linn, *Hitter* (New York: Harcourt Brace & Company, 1993), 295.

623   Ted Williams with John Underwood, *My Turn At Bat*, 205.

624   The problem persisted throughout the season – the season in which he turned 41 years old. He finished the year hitting 90 points below his career average – batting .254 with only 10 home runs and 43 RBIs.

It was during the Saturday afternoon Memorial Day doubleheader that he first cracked .200, going 2-for-4 in both games. He'd started the first game grounding into a double play and then flying out, but he'd salvaged a degree of respectability with a pair of singles. The Red Sox won, 5-4, overcoming an early 3-0 deficit.

625   F. C. Matzek, "Ted Gets HR, 3 Other Hits as Bosox Win Two," *Providence Journal*, May 31, 1959: S-1.

626   Bob Holbrook, "Ted's 1st Homer Aids Sox Sweep," *Boston Globe*, May 31, 1959: 67.

627   Arthur Sampson, "Ted Sparks Sox Twin-Win," *Boston Herald*, May 31, 1959: 55, 56.

628   "Someone told me about the possibility of the 2500th hit that last time up," he said. "but don't worry, I'll have a lot more good days before this season has finished." Henry McKenna, "Williams Fully Confident More Good Days Ahead," *Boston Herald*, May 31, 1959: 56. Sampson mentioned the wind as a factor.

629   He was 0-for-3 the next day, but a double on June 2 got him to 2,500 (and drove in a run.) This May 30 game officially marked the 20th anniversary of Ted Williams in major-league baseball. He had received credit for the years spent in military service, but hadn't achieved the milestone until this date in May because he had been several weeks late in reporting a few years earlier pending divorce proceedings.

630   Green's debut was on July 21, 1959. The Red Sox were the last among the 16 teams to integrate in what was then considered major-league baseball. For a discussion of the subject see Bill Nowlin, ed., *Pumpsie and Progress: The Red Sox, Race, and Redemption* (Burlington, Massachusetts: Rounder Books, 2010).

631   Clif Keane, "Sox Win 6-4 on Homers, *Boston Globe*, June 28, 1959: 61.

632   Henry McKenna, "Red Sox Stop Indians. 6-4," *Boston Herald*, June 28, 1959: 37, 38.

633   McKenna, "Red Sox Stop Indians. 6-4," *Boston Herald*, June 28, 1959.

634   Only once was either of them involved in a play following a switch, when Runnels was thrown out trying to steal second with two outs in the top of the seventh, Brown throwing to Hamner, who had returned to his original post at second base.

635   He'd had the two previous days off, only appearing as a pinch-hitter. The *Boston Herald*'s Henry McKenna began his story about this day's game by writing, "Retirement clouds may be swirling around the head of Ted Williams but No. 9, who will be 41 next Sunday, still has a few sparks left in his booming bat." Henry McKenna, "Baumann Tames Tigers," *Boston Herald*, August 23, 1959: 53.

636   Roger Birtwell, "Baumann Leads Sox Over Tigers," *Boston Globe*, August 23, 1959: 65, 66. This homer was the 491st of Ted Williams' career. It put him within two home runs of tying

Lou Gehrig's mark – though some tabulations at the time had Gehrig with 494. Williams was getting close, but home runs were coming few and far between.

637   Joe Falls, "Ted Hits 491st, Tigers Lose," *Detroit Times*, August 23, 1959: 1-D.

638   The previous year had been discouraging, too, batting just .254, 90 points below his ultimate career average. He felt, correctly, that he had under-performed. That is why he had insisted on taking a pay cut from $125,000 a year down to $90,000 for 1960. That's not something a player's union would have countenanced, but there was no union in those days and Williams was strong-willed. See a brief discussion on his stance in Leigh Montville, *Ted Williams*, 221.

639   Hal Lebovitz, "Ted Almost Quit Two Weeks Ago, Hopes to Finish Year," *Cleveland Plain Dealer*, June 18, 1960: 21.

640   Pinky Higgins was back as manager, brought in to replace Jurges. As to 1960, Joseph Wancho has pointed out that "The 1960 season was the end of an era in the major leagues. It was the last year that both the American and National Leagues would be eight-team leagues." See Joseph Wancho, "June 17, 1960: Ted Williams wallops 500th career home run in Cleveland," SABR Games Project, at https://sabr.org/gamesproj/game/june-17-1960-ted-williams-wallops-500th-career-home-run-in-cleveland/

641   Bob Holbrook, "Ted, Too Tired to Play, Clouts One Over Fence," *Boston Globe*, June 18, 1960: 1.

642   Larry Claflin, "Ted Eyes Ott's Record," *Boston American*, June 18, 1960: 19. Mel Ott had 511 career home runs. With more than three months remaining in the season, that record was perhaps within reach. The only two above Ott were Jimmie Foxx (534) and Babe Ruth (714).

643   Henry McKenna, "Sox Win, 3-1, on Ted's 500th," *Boston Herald*, June 18, 1960: 13, 14.

644   Henry McKenna, "I'm Shooting for 512 Now, Says Ted After 500 Wallop," *Boston Herald*, June 18, 1960: 13.

645   McKenna, "I'm Shooting for 512 Now, Says Ted After 500 Wallop."

646   Ed Rumill, "Ted Williams' 500th Home Run Ball May Someday Reside in Cooperstown," *Christian Science Monitor*, June 18, 1960: 14.

647   Bill McSweeny, "Ted's 506th; Sox By 13-2," *Boston Daily Record*, July 4, 1960: 6. The *Herald* and *Globe* both suggested the home run landed in the second row and barely eluded Hank Bauer.

648   Heller, *Facing Ted Williams*, 78.

649 Harold Kaese, "Athletics Pitch to Ted – WHAM!" *Boston Globe*, July 4, 1960: 57.

650 Before the game, Ted Williams presented both the bat he used and the ball he had hit for home run #500 to William S. Koster of the Jimmy Fund, to be auctioned off as a fundraiser to fight cancer in children.

651 Ralph Wheeler, "Red Sox Bombard A's, 13-2," *Boston Herald*, July 4, 1960: 43.

652 Roger Birtwell, "Sox Unload on A's, 13-2," *Boston Globe*, July 4, 1960: 57.

653 In more recent years, Barry Bonds drew 2,558 walks and Rickey Henderson drew 2,190. Williams ended up with 2,021. He did, of course, miss most of five seasons due to military service.

654 Three other players rank in the top five. In second place is Barry Bonds (.2029), in third is Max "Camera Eye" Bishop (.19955), and in fifth place is Ferris Fain (.1843).

655 Ted Williams and John Underwood, *The Science of Hitting*, 20.

656 Heller, *Facing Ted Williams*, 38. Some charged that Williams was too selfish, turning his nose up at balls that were close but not over the plate, taking a pitch for a ball instead of hitting it and maybe driving in a run. "If I were selfish as charged," he said, "I'd swing for home runs all the time, good pitches or bad. I'd end up with more home runs and fewer walks. But you still have to win the game, and whether certain people believe that or not, that is what I am after." Ed Linn, *Ted Williams: The Eternal Kid* (New York: Thomas Nelson, 1961), 130.

657 Estrada finished the season 18-11, his 18 wins leading the American League.

658 Henry McKenna, "Ted Hits Two 3-Run Homers," *Boston Herald*, August 21, 1960: 53.

659 McKenna, "Ted Hits Two 3-Run Homers."

660 The homers he had hit off Ramos were #388, 409, 418, 430, 482, and this one, #520. The prior game-winners were September 25, 1956; June 2, 1957; and September 28, 1958. It was also, as it happens, the eighth home run Williams had hit on a September 17. See preceding career homers #28, 124, 195, 323, 337, 452, and 478.

661 The start after that, he had lost a 1-0 game in Chicago, Muffett had spent some time with the Cardinals and Giants, and acquired from the Giants in late July 1959. He had fewer than seven innings without a decision for Boston in 1959. He'd joined the Red Sox from Triple A near the end of June and was 5-3 with a 3.36 ERA coming into this game. In seven of his last eight starts, he had not allowed more than two runs.

662   In six of Ramos's prior losses, he had allowed three or fewer runs. He threw a very good game, allowing just five hits and walking no one in the eight innings he worked.

663   Roger Birtwell, "Williams' Homer Rips Nats, 2-1," *Boston Globe*, September 18, 1960: 69.

664   Henry McKenna, "Ted's 520th Home Run Wins, 2-1," *Boston Herald*, September 18, 1960: 59. There is disagreement between newspapers accounts as to whether the count was 2-1 or 1-2.

665   Birtwell, "Williams' Homer Rips Nats, 2-1."

666   Bob Addie, "Nats Still 4th Despite 2-1 Defeat," *Washington Post*, September 18, 1960: C1.

667   Addie, "Nats Still 4th Despite 2-1 Defeat."

668   Ted Williams and John Underwood, *The Science of Hitting*, 48, 49.